Bountiful Blessings

COOKBOOK

Print ISBN 978-1-62416-708-9

Published by Barbour Publishing, Inc., P.O. Box 719, Uhrichsville, Ohio 44683, www.barbourbooks.com

Our mission is to publish and distribute inspirational products offering exceptional value and biblical encouragement to the masses.

Printed in the United States of America.

Contents

Introduction

Of the many bountiful blessings of life, a delicious home-cooked meal is one of the most satisfying.

Old-fashioned home cooking has become a special treat in many households today, with schedules full and time at a premium. A traditional dinner has always been a heartwarming way to encourage family interaction—but getting a full meal to the table can be challenging. That's where the *Bountiful Blessings Cookbook* can help!

We have collected more than 700 recipes for favorite old-fashioned, down-home, family-tested recipes that are delicious, easy, and sure to please. From appetizers to desserts, you'll have a home-cooked meal put together in no time.

We wish you bountiful blessings as you cook from the heart!

Taste and see that the LORD is good.

PSALM 34:8 NIV

Breakfasts

Breakfast Casserole

8 crescent rolls, flattened
Sausage, cooked and drained
1 cup hash browns
6 eggs, beaten
Grated cheese

OVEN 350°

Grease 5x11-inch pan. Layer rolls, sausage, hash browns, and eggs. Top with grated cheese. Bake at 350° for 45 minutes or until done.

Breakfast Casserole

1 pound sausage, cooked and drained
6 eggs, beaten
1 teaspoon salt
1 teaspoon dry mustard
1 cup grated cheese
1 cup milk
2 slices day-old bread, torn

OVEN 350°

Combine all ingredients in 2-quart casserole dish. Bake uncovered at 350° for 45 minutes.

Bacon and Cheese Breakfast Pizza

Pastry for single-crust pie (9 inch)
½ pound bacon, cooked and crumbled
2 cups shredded Swiss cheese
4 eggs
1½ cups sour cream
2 tablespoons chopped fresh parsley

OVEN 450°

Roll pastry to fit into 12-inch pizza pan. Bake at 450° for 5 minutes. Sprinkle bacon and cheese evenly over crust. In bowl, beat eggs, sour cream, and parsley until smooth; pour over pizza. Bake until puffy and light brown.

Breakfast Pizza

1 family-size Boboli (Italian bread)
1 to 2 tablespoons margarine, melted
1 to 2 teaspoons garlic powder
1 can (6 ounce) tomato paste
2 tablespoons picante or salsa
6 to 8 eggs
¼ cup shredded cheddar cheese
10 to 11 slices Canadian bacon, quartered
½ cup grated Parmesan or mozzarella cheese

OVEN 400°

Spread Boboli with melted margarine; add garlic powder. Mix together tomato paste and picante or salsa; spread on bread. Scramble eggs with cheddar cheese, cooking until soft curds. Spread on bread. Arrange quartered bacon slices in rows on pizza. Cover with Parmesan or mozzarella cheese. Bake at 400° for 10 to 15 minutes.

Sausage Cheese Grits Casserole

4 cups water
1 teaspoon salt
1 cup quick grits
4 eggs, slightly beaten
1 pound sausage, browned
1½ cups (6 ounces) grated sharp cheddar cheese, divided
1 cup milk
½ cup margarine

OVEN 350°

Preheat oven to 350°. Grease 3-quart baking dish; set aside. Bring water and salt to boil in large saucepan. Slowly stir in grits. Cook 4 to 5 minutes, stirring occasionally. Remove from heat. Stir small amount of grits mixture into eggs. Return all to saucepan. Add sausage, 1 cup cheese, milk, and margarine. Blend well. Pour into prepared baking dish. Sprinkle with remaining ½ cup cheese. Bake 1 hour or until cheese is golden brown. Let cool 10 minutes.

Grits Casserole

1 cup grits (not instant)
4 cups boiling water
1 stick butter
¼ to ½ pound grated sharp cheese
½ teaspoon garlic salt
½ teaspoon paprika
1 teaspoon salt
2 eggs, beaten

OVEN 375°

Cook grits in boiling water 5 minutes. Add butter, cheese, garlic salt, paprika, salt, and eggs. Pour into greased 9x13-inch baking dish. Bake 40 minutes at 375°.

Overnight Sausage Soufflé

1 pound link pork sausage
6 slices bread, cubed
1 cup grated medium cheddar cheese
4 eggs
2 cups milk
½ teaspoon salt
½ teaspoon dry mustard (optional)

OVEN 325°

Fry sausage and cut into pieces.
Alternate layers of bread cubes, sausage, and cheese in 2½-quart casserole dish.
Beat eggs and add milk; then add salt and dry mustard. Pour egg mixture over other ingredients. Cover and refrigerate overnight. Bake in 325° oven for 45 minutes to 1 hour.

Crepe Peon

Flour tortillas, 1 to 2 per person
1 egg, beaten
⅝ cup milk
2 tablespoons butter

Rather than making your own, or using premade crepes, take any size flour tortilla, dip in beaten egg mixed with ⅝ cup milk, and cook in butter or margarine lightly like French toast. It is sturdier than a "real crepe" and works great.

Variation: Roll any ingredients inside crepe for any occasion: ice cream, cheese with fruit, nuts, veggies, tuna, crab, egg, ham, salad, etc.

Berta's Bavarian Apple Pancakes

3 eggs
1 teaspoon vanilla
4 teaspoons sugar
1 cup milk
1 cup flour
4 apples, peeled and shredded
Lite oil for frying
4 tablespoons cinnamon and sugar mixed for sprinkling

Beat together eggs, vanilla, and 4 teaspoons sugar. Add milk; mix in flour. Stir in apples. Fry in oil in very hot pan. Spoon ⅓ cup mixture into oil. Turn over when edges are dry and bubbles form. Sprinkle with cinnamon and sugar mixture.

Sausage Breakfast Bake

2 cups pancake mix (or 1½ cups prepared baking mix and ½ cup cornmeal)
1¼ cups milk
2 eggs
2 tablespoons salad oil
1 package (8 ounce) smoky links, cut into bite-size pieces
1 jar (14 ounce) spiced apple rings

OVEN 350°

Combine first four ingredients and beat until smooth with rotary beater. Turn into 9x13-inch baking dish. Stir smoky links into batter. Arrange apple rings in batter, in areas where "cake" pieces will be cut. Bake at 350° for 35 minutes. Serve with apple syrup (next column).

Apple Syrup:
Apple syrup from jar of spiced apple rings
4 teaspoons cornstarch
¾ cup maple-flavored syrup
4 teaspoons butter

Pour apple syrup into cup and add water to make ⅔ cup. Pour into saucepan and add cornstarch and maple-flavored syrup. Cook until bubbly and add butter.

Pancakes

1¼ cups flour
1¼ cups buttermilk
1 egg, beaten
1 teaspoon sugar
½ teaspoon salt
½ teaspoon baking soda
1 tablespoon liquid shortening
1 teaspoon baking powder

Mix ingredients and fry on hot griddle.

Doughnut Muffins

1 egg, beaten
½ cup milk
⅓ cup oil
1 teaspoon vanilla
1 teaspoon lemon juice
1½ cups flour
2 teaspoons baking powder
½ cup sugar
1 teaspoon nutmeg
½ teaspoon cinnamon

Topping:
3 teaspoons sugar
¼ teaspoon nutmeg

OVEN 400°

Beat together egg, milk, oil, vanilla, and lemon juice. Add flour, baking powder, sugar, nutmeg, and cinnamon. Pour into muffin tin. Mix together sugar and nutmeg for topping and spread over tops of muffins. Bake at 400° for 20 minutes.

Waffles with Maple Syrup

4 eggs, separated
2 cups milk
3 cups flour, sifted
4 teaspoons baking powder
1 teaspoon salt
2 teaspoons sugar
⅔ cup melted butter or shortening

Using electric mixer, beat egg whites until fluffy; set aside. Beat egg yolks 1 minute; add milk and beat 1 minute. Add sifted dry ingredients and beat 1 minute. Add melted butter and beat 15 seconds. Fold in stiffly beaten egg whites. Pour onto hot waffle iron.

Homemade Maple Syrup:
2 cups sugar
¼ cup brown sugar
32 ounces light corn syrup
1 cup water
1 teaspoon vanilla
1 teaspoon maple flavoring

Mix sugars, corn syrup, and water together and bring just to boiling point (enough to melt sugars). Add vanilla and maple flavoring. Stir well and serve over waffles or pancakes. Keeps well in refrigerator.

Breakfast Granola

7 cups oats (not quick)
1 cup wheat germ
½ cup honey
½ cup oil
½ cup brown sugar
½ cup water
1 teaspoon vanilla or orange flavoring

OVEN 225°

Mix oats and wheat germ. Bring to boil honey, oil, brown sugar, and water. Remove from stove and add flavoring. Pour liquid over oats mixture and mix well. Bake 1 hour at 225° in double cake pan. Stir once or twice during baking. Should be crisp. Add other ingredients to taste such as raisins, dates, dried fruit, coconut, pumpkin, sunflower and/or sesame seeds, orange peel. Applesauce is a good topping.

Breads

Bread Machine Oatmeal Bread

1¼ cups plus 2 tablespoons water
1 tablespoon oil
½ cup molasses (mild)
1 teaspoon salt
3 cups bread flour
1 cup quick-cooking oats
1½ teaspoons yeast

Follow machine instructions.

Yield: 1½-pound loaf.

Bishop's Bread

1½ cups flour, sifted
1½ teaspoons baking powder
¼ teaspoon salt
⅔ cup chocolate chips
2 cups coarsely chopped walnuts
1 cup diced dates
1 cup halved glazed maraschino cherries
3 eggs
1 cup sugar

OVEN 350°

Mix all ingredients together until moist. Mixture will be thick. Put in greased and floured bread pan. Bake at 350° until done, approximately 1 hour.

Chess Bread

½ cup margarine
1 box (1 pound) light brown sugar
3 eggs, well beaten
1 teaspoon vanilla
2 cups self-rising flour, sifted
1 cup chopped nuts (pecans or walnuts)
½ cup chocolate chips (optional)

OVEN 300°

Cream margarine; add sugar, eggs, vanilla, and flour. Add nuts. Pour into 8x12-inch greased baking dish. Bake at 300° for 40 minutes.

Hawaiian Bread

1¼ cups pre-sifted plain flour
1 cup sugar
½ teaspoon salt
1 teaspoon baking soda
½ cup corn oil margarine
3 small ripe bananas, mashed
2 eggs, well beaten

OVEN 350°

Mix together flour, sugar, salt, and baking soda. Using pastry cutter, cut margarine into flour mixture until like cornmeal. Add bananas and eggs. Stir well and pour into 8x8-inch pan sprayed with cooking spray. Bake at 350° for 35 minutes until bread begins to pull away from side of pan. Cool. Cut into 3 loaves. Freezes well.

Variation: Add ¼ cup chopped maraschino cherries and ½ teaspoon almond extract. Add nuts if desired.

Homemade Bread

2 tablespoons yeast (2 packages)
½ teaspoon ginger
3 cups warm water
7 cups flour, whole wheat and unbleached
¼ cup gluten flour
½ cup oil
½ cup honey
2 tablespoons lecithin
2 teaspoons salt

OVEN 250° to 350°

Mix yeast and ginger in water and stir. Add all flour; stir. Let sit 15 minutes. Add remaining ingredients. Stir. Heat just over 1 minute at 250° then turn off. Place dough on lightly floured surface. Knead 7 minutes. Add flour as needed. Place dough in oiled oven-safe bowl. Spray top of dough with cooking spray and cover with towel. Put in oven. Let rise 45 to 60 minutes. Cut and separate dough into 3 equal parts. Roll out then roll into loaf. Tuck ends under and place in loaf pans. Place all 3 pans in oven to rise 30 to 60 minutes, 2 inches above pan. Bake at 350° for 15 to 20 minutes then cover tops with foil and continue baking at 300° for 20 to 25 minutes. Place on cooling racks. Brush lightly with melted butter and cover, for soft crust. Place in plastic bags or wrap and freeze.

Makes 3 loaves.

Banana Nut Bread

⅔ cup sugar
½ cup soft shortening
2 eggs
3 tablespoons sour milk
1 cup very ripe mashed bananas
2 cups sifted flour
1 teaspoon baking powder
½ teaspoon baking soda
½ teaspoon salt
½ cup chopped nuts

OVEN 350°

Mix together sugar, shortening, and eggs. Stir in milk and bananas. Sift together flour, baking powder, baking soda, and salt; stir into other mixture. Blend in nuts. Pour into well-greased loaf pan. Let stand 20 minutes before baking. Bake at 350° for 50 to 60 minutes. Double recipe for two loaves. This bread is very moist.

Country Fair Egg Bread

1½ cups scalded milk
½ cup butter
½ cup sugar
2 (¼ ounce) packages yeast
½ cup lukewarm water
2 eggs, beaten
9 cups sifted flour (approximately)

OVEN 350° to 425°

Pour scalded milk over butter and sugar. Cool. Dissolve yeast in lukewarm water and let stand until it bubbles, about 5 minutes. Add yeast and beaten eggs to cooled milk mixture. Gradually add flour, beating in thoroughly. Do not add any more flour than is necessary to make an easily handled dough, as bread should be light and tender.

Turn out onto floured board and knead until smooth and elastic. Place in greased bowl, cover, and let rise until doubled in size (about 1½ hours). Punch down and turn out onto lightly floured board. Shape into 3 loaves and place in greased 8-inch loaf pans. Cover and let rise until dough is just to tops of pans. Bake in 425° oven for 10 minutes, then lower heat to 350° and bake 40 minutes longer, or until bread is done.

Makes 3 loaves.

Banana Nut Pudding Bread

1 package banana cake mix
1 package banana instant pudding mix (or vanilla)
½ cup vegetable oil
1 cup water
4 eggs
2 bananas, mashed
Chopped nuts

OVEN 350°

Blend all ingredients in large bowl. Bake at 350° in loaf pan about 30 minutes.

Sour Cream Nut Bread

2½ cups buttermilk biscuit mix
⅔ cup sugar
1 cup chopped nuts
1 cup sour cream
⅓ cup milk
2 eggs, lightly beaten
1 teaspoon vanilla

OVEN 350°

Preheat oven to 350°. Grease bottom of loaf pan. In large bowl, combine biscuit mix, sugar, and nuts. Stir in sour cream, milk, eggs, and vanilla, blending well. Pour into prepared pan. Bake for 50 to 55 minutes. Cool in pan 10 minutes. Remove from pan; cool on wire rack.

Irish Brown Bread

1¾ cups flour (whole wheat, or half white and half whole wheat)
1 cup oats (or ⅓ cup bran; ⅓ cup cracked wheat; ⅓ cup wheat germ)
½ cup brown sugar plus 1 tablespoon molasses
½ teaspoon baking soda
1 teaspoon salt
5½ tablespoons margarine (or butter)
1 egg, beaten
Buttermilk or regular milk
Raisins (optional)

OVEN 400°

Mix dry ingredients. Rub in margarine. Mix in egg and enough milk to make stiff, not liquid, dough. Spoon into greased loaf pans (one regular size or two small) and bake uncovered for 45 minutes at 400°. The small loaf pans turn out nice loaves with lots of crust. Great for parties and holiday meals. Serve with butter, sharp cheddar cheese, and lots of strong, hot Irish tea.

Julekage (Christmas Bread)

1 cup milk (¾ cup milk and ¼ cup water if dry yeast is used instead of cake yeast)
2 cakes or 2 (¼ ounce) packages yeast
½ cup sugar
2 eggs, slightly beaten
1 teaspoon salt
6 cardamom seeds, ground
4 cups flour, divided
⅛ pound butter
⅔ package candied fruit
Dark raisins
Golden raisins

FROSTING:
3 cups powdered sugar
⅓ cup butter, softened
1½ teaspoons almond flavoring
2 tablespoons milk

OVEN 350°

Scald and cool milk. When milk is lukewarm, dissolve yeast in milk. Mix in sugar, eggs, salt, cardamom, and 2 cups flour. Melt butter and add to mixture. Mix well. Add remaining flour, but keep dough "sticky." Mix in candied fruit and a good handful each of dark and golden raisins, packing in as much fruit as mixture will hold. Knead on floured board until smooth. Put into greased bowl to raise. (Dough should rise to twice its original size. Due to fruit, this can take 2 hours or longer.)

After dough is risen, cut dough down with knife while dough is in bowl, instead of punching or kneading. Let rise again, about 45 minutes. Divide dough into two parts and pound down. Shape into loaves and let rise to about twice its size again. Bread can be baked in bread pans or formed into round loaves and baked on greased cookie sheet or in greased pie pan. Bake 30 to 40 minutes at 350°.

Bread may be frosted with powdered sugar frosting while still warm.

Frosting: Cream together sugar and butter. Stir in flavoring and add milk until desired consistency is reached.

Peach Bread

½ cup butter, room temperature
1 cup sugar
2 eggs
1 teaspoon vanilla
1 cup mashed peaches (drained well, if canned)
¼ cup sour cream
1¾ cups flour
1 teaspoon baking soda
1 teaspoon baking powder
½ teaspoon salt
½ cup ground almonds

OVEN 350°

Preheat oven to 350°. Grease and flour 8½x5½-inch loaf pan. Cream butter and sugar until fluffy. Add eggs, vanilla, peaches, and sour cream; mix well. Add dry ingredients and mix well. Pour into prepared pan and bake 50 minutes, or until toothpick inserted in center comes out clean.

Strawberry Bread

3 cups flour
1 teaspoon salt
1 teaspoon baking soda
1 tablespoon cinnamon
2 cups sugar
3 eggs, well beaten
1¼ cups oil
2 packages frozen strawberries, thawed and drained
1¼ cups chopped nuts
Red food coloring, if desired

OVEN 350°

Combine dry ingredients. Make well in center. Pour in eggs and oil. Stir until dry ingredients are moistened. Add berries and nuts. Mix well. Pour into lightly greased 8-inch loaf pans and bake at 350° for 60 to 70 minutes.

Makes 2 loaves.

Pineapple Nut Bread

¾ cup sugar
2 eggs
½ cup margarine or shortening
2 cups flour
1 teaspoon baking powder
1 teaspoon baking soda
½ teaspoon nutmeg
½ teaspoon salt
1 teaspoon vanilla
½ cup chopped nuts
1 (16 ounce) can crushed pineapple, drained

OVEN 350°

Mix ingredients in order listed. Stir just until moist. Bake in greased loaf pan at 350° for 35 to 40 minutes. Garnish with chopped maraschino cherries if desired.

Cranberry Apple Bread

2 cups chopped, peeled apples
¾ cup sugar
2 tablespoons oil
1 egg
1½ cups flour
1½ teaspoons baking powder
½ teaspoon baking soda
1 teaspoon cinnamon
1 cup fresh or frozen cranberries
½ cup chopped walnuts

OVEN 350°

Preheat oven to 350°. Grease loaf pan. Combine apples, sugar, and oil in medium bowl. Add egg and mix well. Combine dry ingredients in separate bowl. Add apple mixture, mixing just until dry ingredients are moist. Stir in cranberries and walnuts. Spread batter evenly in loaf pan. Bake for 1 hour or until toothpick inserted in center comes out clean.

No Knead Bread

1½ cups scalded milk
½ cup shortening
½ cup sugar
1 teaspoon salt
1½ cups water
3 (¼ ounce) packages dry yeast
½ teaspoon malt powder
3 eggs
9 cups flour, divided

OVEN 350°

Mix together scalded milk, shortening, sugar, and salt; cool to lukewarm by adding water. Add dry yeast. Stir. Add malt powder, eggs, and 4 cups flour. Mix on low speed until blended; then mix on high for 3 minutes. Work in 5 more cups flour. Shape into loaves to rise—OR—roll out divided dough one-fourth at a time and spread with melted butter, brown sugar, and cinnamon to taste. Roll up and seal with water. Let rise in loaf pans and bake at 350° for 1 hour to 1 hour and 15 minutes.

Becky's Lemon Bread

Lemon peel and pulp from 1 lemon, chopped finely
1 cup sugar
½ cup shortening
2 eggs (or 4 egg whites)
1¼ cups flour
1 teaspoon baking powder
¼ teaspoon salt
½ cup milk
1½ cups chopped nuts

Glaze:
½ cup sugar
Lemon juice

OVEN 350°

Prepare and set aside lemon juice, peel, and pulp. In mixing bowl, cream sugar, shortening, and eggs, one at a time. Mix together flour, baking powder, and salt. Add to egg mixture alternately with milk. When mixture is creamy, add chopped lemon and nuts. Spoon into greased and floured loaf pan. Bake at 350° for 1 hour. While bread is baking, make glaze from lemon juice and sugar. When bread is done, prick holes in top with fork and pour glaze over bread while it's hot.

Hardtack

1½ cups buttermilk
¾ cup oil
1 teaspoon baking soda
½ cup sugar
2 cups quick-cooking oats
3 cups flour
½ teaspoon salt

OVEN 400°

Mix all ingredients together and let stand for 20 minutes or so. Using about 1 cup mixture at a time, roll out very thin. Prick with fork or roll with spiked rolling pin. Cut into roughly 2x4-inch pieces. Put on greased cookie sheet and bake until light brown. Watch closely.

German Sweet Bread

¼ pound margarine (or butter)
1 cup sugar
2 cups flour (some can be whole wheat flour)
1 cup milk
1 teaspoon baking powder
2 eggs
Cinnamon (optional)

OVEN 350°

Cream together margarine and sugar. Add flour then other ingredients and mix well. Pour into greased bread pan (loaf pan). Bake at 350° for 1 hour. Serve hot or cold.

Grandma's Sweet Bread

1 cup sugar
½ cup margarine
½ cup sour cream
½ cup half-and-half
3 cups flour
1 teaspoon baking soda
1 teaspoon baking powder
1 teaspoon vanilla
Nutmeg

OVEN 375°

Cream sugar and margarine. Add sour cream and half-and-half. Add remaining ingredients; mix well. Chill in refrigerator overnight. Roll in figure eight shapes. Bake on ungreased cookie sheet at 375° until light brown.

Makes 3½ to 4 dozen.

Rosetta's and Laura's Pumpkin Bread

1½ cups sugar
1½ cups flour
1 teaspoon baking powder
1 teaspoon baking soda
1 teaspoon salt
¼ teaspoon cinnamon
Cloves
Nutmeg
2 eggs
½ cup salad oil
½ cup water
1 cup pumpkin
1 tablespoon applesauce
½ cup chopped nuts

OVEN 350°

Sift dry ingredients together. Beat eggs; stir in oil, water, pumpkin, and applesauce. Add this mixture to dry ingredients; mix thoroughly. Add nuts. Bake in greased and floured 9x5x3-inch loaf pan for 1 hour in 350° oven.

Pumpkin Loaf

3 cups sugar
1 cup oil
3 eggs, beaten
2 cups or 1 can pumpkin
3 cups self-rising flour
1 teaspoon nutmeg
1 teaspoon cloves
1 teaspoon cinnamon
½ teaspoon salt

OVEN 350°

Blend sugar and oil; add beaten eggs. Add pumpkin then dry ingredients. Pour into two greased loaf pans. Bake at 350° for 1 hour to 1 hour and 15 minutes.

Pumpkin Roll

3 eggs
1 cup sugar
⅔ cup pumpkin
Lemon juice
¾ cup flour
1 teaspoon baking powder
2 teaspoons cinnamon
1 teaspoon ginger
½ teaspoon nutmeg
½ teaspoon salt
1 cup chopped nuts

Filling:
1 cup sifted powdered sugar
8 ounces cream cheese, softened
4 tablespoons butter, softened
½ teaspoon vanilla

OVEN 375°

Beat eggs on high speed. Blend in sugar, pumpkin, and lemon juice. Stir in dry ingredients. Spread on waxed paper–lined cookie sheet. Top with nuts and bake at 375° for 15 minutes.

Heavily dust clean dish towel with powdered sugar, peel off waxed paper from pumpkin roll, and roll it and towel up together like cinnamon roll. Allow to cool for 1 to 1½ hours. Blend filling ingredients until smooth. Unroll towel and roll; spread filling evenly over flat surface. Then re-roll without towel. Should resemble jelly roll. The powdered sugar coating makes it very attractive.

Pumpkin Nut Bread

4 eggs
1 cup water
3 cups flour
1 teaspoon ground cloves
½ teaspoon baking powder
1 cup chopped pecans
1 cup cooked pumpkin
3 cups sugar
½ teaspoon salt
1 teaspoon cinnamon
2 teaspoons baking soda

OVEN 325°

Mix all ingredients together. Pour into bread pans; bake at 325° for 45 minutes to 1 hour.

Pumpkin Bread

2⅔ cups sugar
⅔ cup shortening
4 eggs
2 cups canned pumpkin
⅔ cup water
3⅓ cups flour
2 teaspoons baking soda
1½ teaspoons salt
½ teaspoon baking powder
1 teaspoon cinnamon
1 teaspoon cloves
⅔ cup coarsely chopped nuts
⅔ cup raisins

OVEN 350°

Preheat oven to 350°. Grease bottoms of two 9x5x3-inch loaf pans, or three small loaf pans. Mix sugar and shortening in large bowl. Mix in eggs, pumpkin, and water. Blend in flour, baking soda, salt, baking powder, cinnamon, and cloves. Stir in nuts and raisins. Pour into pans. Bake about 1 hour and 10 minutes, or until done.

Zucchini Bread

3 eggs
2 tablespoons vanilla
1 cup salad oil
2 cups sugar
3 cups shredded zucchini
3 cups flour
½ tablespoon baking powder
1 teaspoon salt
1 teaspoon baking soda
1 teaspoon cinnamon

OVEN 350°

Mix together, eggs, vanilla, oil, sugar, and zucchini. Add flour, baking powder, salt, baking soda, and cinnamon. Blend well. Pour into two greased loaf pans. Bake at 350° for 1 hour, or until toothpick inserted in center comes out clean.

Zucchini Bread

3 eggs
2 cups sugar
1 cup oil
2 cups grated zucchini
2 teaspoons vanilla
3 cups flour
1 teaspoon salt
1 teaspoon baking soda
¼ teaspoon baking powder
3 teaspoons cinnamon
1 cup coarsely chopped walnuts or raisins

OVEN 350°

Beat eggs until light and fluffy. Add sugar, oil, zucchini, and vanilla.
Mix lightly but well. Combine dry ingredients in separate bowl; add to egg and zucchini mixture. Stir until well blended. Stir in nuts or raisins. Pour into two greased and floured 9x5-inch bread pans. Bake for 60 minutes or until toothpick inserted in center comes out clean. Cool on racks slightly before removing from pans.

Zucchini Bread with Peanut Butter

3 eggs
2½ cups sugar
1 cup oil
½ cup peanut butter
3 cups flour
3 teaspoons cinnamon
1 teaspoon salt
1 teaspoon baking soda
1 teaspoon baking powder
3 teaspoons vanilla
2 cups grated zucchini
1 cup chopped nuts

OVEN 350°

Combine ingredients. Bake at 350° for 50 to 60 minutes. Can be baked as bread or as muffins.

Zucchini Pineapple Bread

3 eggs
1 cup oil
1 to 2 cups sugar
2 teaspoons vanilla
3 cups flour
2 teaspoons baking soda
1 teaspoon salt
¼ to ½ teaspoon baking powder
1½ teaspoons cinnamon
¾ teaspoon nutmeg
2 cups shredded zucchini
1 cup (8¼ ounce can) crushed pineapple, well drained
1 cup raisins or currants
1 cup chopped nuts

OVEN 325°

Do not preheat oven. In large mixing bowl, beat eggs, oil, sugar, and vanilla until thick. Sift flour, baking soda, salt, baking powder, and spices together and stir into first mixture. Stir in remaining ingredients. Pour into two greased and floured 5x9-inch loaf pans and bake at 325° for 1 hour, or 45 minutes for small loaf pans, or until toothpick comes out clean. When completely cooled, wrap in foil. Keep in refrigerator, or freeze.

Makes 2 loaves.

Dark Zucchini Bread

3 eggs
1 cup vegetable oil
1½ cups sugar
2 cups grated zucchini
2 teaspoons vanilla
2 cups flour
¼ teaspoon baking powder
3 teaspoons cinnamon
1 teaspoon salt
2 teaspoons baking soda
1 cup chopped nuts

OVEN 350°

Stir together all ingredients. Pour into small loaf pans and bake at 350° for 20 to 30 minutes.

Lena's Corn Bread

⅔ cup cornmeal
1⅓ cups flour
⅓ cup sugar
1 teaspoon salt
4 teaspoons baking powder
1 cup milk
1 egg
¼ cup oil

OVEN 375°

Combine dry ingredients. In mixing bowl, mix milk, egg, and oil. Stir dry ingredients into liquids. Bake at 375° for about 15 minutes if making muffins. Can also pour into square cake pan and bake about 25 minutes.

Broccoli Corn Bread

1 box corn bread mix
3 eggs, beaten
1 onion, diced
1 cup cottage cheese
1 (10 ounce) package taco cheese
½ cup butter, melted
1 box frozen chopped broccoli

OVEN 350°

Mix all ingredients together. Put in 9x13-inch pan. Bake at 350° for 45 minutes. Delicious served with soup or salad.

Jalapeño Corn Bread

3 cups corn bread mix
½ cup vegetable oil
1 large onion, grated
1½ cups grated cheddar cheese
2 cups whole or evaporated milk
3 eggs
1 cup canned cream-style corn
½ cup chopped jalapeño peppers (may be omitted)
1 (3½ ounce) jar pimentos, chopped

OVEN 400°

Preheat oven to 400°. Mix all ingredients well. Pour into greased 9x13-inch pan. Bake until brown, about 45 minutes.

Yield: 24 squares.

Mexican Corn Bread

1 cup cornmeal
¼ cup sugar
1 teaspoon salt
1 cup flour
1 egg
1 cup milk
¼ cup vegetable oil
1 can cream-style corn
1 cup cottage cheese
1 (4 ounce) can diced green chilies
½ pound grated longhorn cheese

OVEN 450°

Combine dry ingredients; add egg, milk, oil, corn, and cottage cheese. Stir lightly and pour half of batter into well-greased 9x13-inch pan. Layer green chilies and cheese on top of batter. Add rest of batter and bake at 450° for 20 to 25 minutes.

Sopapillas (Fry Bread)

4 cups flour
1 teaspoon salt
4 teaspoons baking powder
2 tablespoons shortening
1½ cups water (approximately)
Vegetable oil for frying

Mix flour, salt, and baking powder. Work shortening into flour mixture, add enough water to make soft dough (not sticky). Knead well; let stand 30 minutes. Halve dough; roll out until ⅛-inch thick. Cut into 3-inch squares. Fry at 365°. When grease is hot, drop in squares and hold or keep dunking until square puffs up. Fry until golden brown then turn over and fry other side. Serve with honey or shake in cinnamon and sugar until coated. Just great served with pinto beans and Mexican food.

Navajo Fry Bread

2 cups flour
2 teaspoons baking powder
½ teaspoon salt
½ cup powdered milk
Warm water
½ inch melted lard or shortening

Sift together flour, baking powder, and salt. Blend in powdered milk. Add enough warm water to make soft dough. Knead until dough is not sticky. Cover and let stand for 1 hour. Pinch off handful of dough and roll into circle ½- to ¼-inch thick. Fry in lard or shortening in heavy skillet. Brown both sides. Should brown quickly. Drain on paper towels.

May be served plain or with honey, or roll hot dog in circle of dough to cook in skillet. Recipe may be doubled.

Grandma's Popovers

1½ cups flour
1½ cups milk
¾ teaspoon salt
3 eggs
6 tablespoons butter, margarine, or drippings

OVEN 450°

Combine ingredients in blender. Mix on high until smooth and creamy. Pour into oven-safe glass custard cups filled half full or muffin tins preheated with about ½ tablespoon butter or margarine, or drippings from roast beef. Bake at 450° for 15 minutes. Reduce heat to 350°; bake until "popped" high and golden brown. May be pricked with fork to let steam escape and returned briefly to oven.

Yield: 12 popovers.

Blueberry Muffins

2 cups flour
½ cup sugar
3 teaspoons baking powder
1 egg, slightly beaten
1 cup milk
⅓ cup vegetable oil
1 cup blueberries

OVEN 350°

Mix flour, sugar, and baking powder. In separate bowl, beat egg; add milk and oil; mix with fork. Make well in flour mixture and pour in milk and oil mixture. Stir well. Add blueberries. Spoon batter into greased muffin tins or, for easier cleanup, use paper muffin cups. Sprinkle with sugar. Bake at 350° until golden. Serve with butter.

Makes 12 large muffins.

Yeast Biscuits

1 (¼ ounce) package yeast
1 cup hot water (115°)
2 tablespoons oil
1 tablespoon honey
1 teaspoon salt
2¼ cups flour

OVEN 350°

Preheat oven to 350°. Dissolve yeast in water. Add all other ingredients. Mix well. Make into biscuits. Let rise until double. Bake 30 minutes.

Balloon Biscuits

½ cup sugar
¼ cup cinnamon
2 packages (10 each) refrigerated biscuits
20 large marshmallows
4 tablespoons butter, melted

OVEN 425°

Spray large baking sheet with nonstick vegetable oil spray. Mix sugar and cinnamon in small bowl. Roll or pat each biscuit to enclose marshmallow. Pinch to seal; coat with butter then with sugar. Place seam down on baking sheet. Bake on middle rack of oven at 425° for 8 to 10 minutes until golden brown. When done, marshmallows will have disappeared, leaving sweet hollow shell.

Variation: Use chunks of banana instead. The bottom will be sticky, chewy, and yummy!

Favorite Biscuits

2 cups flour
1 tablespoon baking powder
½ teaspoon salt (optional)
1 tablespoon honey (optional)
4 tablespoons margarine
1 cup yogurt (plain)

OVEN 450°

Combine dry ingredients. Add honey if desired. Cut up margarine. Use fork to chop and combine thoroughly. Add yogurt. Knead and pat out on floured board. Cut and bake in 450° oven for 10 minutes.

Rich Muffins

2 cups flour
½ cup sugar
1 tablespoon baking powder
½ teaspoon salt
2 eggs, beaten
½ cup oil
½ cup milk

OVEN 400°

Sift flour with sugar, baking powder, and salt into mixing bowl. Combine eggs, oil, and milk in separate bowl. Make well in center of dry ingredients. Add liquids all at once. Mix only until dry ingredients are moist. Fill well-greased muffin tins ⅔ full. Bake at 400° for 15 to 20 minutes or until golden brown.

Makes 12.

Corn Muffins

1½ cups cornmeal
½ cup flour
2 tablespoons sugar
2 teaspoons baking powder
½ teaspoon baking soda
½ teaspoon salt
1¼ cups buttermilk
¼ cup unsweetened applesauce
2 egg whites
2 tablespoons vegetable oil

OVEN 400°

In large bowl combine first six ingredients. Combine milk, applesauce, egg whites, and oil. Stir into dry ingredients just to moisten well. Fill greased muffin cups ⅔ full. Bake at 400° for 18 to 20 minutes. Cool in pan 8 to 10 minutes.

Whole Wheat Banana Muffins

⅓ cup oil
½ cup honey
3 extra-ripe bananas
2 eggs, beaten
¼ cup hot water
1¾ cups whole wheat flour
½ teaspoon salt
1 teaspoon baking soda
½ cup nuts or raisins, or both (optional)

OVEN 350°

Beat oil, honey, bananas, and eggs; add water. Mix in dry ingredients. Bake at 350° for 20 minutes in muffin tins. Use cupcake liners to avoid extra cleanup!

Applesauce Muffins

1 cup margarine, softened
2 eggs
2 cups applesauce
1 teaspoon vanilla
4 cups flour
2 cups sugar
2 teaspoons baking soda
3 teaspoons cinnamon
1 teaspoon ground cloves
2 teaspoons allspice

OVEN 375°

Mix softened margarine with eggs. Add applesauce, vanilla, and dry ingredients to this. Bake in muffin tins at 375° until brown, 10 to 15 minutes. Can keep batter in refrigerator two weeks.

Makes 4 to 5 dozen.

Variation: Nuts and raisins can be added just before baking.

Aebleskiver (Danish Apple Pancake Muffins)

2 eggs, separated
2 tablespoons sugar
2 cups milk
2 cups flour
2 teaspoons baking powder
¼ teaspoon salt
¼ cup melted butter
1 apple, diced

Beat egg yolks. Add sugar and milk. Sift together flour, baking powder, and salt. Add to egg mixture. Stir in melted butter. Fold stiffly-beaten egg whites into batter, leaving it lumpy. Don't stir batter after adding egg whites. Heat monk's pan, or a heavy-duty muffin pan with deep wells, with 1 teaspoon butter in each muffin cup. When butter is bubbling, add batter. When outside of batter is crusty, add a cube of apple; use something sharp to flip each aebleskiver. Done when brown on both sides. Serve with butter and syrup.

Pumpkin Muffins

1¼ cups sugar
1¼ cups pumpkin
½ cup margarine, melted
2 eggs
1½ cups flour
2 teaspoons baking powder
1 teaspoon cinnamon
¼ teaspoon ground nutmeg
¼ teaspoon salt
1 cup milk
½ cup raisins
¼ cup chopped pecans or walnuts

OVEN 400°

Combine sugar, pumpkin, and margarine. Blend in eggs. Combine dry ingredients and add alternately with milk, mixing well after each addition. Stir in raisins and nuts. Spoon into well-greased miniature muffin cups. Pour filling ⅔ full. Sprinkle with combined 2 tablespoons sugar and ¼ teaspoon cinnamon. Bake for 25 minutes.

Makes approximately 5 dozen.

Sweet Blueberry Muffins

1½ cups flour
½ cup sugar
2 teaspoons baking powder
½ teaspoon salt
¼ cup vegetable oil
1 egg
½ cup milk
¾ cup blueberries

OVEN 400°

With electric mixer, mix all ingredients except berries thoroughly. Stir in berries. Bake in greased muffin tins at 400° for 25 minutes.

Banana Chocolate Chip Muffins

⅔ cup sugar
1 tablespoon baking powder
½ teaspoon salt
2 cups flour
⅓ cup butter, melted
1 egg, beaten
1 cup milk
2 or 3 bananas, chopped
1 cup mini chocolate chips

OVEN 375°

Sift together dry ingredients. Stir in butter, egg, and milk until blended. Fold in bananas and chocolate chips. Spoon into greased or paper-lined muffin tins. Bake at 375° for 15 to 20 minutes.

Yield: 1 to 1½ dozen.

Cherry Chocolate Chip Muffins

2 cups flour
½ cup sugar
1 teaspoon baking soda
½ teaspoon cinnamon
¾ cup vegetable oil
2 eggs
2 teaspoons vanilla
1 (20 ounce) can cherry pie filling
½ cup milk chocolate chips
⅓ cup chopped nuts

OVEN 350°

Combine all ingredients; fill muffin cups a little over half full. Bake at 350° for 30 minutes.

Makes about 20 muffins.

Cornmeal Rolls

⅓ cup cornmeal
½ teaspoon salt
¼ cup sugar
2 cups milk
½ cup butter or margarine
1 (¼ ounce) package dry yeast
⅓ cup water
2 eggs, beaten
4 cups flour
Melted butter

OVEN 350°

Mix cornmeal, salt, sugar, and milk. Cook until slightly thick. Remove from heat; add butter or margarine and cool. Dissolve yeast in warm water. Add to mixture. Add eggs and flour a little at a time. Turn out onto floured board and knead. Let rise until double. Pan to preference. Bake at 350° about 15 minutes, or until golden brown. Dip in butter.

Stoneground Cornmeal Rolls

⅓ cup stoneground cornmeal
½ cup sugar
2 teaspoons salt
½ cup shortening
2 cups milk
1 (¼ ounce) package active dry yeast
¼ cup warm water
2 eggs, beaten
4 cups flour
Melted butter

OVEN 375°

Cook cornmeal, sugar, salt, shortening, and milk in medium saucepan until as thick as cooked cereal. Cool to lukewarm. Add yeast dissolved in lukewarm water, then eggs. Beat. Add flour to form dough. Knead. Place in covered bowl and let rise 1 hour. Punch down. Knead. Roll and cut out biscuits. Sprinkle butter and cornmeal on top. Bake at 375° for 15 minutes.

Feather Rolls

1½ cups warm water
¼ cup sugar
½ cup mashed potatoes (hot)
⅓ cup oil
1 teaspoon salt
1 tablespoon instant yeast
4½ to 5 cups bread flour, divided

OVEN 350°

In large bowl mix water, sugar, potatoes, oil, salt, yeast, and 2 cups flour. Add remaining flour and stir by hand. Dough should be a little bit sticky. Cover and put in refrigerator overnight. Three hours before serving, take out of refrigerator with oiled hands; form into 20 to 24 small rolls. Place on greased cookie sheet. Let rise until doubled. Bake at 350° until golden, 15 to 20 minutes. Do not overbake. Brush tops with margarine. Very fluffy and light rolls.

Perfect Sunday Dinner Rolls

½ cup sugar
1 (¼ ounce) package dry yeast, dissolved in ¼ cup warm water
2 eggs
1 cup warm water
½ cup oil
1 teaspoon salt
4 cups flour

OVEN 375°

Add sugar to yeast and water. Beat eggs in warm water; add oil and salt. Add to yeast and sugar mixture. Gradually add flour. This will be a sticky dough and will rise at least twice its size, so use a large bowl. Let stand overnight and make out dough in the morning by dividing in 4 parts. Roll out each part onto floured surface to make circle. Cut like pizza and roll from large end to small. Place on greased pan; let stand until you return home from church. Bake at 375° for 8 minutes.

No Knead Refrigerator Rolls

2 (¼ ounce) packages active dry yeast
2 cups warm water (110° to 115°)
½ cup sugar
2 teaspoons salt
6½ to 7 cups flour
1 egg
¼ cup soft shortening or oil

OVEN 400°

Dissolve yeast in water. Add sugar, salt, and half of flour to yeast. Beat egg with shortening and remaining flour until smooth. Add to yeast mixture. Cover and place in refrigerator at least 2 hours. Two hours before baking, cut off amount needed and shape into rolls. Place on greased baking sheet. Let rise 1½ to 2 hours. Heat oven to 400°. Bake 12 to 15 minutes. Dough will keep in refrigerator for 5 days.

Scones

1½ teaspoons baking powder
1½ teaspoons salt
½ teaspoon ground ginger
2 cups flour (plus extra for dusting)
½ cup sugar
¾ cup unsalted butter, cut into small pieces
1 cup sultanas (golden raisins) or any dried fruit, such as cherries, cranberries, or diced apricot
2 large eggs, beaten
3 to 4 teaspoons milk

Sift dry ingredients in bowl and stir in sugar. Rub in butter until mixture is like fine bread crumbs. Stir in dried fruit. Add eggs. Stir in just enough milk to make firm but sticky dough. Turn dough onto floured board, sprinkle with flour, and roll to ½-inch thickness. Cut into rounds. Re-roll trimmings and cut more rounds. Brush heavy frying pan with oil and heat over medium heat. Fry scones for about 5 minutes on each side until well browned. Serve warm with butter or preserves. Also good plain. You may store and eat them cold as well.

Cheese Scones

½ cup butter
3 cups flour
5 teaspoons baking powder
¼ teaspoon salt
4 teaspoons sugar
Grated cheddar cheese (approximately 1½ cups)
1¾ cups milk

OVEN 425°

Preheat oven to 425°. Blend butter into dry ingredients; add cheese and stir with fork. Add milk. Scoop onto baking sheet with greased ice-cream scoop. Bake approximately 15 minutes.

Caramel Rolls

2 teaspoons cinnamon
½ cup sugar
4 cans refrigerator biscuits
½ cup ice cream
½ cup brown sugar
½ cup margarine

OVEN 350°

Cut biscuits in half and roll in cinnamon and sugar. Put in 9x13-inch pan sprayed with cooking spray; combine rest of ingredients and microwave until melted. Pour over biscuits and bake at 350° for 25 to 30 minutes or until brown. Invert on large pan and enjoy!

Quick Mix Cinnamon Rolls

2¼ cups prepared baking mix
⅔ cup milk
2 teaspoons cinnamon
1 cup sugar

OVEN 450°

Heat oven to 450°. Stir ingredients until soft dough forms. Turn onto surface dusted with baking mix. Knead 10 times. Roll dough ½-inch thick. Butter surface entirely. Sprinkle cinnamon and sugar mixture onto buttered dough. Starting with dough closest to you, roll into long tube. Seal with water. Cut into 1 dozen rolls. Bake 10 minutes on ungreased cookie sheet.

Easy Cinnamon Rolls

1 package yellow cake mix
5 cups flour
3 (¼ ounce) packages yeast
2½ cups warm water
Butter, melted
Sugar and cinnamon

OVEN 350°

Mix cake mix and flour in large bowl. Dissolve yeast in warm water and add to flour mixture. Mix well. Place in large greased bowl and let rise until doubled. Punch down and divide in half. Roll out on floured board in rectangle shape to ¼-inch thickness. Brush with melted butter then sprinkle with sugar and cinnamon. (Optional: add chopped nuts and coconut.) Roll up and seal; cut into 1-inch rolls. Put on ungreased cookie sheet or baking dish. Cover and let rise again until double. Bake in 350° oven for approximately 15 to 20 minutes. Let cool slightly and frost with icing.

Icing:
1 pound powdered sugar
Milk
½ teaspoon vanilla

Mix powdered sugar with small amount of milk, just to make spreadable. Add vanilla. Spread on top of rolls while still warm.

Mayonnaise Rolls

2 cups self-rising flour
1 cup milk
4 tablespoons mayonnaise

OVEN 400°

Stir all ingredients together. Fill muffin cups about ¾ full and bake at 400° for 20 minutes.

Makes 1 dozen.

Variation: Add garlic and cheese or herbs.

Holiday Buns

4 cups warm water
1 cup sugar
1 (¼ ounce) package yeast
1 egg
3 teaspoons salt
1 cup oil
10 cups flour

OVEN 350°

Combine water, sugar, and yeast. Let stand 10 minutes, covered. Mix in remaining ingredients and let rise until doubled. Put in baking pans, for round rolls. Bake at 350° for 20 minutes.

Variation: For raisin bread, add 1 cup raisins and 2 teaspoons cinnamon.

Pineapple Sweet Rolls

1 (¼ ounce) package yeast
2 tablespoons warm water
1 cup milk
½ cup sugar
1½ teaspoons salt
¼ cup shortening
1 egg, beaten
3½ cups flour

Filling:
1 can crushed pineapple
½ cup brown sugar
¼ teaspoon cinnamon
4 teaspoons cornstarch
1 tablespoon butter
1 cup toasted, grated coconut

OVEN 350°

Dissolve yeast in warm water. Heat milk to boil. Remove from heat. Add sugar, salt, and shortening, stirring well. Let cool. Add dissolved yeast, beaten egg, and flour, beating well. Knead dough lightly. Let rise in warm place for 1 hour. Roll out into rectangle. Spread with pineapple filling.

Filling: Combine pineapple, brown sugar, cinnamon, and cornstarch; heat until thick and clear. Remove from heat and add butter and coconut. Let filling cool before spreading over dough. After filling is spread over dough, roll up. Slice; place slices in greased pan. Let rise for 1 hour. Bake at 350° for 20 minutes.

Makes 18 to 20 rolls.

Appetizers

Chicken Fingers

3 cups cornflakes
½ teaspoon poultry seasoning
¼ teaspoon ground black pepper
3 tablespoons fat-free egg substitute
3 tablespoons skim milk
1 pound boneless skinless chicken breasts
Nonstick cooking spray

OVEN 400°

Place cornflakes in food processor and process into crumbs. Combine cornflake crumbs, poultry seasoning, and pepper. Stir to mix well; set aside. Combine egg substitute and skim milk in dish. Mix well and set aside. Cut chicken breasts into strips. Dip in egg mixture first and then in cornflake mixture. Coat large baking sheet with nonstick cooking spray. Spray strips lightly with cooking spray. Bake at 400° for 15 minutes.

Barbecue Beef Cups

¾ cup chopped beef
1 teaspoon onion flakes or fresh onion
½ cup barbecue sauce
1 can refrigerator biscuits (10 count)
¼ cup shredded cheddar cheese

OVEN 400°

In large skillet, brown beef; drain excess grease. Add onion flakes and sauce. Separate biscuits and place in ungreased cups of muffin pan. Press each biscuit in middle to form a cup. Spoon a drop of beef mixture into each biscuit cup and top with cheese. Bake in 400° oven for 8 to 10 minutes.

Deviled Eggs

14 hard-cooked eggs
¾ cup low-fat or fat-free mayonnaise or salad dressing
4 packets sugar substitute sweetener
½ teaspoon vinegar
½ teaspoon mustard
¼ teaspoon salt
Paprika

When eggs are cool, cut in half lengthwise. Mix yolks with all other ingredients except paprika. Fill egg whites with mixture. Sprinkle yolk filling with paprika.

Bologna Sandwhich Spread

1 pound bologna (or ham)
2 hard-cooked eggs
½ cup Colby cheese (optional)
½ cup pickle relish
½ cup mayonnaise or salad dressing
2 teaspoons mustard

Grind together bologna, eggs, and cheese. When everything is finely ground, mix in relish, salad dressing, and mustard. Serve chilled on your favorite bread.

Pizza Pinwheels

2 (10 ounce) packages refrigerator pizza dough
½ cup bottled pizza sauce
2 ounces shredded mozzarella cheese (about ½ cup)
4 cherry tomatoes, halved
1 egg yolk

OVEN 425°

Preheat oven to 425°. Lightly oil 1 or 2 baking sheets. On lightly floured surface, unroll each package of dough, forming two squares. Cut each square into 4 smaller squares; transfer to baking sheets. Spread pizza sauce evenly over squares to within ½ inch of edges. Starting from corners of squares, cut toward middle of dough; stop ½ inch from center. Fold every other point into center; press to secure. Over each pinwheel center sprinkle 1 tablespoon cheese and top with tomato half. Combine egg yolk with 1 tablespoon water; brush over dough. Bake 12 to 15 minutes, until crust is golden and cheese bubbles.

Tequitas

3 to 6 pounds extra-lean ground beef
1 package French's Chili-O mix
1 package Williams chili mix
1 family-size can tomato sauce
8 ounces Velveeta cheese
Approximately 12 dozen corn tortillas (depends how much meat is in each tequita)

Brown ground beef. Add chili mixes and tomato sauce. Simmer 20 to 30 minutes. Add chunks of cheese; stir until melted. Turn off heat. Heat tortillas by placing them (one or two at a time) in hot vegetable oil, turn, and remove immediately; drain on paper towels. Roll meat mixture in tortilla and fasten with toothpick. Store in freezer until ready to cook; then drop frozen tequitas in deep oil and cook until crispy. Serve with a side of taco sauce or salsa to dip tequitas in.

White Toruntila Roll

8 ounces cream cheese, softened
1 (4 ounce) can mild chopped green chilies
Very thinly sliced ham, turkey, or other meat, chopped very fine to resemble deviled meat consistency
Picante sauce or pimientos to taste
4 white flour tortillas, burrito size

Mix cream cheese, chilies, chopped meat, picante, and/or pimiento well. Spread filling to about ½ inch of edge of tortillas. Roll tortillas and wrap in plastic wrap. Chill well. Slice in ½-inch slices and serve. (Best when chilled overnight.)

Mexican Hors D'oeuvres

8 ounces cream cheese, softened
1 ripe avocado, mashed
1 tablespoon lemon juice
2 tablespoons mayonnaise
½ cup sour cream

Topping suggestions:
Finely chopped green onions
Shredded lettuce
Chopped tomatoes
Sliced green olives
Shredded cheddar cheese

Mix together until smooth. Spread on large plate or tray; chill. Add toppings of your choice. Sprinkle with chili powder. Serve with tortilla chips.

Stuffed Mushrooms

½ cup butter, melted
¾ cup Italian-style bread crumbs
¼ cup grated Parmesan cheese
1 pound fresh mushrooms, washed, stems removed
4 ounces shredded mozzarella cheese

OVEN 375°

Combine butter, bread crumbs, and Parmesan cheese with fork. Stuff each mushroom cap with bread crumb mixture until all is used. Top each cap with mozzarella cheese. Arrange caps on lightly greased baking sheet and bake at 375° until mozzarella is melted and golden. Serve hot.

Stuffed Mushrooms

1 (8 ounce) box large mushrooms
½ cup butter
1 can crabmeat
1½ cups bread crumbs
1 lemon

OVEN 350°

Clean mushrooms. Chop stems into small pieces; sauté in melted butter in saucepan with crabmeat until tender. Remove pan from heat; add bread crumbs. Fill mushroom caps with mixture. Bake at 350° for 10 minutes. Sprinkle with juice of lemon.

Rye Hors D'oeuvres

1 pound sausage
1 pound ground beef
1 pound processed cheese, melted
1 tablespoon oregano
½ teaspoon garlic salt
½ teaspoon Worcestershire sauce
2 packages party-style rye bread

Brown meats and drain on paper towel. Mix all ingredients together (except bread). Spread rye bread slices on cookie sheets. Spread meat mixture on bread and broil until meat mixture is bubbly. Freezes well.

Salmon Puffs

1 small onion, chopped
1 can salmon, deboned
1 (10¾ ounce) can cream of chicken soup
1 egg
¾ cup self-rising cornmeal
¾ cup self-rising flour
Black pepper to taste

Mix all ingredients well. Drop by teaspoonfuls into frying pan with 350° oil. Brown on both sides of puffs. Remove from frying pan and place on platter padded with paper towels to drain.

Serves large number.

Mini Ham Puffs

1 (2½ ounce) package processed ham
1 small onion
½ cup shredded Swiss cheese
1 egg
⅛ teaspoon ground black pepper
1½ teaspoons Dijon mustard
1 (8 ounce) tube refrigerated crescent rolls

OVEN 350°

Preheat oven to 350°. Chop ham and onion finely. Place in bowl and stir in cheese, egg, pepper, and mustard. Spray mini-muffin pan with vegetable oil spray. Unroll crescent rolls and press dough into one large rectangle. Cut rectangle into 24 pieces. Place dough pieces in muffin cups. Use small scoop when filling cups. Bake for 15 minutes, or until lightly browned.

Makes 24 appetizers.

Variation: Mini Ham Squares. Spread crescent roll dough on 13-inch baking stone. Pinch seams to seal. Spread ham mixture on crust and bake at 350° for 20 minutes. Cut into small squares to serve.

Sugar Dogs

3 packages hot dogs, cut in thirds
1 pound bacon, each piece cut in half
2 pounds brown sugar

Wrap piece of hot dog in bacon strip. Secure with toothpick. Put hot dogs in slow cooker. Pour bag of sugar over top. Cook on low until sugar melts. Serve hot.

Mapley Appetizers

16 ounces smoked sausage links
4 teaspoons cornstarch
½ teaspoon salt
1 (13½ ounce) can pineapple chunks, drained (reserve juice)
½ cup maple syrup
⅓ cup water
⅓ cup vinegar
1 large green pepper, cut into small squares
1 jar maraschino cherries, drained

OVEN 250°

Cut sausage into small pieces and brown in skillet. Blend cornstarch, salt, pineapple juice, maple syrup, water, and vinegar. Heat to boiling, stirring constantly. Add pineapple, sausage, green pepper, and cherries. Cook 5 minutes. Keep warm for serving.

Holiday Crackers (Oyster Snack Crackers)

1 package dry ranch dressing mix
¾ to 1 cup salad oil or olive oil
½ to 1 teaspoon dill weed
¼ to ½ teaspoon garlic powder
¼ to ½ teaspoon lemon pepper seasoning
16 ounces plain oyster crackers

Combine ranch dressing mix and oil; add dill weed, garlic powder, and lemon pepper. Pour over crackers; stir well to coat. Place in warm oven for 20 minutes. Stir well halfway through. Place in airtight container. Great with soups or just to eat as a snack!

Salmon Party Ball

1 (16 ounce) can salmon
8 ounces cream cheese, softened
1 tablespoon lemon juice
2 teaspoons grated onion
1 teaspoon prepared horseradish
¼ teaspoon salt
¼ teaspoon liquid smoke
½ cup chopped pecans
3 tablespoons snipped parsley
Assorted crackers

Drain and flake salmon, removing bones and skin. Combine salmon, cheese, lemon juice, onion, horseradish, salt, and liquid smoke; mix. Chill several hours. Combine pecans and parsley. Shape salmon mixture into ball; roll salmon ball in nut mixture. Chill. Serve with assorted crackers. Trim plate with cherry tomatoes and parsley if desired.

Makes 3 cups of spread.

Cheddar Cheese Crackers

1 cup flour
¼ teaspoon cayenne or red pepper
½ teaspoon dry mustard
½ cup margarine, softened
½ pound shredded cheddar cheese (2 cups)
3 tablespoons toasted sesame seeds

OVEN 350°

Preheat oven to 350°. Toast sesame seeds in skillet over low heat. Combine flour, pepper, mustard, margarine, and cheese; work with hands or spoon into stiff dough. Roll into small balls, about 1 tablespoon. Dip balls into sesame seeds. Place on ungreased cookie sheet. Press flat with glass dipped in flour. Bake until light golden brown.

Cheese Ball

2 (8 ounce) packages cream cheese, softened
1 bunch green onions, chopped
1 small can chopped black olives
1 small can prepared ham, crumbled with broth
1 cup chopped pecans
1 (10 ounce) package shredded cheddar cheese

Mix cream cheese in medium-size bowl with onions, black olives, and crumbled ham. Add about half of chopped pecans and shredded cheese. Shape into 2 balls. Pour remainder of pecans and cheese on plate and roll balls in it until covered. Chill and serve with crackers of your choice.

Apricot Cheese Ball

8 ounces cream cheese, softened
⅓ cup apricot preserves
1 to 2 tablespoons chopped chives
2 teaspoons minced dried onions
Dash parsley
Chopped walnuts

Combine all ingredients except nuts. Roll cheese ball in nuts.

Cheese Ball

2 (8 ounce) packages cream cheese, softened
1 cup butter
4 cups grated cheese
2 packages dry ranch mix dressing
Nuts

Mix all together except nuts; shape into balls. Roll in nuts.

Hawaiian Cheese Ball

2 (8 ounce) packages cream cheese, room temperature
½ cup shredded cheddar cheese
1 teaspoon seasoned salt
2 tablespoons finely chopped onion
2 tablespoons finely chopped green pepper
1 (8 ounce) can crushed pineapple, well drained
½ cup chopped pecans

Blend all ingredients except pecans. Shape into balls. Roll balls in pecans. Serve with assorted crackers.

Cheese Ball

8 ounces cream cheese, softened
1 tablespoon milk
2 teaspoons Worcestershire sauce
½ medium onion
1 tablespoon margarine
½ teaspoon garlic salt
Dash salt and pepper
½ pound grated sharp cheddar cheese
Chopped pecans (optional)
Parsley (optional)

Mix all ingredients together and shape into ball. Roll in chopped pecans or parsley.

Party Mix

1 bag Cheetos crunchy corn curls
1 box Cheez-It crackers
1 bag pretzel sticks
1 bag corn chips
1 box fish crackers
1 can cocktail peanuts
1½ cups melted butter
4 tablespoons Worcestershire sauce
1 tablespoon Accent seasoning
1 tablespoon seasoned salt
½ teaspoon celery salt

OVEN 200°

Mix first six ingredients together. In small pan combine butter, Worcestershire sauce, Accent, seasoned salt, and celery salt. Add to dry ingredients. Spread into single layer on cookie sheets. Bake at 200° for 2 hours. Stir every 20 minutes while baking.

Hot Spinach Balls

4 large eggs, beaten
2 (10 ounce) packages frozen chopped spinach (squeeze dry)
1 cup minced onion
¾ cup grated Parmesan or Romano cheese
¾ cup butter or margarine, melted
½ teaspoon thyme
¼ teaspoon nutmeg
¼ teaspoon pepper
½ teaspoon garlic salt
2½ cups herb-seasoned stuffing mix (crumb type)

OVEN 350°

Stir all ingredients, except stuffing, until well blended. Add stuffing mix. Let stand 20 minutes until slightly firm. Shape into balls using rounded teaspoon for each ball. Arrange on ungreased cookie sheet. Bake at 350° for 20 minutes, until lightly browned.

Balls may be cooled, wrapped, and frozen. Reheat on cookie sheet at 350° for approximately 10 minutes.

Makes approximately 112 balls.

Easy Salsa

2 (14 or 16 ounce) cans diced tomatoes
1 (4 ounce) can diced green chilies
1 teaspoon cumin
1 teaspoon seasoned salt
½ teaspoon garlic powder
½ teaspoon lemon or lime juice
½ green bell pepper
½ onion
½ jalapeño pepper
Few sprigs fresh cilantro

Place all ingredients in blender and process quickly until vegetables are chopped. Refrigerate for 2 hours to blend flavors. Serve with tortilla chips.

Granola

6 cups oats
2 cups whole wheat flour
1 teaspoon salt
2 teaspoons cinnamon
½ cup sunflower, pumpkin, or sesame seeds
1 cup ground nuts (optional)
1 teaspoon maple flavoring
1 tablespoon vanilla
1 teaspoon almond extract
1 to 1½ cups fruit juice
¾ cup mashed ripe bananas
½ cup dried fruit (optional)

OVEN 170°

Combine dry ingredients. Combine liquids, then add to dry ingredients. Mix with hands until evenly moistened and crumbly/chunky. Spread in single layer on cookie sheet. Bake at 170° overnight (8 hours). Add fruit during last half hour.

Makes 13 cups.

Salsa

12 cups tomatoes, peeled and chopped
4 large green peppers
2 jalapeño peppers
5 medium yellow onions
2 bunches green onions
2 tablespoons onion salt
2 (10 or 12 ounce) cans tomato paste
1 tablespoon salt
2 tablespoons garlic salt
4 tablespoons lemon juice
⅓ cup brown sugar
1½ cups vinegar
3 tablespoons black pepper

Chop fine; put in large kettle. Boil 20 minutes at medium heat. Pour into hot jars.

Makes 9 to 12 pints.

Taco Dip

8 ounces cream cheese, softened
1 pound hamburger, browned, drained
1 cup salsa
1 (16 ounce) can refried beans
1 cup shredded cheddar cheese
Sliced olives

OVEN 350°

Spread cream cheese in bottom of 9-inch pie pan. Mix browned hamburger with salsa and put on top of cream cheese. Spread beans on top; sprinkle shredded cheese over beans. Top with sliced olives and bake at 350° for 25 minutes. Serve with tortilla chips.

Mexican Dip

8 ounces cream cheese, softened
1 ripe avocado, peeled and mashed
1 tablespoon lemon juice
2 tablespoons mayonnaise
4 ounces sour cream

Toppings:
Green onions, finely chopped
Lettuce
Tomatoes
Shredded cheddar cheese
Green olives, sliced

Blend all ingredients together until smooth; chill. Spread on large plate then layer with suggested toppings. Sprinkle with chili powder to taste. Serve with your favorite corn chips.

Bean-Beef Dip

1 can roast beef in gravy
1 (16 ounce) can refried beans
1 small jar chunky salsa
1 (4 ounce) can diced chilies

Shred roast beef; mix with other ingredients. Heat and serve with tortilla chips.

Bean Dip

8 ounces cream cheese, softened
1 can Hormel chili with no beans
Shredded cheddar cheese

Mix cream cheese with chili. Sprinkle with shredded cheddar and microwave until cheese melts. Serve with tortilla chips.

Creamy Taco Cheese Dip

½ pound ground beef
1 small onion
½ can Rotel diced tomatoes
½ block Velveeta cheese
1 can ranch-style beans
8 ounces sour cream
½ (1¼ ounce) package taco seasoning
1 can pitted black olives

Brown beef and small onion; drain well and set aside. Heat tomatoes until bubbling hot. Add cheese, beans, sour cream, and taco seasoning. When mixture is hot, mix in browned beef, onion, and olives.

Beef Dip

1 cup sour cream
2 (8 ounce) packages cream cheese, cut up
2 (2½ ounce) packages chipped dried beef
2 tablespoons minced onion
4 tablespoons milk
½ cup chopped green pepper
Garlic to taste
Pepper to taste
Crackers of choice
Butter or margarine
Chopped nuts

OVEN 350°

Mix first eight ingredients in blender. Pour into 8x8-inch glass dish. Top with crumbled crackers and nuts coated in margarine or butter. Bake at 350° for 35 minutes.

Holiday Spinach and Artichoke Dip

16 ounces sour cream
1 (14 ounce) can artichokes, drained and chopped
1 (2 ounce) jar diced pimientos, rinsed and drained
2 (10 ounce) packages frozen chopped spinach, thawed and well drained
2 round loaves sourdough bread
1 package ranch dip mix

OVEN 400°

Mix sour cream, artichokes, pimientos, and spinach; set in refrigerator 1 hour. Cut top off bread and clean out inside, being careful not to tear open. Save filling; cut up and toast for dippers. Spoon mix into hollowed bread. Bake at 400° for 20 to 25 minutes. Cover with foil if browning too much. Serve hot or cold. Great next day.

Shrimp Mousse

1 (10¾ ounce) can tomato soup, diluted
2 (8 ounce) packages cream cheese, softened
½ cup mayonnaise
1 (8 ounce) can small shrimp, chopped
3 ounces lemon-flavored gelatin
½ cup hot water
1 cup finely chopped celery
½ cup chopped green (or winter) onions

Heat soup. Whip cream cheese and mayonnaise. Add chopped shrimp and soup to cheese mixture; blend well. Separately dissolve gelatin in hot water. Combine all ingredients and mix well. Chill in 5-cup mold. Serve with favorite dipping vegetables, crackers, and chips.

Fruit 'n' Sauce

2 cans pineapple chunks
2 cans sliced peaches
2 cans mandarin oranges
3 or 4 bananas
1 small box vanilla pudding mix
(not instant)

Drain pineapple, peaches, and oranges, reserving 2 cups juice. Pour juices in pot with pudding mix. Bring to boil and remove from heat. Cool and pour over fruit. Chill.

Refrigerator Pickles

1 cup sugar
1 cup vinegar
1 tablespoon salt
2 cucumbers (approximately)

Mix sugar, vinegar, and salt in pan. Bring to boil. Boil just until sugar and salt are dissolved, about 1 minute. Remove from heat. Cool. Slice cucumbers into thin slices. Put in quart jar. Pour in cooled vinegar solution. Put in refrigerator. The cucumbers will fill jar. The brine might not come to top of jar, but in a few hours the cucumber slices will "wilt" a bit so all will be covered. Tip jar upside down a couple of times during first 3 or 4 hours. Keep refrigerated until gone.

Apple Butter

16 cups cooked apple pulp
1 cup cider vinegar
9 cups sugar
4 cinnamon sticks (approximately
2 inches each)

OVEN 350°

Boil all ingredients in slow cooker until thick, several hours. Or put ingredients in roaster pan and cook in 350° oven. Stir often and be careful as mixture pops very easily.

Cassia Bud Sweet Dills

1 (43 to 46 ounce) jar kosher dill pickles, drained and sliced
2 cups sugar
½ cup vinegar
¼ cup water
1 top cassia buds or ½ crushed cinnamon stick
½ teaspoon pickling spice

Put dill slices in jar or container. Boil sugar, vinegar, and water until clear; watch closely. To pickle slices add cassia buds or cinnamon stick. Then add pickling spice. Pour syrup over pickles. Refrigerate. Pickles will be ready the next day.

Fruit Slush

1 medium can frozen orange juice
½ cup lemon juice
2 cans crushed pineapple, with juice
3 cups water
2 cups sugar
3 to 4 bananas, diced
1 (10 ounce) jar maraschino cherries

Mix together and put in freezer until slushy or freeze and take out and thaw until slushy.

Lime Sherbet Punch

1 (46 ounce) can pineapple juice
1 large bottle ginger ale
1 pint lime sherbet

Pour juice and ginger ale into punch bowl. Add scoops of lime sherbet.

Frozen Slushy

1 can fruit juice (can mix several kinds together)

Pour juice into freezer container and freeze. Take out about half hour before using to allow to thaw. Do not thaw to liquid stage. Thaw until fruit juice is slushy. Serve in small containers, dishes, or 3-ounce paper cups.

Hot Chocolate

1 (1 pound) can Nesquik, or powdered chocolate drink mix
1 pound sugar
1 (8 quart) box powdered sugar
1 (3 to 6 ounce) jar powdered creamer

Stir all ingredients together and store in container. Put 4 heaping teaspoons in 1 cup boiling water.

Fruit Slush with Apricots

1 can frozen orange juice, thawed
6 bananas
1 can apricots
1 can crushed pineapple
1 jar maraschino cherries or 16-ounce package strawberries, juice included

Mix juice (adding no water or sugar), bananas, and apricots in blender. Add remaining ingredients and stir in large bowl. Put in 9-ounce clear plastic cups and freeze. Microwave 15 to 30 seconds to serve. Amounts and ingredients are flexible according to your needs.

1979 Cranberry Tea

1 (1 pound) package cranberries, or 1 quart cranberry juice
3 quarts water, divided
1 cup hot cinnamon candy
½ cup lemon juice
1¼ cups orange juice
2 cups sugar, or sweetened to your taste
10 cloves (whole)

Cook cranberries in 1 quart water until tender; strain and use juice. Add 2 quarts more water. Add other ingredients, heat together, and serve.

Orange Spiced Tea

1 cup powdered orange drink mix
1 heaping cup lemon instant tea (unsweetened)
3 cups sugar (or sugar substitute)
1 teaspoon cinnamon
½ teaspoon nutmeg (can substitute cloves)

Mix all ingredients together. Put 3 heaping teaspoons of mix to one medium mug of hot water (boiling water is best). Use more or less to suit your taste.

English Wassail

3 oranges
Whole cloves
3 quarts apple cider
2 cinnamon sticks (3 inches long)
½ teaspoon nutmeg
½ cup honey
⅓ cup lemon juice
2 teaspoons lemon rind
5 cups pineapple juice

OVEN 325°

Stud oranges with cloves about ½ inch apart. Place in baking pan with a little water; bake at 325° for 30 minutes. Heat cider and cinnamon sticks in large saucepan. Bring to boil. Simmer, covered, 5 minutes. Add remaining ingredients and simmer uncovered, 5 minutes longer. Pour into punch bowl; float spiced oranges on top. Use cinnamon sticks for stirring. Or put in slow cooker on high to keep hot.

Perky Punch

1 small can frozen orange juice
1 small can frozen lemonade
1 package strawberry Kool-Aid
1 package cherry Kool-Aid
1 tall can Hawaiian punch
2 (12 ounce) bottles ginger ale

Prepare orange juice and lemonade according to directions on cans. Add Kool-Aid using half amount of water and all 2 cups sugar required. Add Hawaiian punch. Pour into punch bowl; add ginger ale and ice cubes.

Rhubarb Strawberry Sauce

2 cups water
2 cups diced rhubarb
¾ cup sugar
1 (3 ounce) box wild strawberry–flavored gelatin

Put water, rhubarb, and sugar in saucepan and cook until rhubarb is soft. After rhubarb is boiled, remove from heat and add gelatin. Mix well. Put in bowl and cool. Refrigerate until firm. Serve with dinner.

Serves 8.

Fresh Cranberry Sauce

1 pound fresh cranberries (4 cups)
2 cups water
2 cups sugar

Cook cranberries in water 5 to 10 minutes or until all skins pop open. Strain through fine sieve to remove skins and seeds, pressing pulp through with juice. Stir sugar into pulp; boil about 3 minutes. Refrigerate.

Makes about 1 quart.

Cranberry Relish

2 cups sugar
2 (12 ounce) bags cranberries
1 cup orange juice
1 (16 ounce) can sliced peaches, drained
1 cup crushed walnuts
1 (8 ounce) can crushed pineapple
1 cup golden raisins

Bring sugar, cranberries, and orange juice to boil, stirring constantly. Reduce heat. Simmer uncovered until berries pop open. Remove from heat. Cut up peaches and add with nuts, pineapple, and raisins. Store covered and refrigerated.

Makes 2 quarts.

Squash Relish

12 cups grated squash
5 tablespoons salt
4 cups chopped onions
2 cups chopped bell peppers
5 cups sugar
2½ cups white vinegar
2 teaspoons pickling spices
1 teaspoon celery seeds
1 teaspoon turmeric

Combine squash and salt; let stand overnight. Rinse. Mix spices in little bag; add to rest of ingredients and let boil 5 minutes.

Makes about 6 pints.

Peach Marmalade

5 cups mashed peaches
5 cups sugar
1 small can crushed pineapple
1 (6 ounce) package apricot-flavored gelatin

Boil peaches, sugar, and pineapple for 15 minutes. Stir in gelatin and boil until dissolved. Pour into containers and freeze.

Strawberry Fig Jam

3½ cups mashed figs
3 cups sugar
1 small package strawberry-flavored gelatin

Mix well, bring to boil, and cook 5 minutes. Pour into sterilized jars and seal.

Strawberry Preserves

2 quarts strawberries, heaping
6 cups sugar, divided

Cover strawberries with boiling water and let stand 2 minutes; drain. Put in kettle with 4 cups sugar and boil for 2 minutes. Once rolling boil starts, set kettle aside and let bubbling stop. Add 2 cups sugar; cook at rolling boil for 15 minutes. Leave in kettle 15 minutes then pour into shallow pan. Shake pan often. Preserves should not be more than 1½ inches deep. Let stand overnight. Pack cold in sterilized jars and seal.

Blushing Peach Jam

¼ cup lemon juice, divided
1½ pounds (2 cups) peaches, peeled, pitted, crushed
2 cups red raspberries (measure before crushing)
1½ teaspoons margarine
1 package powdered Sure-Jell
7 cups sugar

Add 2 tablespoons lemon juice to crushed peaches. Let stand. Crush berries and add remaining 2 tablespoons lemon juice. Combine peaches and raspberries. Add margarine. Put in heavy kettle. Add Sure-Jell. Bring to full rolling boil. Add sugar and follow Sure-Jell instructions from there.

Jalapeño Pepper Jelly

1½ cups chopped green peppers
½ cup chopped fresh jalapeño peppers
1½ cups white vinegar
6 cups sugar
4 drops green food coloring
6 ounces Certo or Sure-Jell

Mix green peppers, jalapeños, and white vinegar in blender until mushy. The more jalapeño pepper seeds used, the hotter the jelly. Put mush into large cooking pot. Add sugar and bring to boil, stirring often. Remove from heat, add food coloring, and let stand 10 minutes. Stir in Certo and pour into sterilized jars.

Baker's Note:
Before handling jalapeños, spray hands with cooking spray or use rubber gloves.

Barbecue Sauce

6 tablespoons margarine
1 teaspoon Tabasco sauce
2 cups ketchup
⅔ cup concentrated lemon juice
2 tablespoons mustard
2 teaspoons onion powder
2 teaspoons Accent (optional)
¼ cup Worcestershire sauce
¼ cup molasses
½ teaspoon salt

Combine ingredients in saucepan and simmer 15 minutes. Refrigerate. Great on chicken, beef, pork, and hot dogs.

Makes 1 quart.

Salads

Freeda's Cherry Salad

1 (14 ounce) can sweetened condensed milk
1 (16 ounce) container whipped topping
1 (20 ounce) can cherry pie filling
1 (16 ounce) can crushed pineapple
1 cup chopped pecans
2 cups miniature marshmallows

Mix ingredients together. Chill and serve.

Salad Dressing

1 cup sugar
2 teaspoons salt
4 teaspoons prepared mustard
¼ cup celery
¼ cup onion
½ cup vinegar
1 cup salad oil

In blender, chop or grind until mixed well. Keeps several weeks in refrigerator.

Cherry Pie Salad

1 (14 ounce) can sweetened condensed milk
1 large can crushed pineapple, drained
2 (20 ounce) cans cherry pie filling
½ cup chopped nuts (optional)
1 (16 ounce) container whipped topping

In large bowl, mix condensed milk and drained pineapple together. Add cherry pie filling and nuts. Mix well. Fold in whipped topping. Refrigerate until time to serve.

Cherry Salad

1 (20 ounce) can cherry pie filling
1 large can crushed pineapple, drained
1 (8 ounce) container whipped topping
1 (14 ounce) can sweetened condensed milk
1 (3 ounce) package dry cherry pie filling (no water)
Small package marshmallows (optional)

Mix all ingredients together. Chill and serve.

Lime and Cottage Cheese Salad

1 package lime gelatin
1 cup canned milk, undiluted
1 tablespoon lemon juice
1 cup cottage cheese
½ cup finely chopped celery
¾ cup boiling water
1 (9 ounce) can crushed pineapple, with juice
½ cup mayonnaise
½ cup broken nut meats (optional)

Dissolve gelatin in boiling water. Cool slightly; then stir in milk and cool until syrupy. Fold in other ingredients and chill until firm. Cut into squares and serve on lettuce leaf.

Summer Delight Gelatin Salad

1 package lemon gelatin
2 cups boiling water
¼ teaspoon salt
2 tablespoons lemon juice or vinegar
2 cups crushed pineapple
1 cup evaporated milk
2 tablespoons horseradish
1 cup chopped nuts
1 cup Miracle Whip
¾ cup cottage cheese
1 package lime gelatin
Paprika

Mix together lemon gelatin mix, water, salt, and lemon juice. Cool; then add pineapple and milk. Add horseradish, nuts, Miracle Whip, and cottage cheese; let set. When set, add 2 cups hot water to lime gelatin. Let set until cool. Pour over salad. Sprinkle with paprika.

Lite Lime Salad

1 (24 ounce) carton lime Light n' Lively cottage cheese
2 (3 ounce) packages sugar-free lime gelatin
1 (20 ounce) can crushed pineapple, well drained
2 (8 ounce) containers lite whipped topping

Place cottage cheese in large mixing bowl. Stir in powdered contents of gelatin packages. Add pineapple and whipped topping. Mix well. Refrigerate.

Orange-Pineapple Salad

1 (15 ounce) can crushed pineapple, undrained
1 (6 ounce) package orange gelatin
2 cups buttermilk
1 cup flaked coconut
1 cup chopped pecans
1 (12 ounce) carton whipped topping

Place pineapple and juice in saucepan; bring to boil, stirring constantly. Remove from heat. Add gelatin and stir until completely dissolved. Stir in buttermilk, coconut, and pecans. Cool. Fold in whipped topping and pour into 9x13-inch casserole dish. Chill until firm.

Orange Salad

1 (3 ounce) package vanilla pudding (cooked type)
1 (3 ounce) package tapioca pudding (cooked type)
1 (3 ounce) package orange gelatin
3 cups water
1 large can mandarin oranges, drained
1 (20 ounce) can crushed pineapple, drained
1 (12 ounce) container whipped topping

Bring pudding mixes, gelatin, and water to boil. Cool. Add fruit and fold in whipped topping.

Gail's Orange Salad

1 small package orange gelatin
1 large container whipped topping
1 small container cottage cheese
1 can mandarin oranges, drained
Pineapple
½ small package miniature marshmallows

Pour dry gelatin over whipped topping; mix well. Add cottage cheese and fold in oranges, pineapple, and marshmallows.

Orange-Carrot Gelatin Salad

1 (3 ounce) package orange gelatin
1 cup boiling water
1 (8 ounce) can crushed pineapple
1 (11 ounce) can mandarin oranges, drained
1 cup grated carrots

Dissolve gelatin in boiling water. Drain pineapple, reserve juice. Add enough cold water to juice to measure 1 cup. Stir in gelatin. Chill until partially set. Add pineapple, oranges, and carrots. Pour into serving bowl. Chill until firm.

Serves 4 to 6.

Orange Salad

1 large can pineapple chunks or tidbits, with juice
2 cans mandarin oranges, with juice
2 (3 ounce) packages tapioca pudding
1 (3 ounce) package orange gelatin
1 teaspoon orange drink mix (optional, but makes nice color)
1 to 2 teaspoons lemon juice (optional)
2 bananas, sliced (optional)

Drain fruit. Heat approximately 3 cups of juice in large pan, add water if you don't have enough liquid. Combine pudding mix with another 1¼ to 1½ cups juice/water mixture. Pour pudding/juice mixture into hot juice; stirring continuously, cook until almost clear. Add gelatin, orange drink mix, and lemon juice; stir well. Cool slightly. Add pineapple and oranges. Allow to cool completely for several hours. Add bananas just before serving.

Serves 8.

Orange-Apricot Salad

2 (3 ounce) packages orange gelatin
2 cups boiling water
1 (12 ounce) can apricot nectar
1 can mandarin oranges, drained
1 cup whipped topping

Dissolve gelatin in boiling water. Add apricot nectar. Chill until it begins to set. Fold oranges and whipped topping into gelatin mixture. Pour into mold and chill.

Apricot Gelatin

2 (3 ounce) packages apricot gelatin
¾ cup sugar
2 small jars strained apricot baby food
1 can crushed pineapple
8 ounces cream cheese, softened to room temperature
2 small packs whipped topping mix

Heat gelatin, sugar, apricots, and undrained pineapple until gelatin is dissolved. Do not boil! Beat cream cheese. Pour gelatin mixture into cream cheese and beat together. Allow to cool. Prepare whipped topping according to directions on package. Fold into cooled gelatin and cream cheese mixture. Pour into 9x13-inch dish and refrigerate overnight.

Glenda's Blueberry Salad

2 (3 ounce) or 1 (6 ounce) blackberry or raspberry gelatin
2 cups boiling water
1 (2 ounce) can crushed pineapple, undrained
1 (21 ounce) can blueberry pie filling

Topping:
8 ounces cream cheese, softened
1 pint sour cream
½ cup sugar
1 teaspoon vanilla

Dissolve gelatin in boiling water. Add pineapple. Stir in pie filling. Pour into large glass bowl or individual serving cups and refrigerate until jelled. To prepare topping, mix together cream cheese and sour cream. Stir in sugar and vanilla. Spread topping over salad.

Caramel Apple Salad

1 (3 ounce) package butterscotch instant pudding
1 (8 ounce) container whipped topping
1 (10 ounce) can pineapple, crushed or tidbits, with juice
1 cup miniature marshmallows
3 cups chopped apples

Mix all ingredients together, refrigerate, and enjoy.

"Best Ever" Dressing

2 tablespoons sugar or 2 teaspoons sugar substitute
2 tablespoons vinegar
¼ cup orange juice
2 tablespoons vegetable oil (can use light mayonnaise instead)
2 tablespoons ketchup
Garlic powder and salt and pepper

Blend all ingredients and chill.

English Walnut Apple Salad

1 cup sugar
2 tablespoons flour
1 tablespoon butter
1 cup water
1 tablespoon vinegar
Few drops red food coloring
4 or 5 large, sweet apples, sliced
¾ cup chopped English walnuts

Mix sugar, flour, butter, and water in saucepan; cook until thick. Remove from heat and cool. When cooled add vinegar and food coloring. Pour over apples and nuts. Mix. Cover and store in refrigerator until ready to serve.

Marshmallow Apple Salad

3 apples, cut up in cubes, skins on
½ to 1 cup grapes, cut in half
½ cup chopped nuts
1 cup miniature marshmallows
1 cup whipped topping

Dressing:
1 cup pineapple juice
1 tablespoon butter
1 heaping tablespoon flour
¾ cup sugar
2 eggs, separated

Combine all salad ingredients except whipped topping. To make dressing, heat juice and butter until warm. Blend flour, sugar, and egg yolks; add egg whites, beaten stiff, and pineapple juice. Cook on medium-low heat or use double boiler until thick. Cool. Add dressing to apple mixture at least half hour before serving.

Add 1 cup whipped topping to salad just before serving.

Taffy Apple Salad

1 (8 ounce) can crushed pineapple with juice
2 tablespoons flour
½ cup sugar
5 Granny Smith (sour) apples, diced with skins on
1 (16 ounce) container whipped topping
½ to 1 cup Spanish peanuts, with skins

Cook pineapple with juice, flour, and sugar until thick. Cool completely in refrigerator. Add apples, whipped topping, and peanuts.

Grape Salad

10 ounces peas, cooked slightly, drained
½ to 1 cup finely diced celery
1 to 2 cups diced turkey, chicken, ham
½ pound each, red and green seedless grapes
1 cup salad dressing
1 teaspoon ginger
2 tablespoons lemon juice
Small package almonds, sliced or slivered

Mix all ingredients together except almonds. Set at least 1 hour before serving. Add slivered or sliced almonds just before serving.

Cinnamon Salad

1 (4 ounce) package cherry or raspberry gelatin
1 cup hot water
½ cup red cinnamon candies
½ cup boiling water
1 cup chopped apples
1 cup chopped celery
¾ cup chopped pecans

Dissolve gelatin in 1 cup hot water. Add cinnamon candies to ½ cup boiling water; stir to dissolve. Add enough water to make 1 cup liquid. Combine gelatin and candy mixture. Chill until partially set. Add remaining ingredients. Chill until firm. Can be doubled for more.

Paradise Salad

24 ounces regular or low-fat cottage cheese
1 (6 ounce) package gelatin
1 (12 ounce) container regular or fat-free whipped topping
2 (20 ounce) cans crushed pineapple, drained well

Mix cottage cheese and dry gelatin, then mix in whipped topping. Add pineapple. Mix well and chill.

Make the night before you want to serve it for full flavor. Keeps in the refrigerator for 2 weeks. Use low-fat cottage cheese and fat-free whipped topping for a great low-fat salad.

Strawberry Nut Salad

2 (3 ounce) packages strawberry gelatin
1 cup boiling water
1 cup chopped pecans
16 ounces frozen strawberries
1 (20 ounce) can crushed pineapple, drained
3 bananas, chopped
8 ounces sour cream
¼ cup mayonnaise or salad dressing

Combine gelatin and boiling water; stir in nuts, strawberries, and pineapple; set aside. Stir bananas into gelatin mixture; spoon half of mixture into 7x11-inch baking dish, and refrigerate until almost jelled. Combine sour cream and mayonnaise; spread over strawberry layer then top with remaining strawberry mixture. Refrigerate.

Tangy Fruit Salad

1 (20 ounce) can pineapple chunks, juice drained and reserved
3 (4 ounce) packages vanilla instant pudding mix
½ cup powered orange drink mix
1 (11 ounce) can mandarin oranges, drained
1 (16 ounce) can fruit cocktail, drained
2 bananas, sliced
1 apple or pear, cut into chunks

In small bowl, combine reserved pineapple juice, pudding mix, and drink mix; set aside. In large bowl combine all fruit. Fold juice mixture into fruit. Refrigerate before serving.

Yield: 6 to 8 servings.

Crunchy Fruit Salad

2 bananas
2 oranges, pared and sectioned
1 cup strawberries, cut into halves
½ cup sour cream
Honey
1 tablespoon orange juice
1 cup granola

Slice bananas into 1-quart bowl. Cover completely with oranges and strawberries. Cover and refrigerate at least 1 hour, but no longer than 24 hours. Just before serving, mix sour cream, honey, and orange juice. Fold into fruit until well coated. Sprinkle with granola.

Cheesy Fruit Salad

1 tablespoon cornstarch
1 egg, beaten slightly
¼ cup sugar
1 tablespoon mayonnaise or salad dressing
¼ pound American cheese, diced
1 (4 ounce) package marshmallows, cut up, or 2 cups miniature marshmallows
2 bananas, diced
1 (20 ounce) can pineapple chunks, drained

Mix together cornstarch, egg, and sugar; cook until thick. Cool; add mayonnaise, cheese, marshmallows, bananas, and pineapple chunks. Mix all together. Refrigerate.

Serves 6 to 8.

Fruit Salad

1 (20 ounce) can chunk pineapple juice drained and reserved
7 tablespoons sugar
2 tablespoons flour
2 eggs, beaten
½ teaspoon prepared mustard
1 tablespoon butter
1 small bottle maraschino cherries, cut in half
12 marshmallows, cut up
1 or 2 bananas, sliced

Take juice of pineapple, sugar, flour, eggs, and mustard and boil in saucepan until thick (use medium heat and stir often so it will not scorch). When thickened remove from heat and add butter and cool. When cool, mix with pineapple, marshmallows, cherries, and bananas (added last for they turn dark).

Molded Fruit Salad

2 (3 ounce) packages orange or lime gelatin
2 cups boiling water
1 (8 ounce) package cream cheese (low-fat works fine)
1 cup miniature marshmallows
½ cup mayonnaise
1 (15 or 16 ounce) can crushed pineapple or fruit cocktail, with juice

Dissolve gelatin in boiling water. Add cream cheese, marshmallows, and mayonnaise. Will be smooth and creamy if mixed in blender. After blended, add pineapple or fruit cocktail, including juice. Spray 4- to 5-cup mold with vegetable oil. Cool salad in mold until completely jelled.

Fruit Grapes

¾ cup brown sugar
½ large tub whipped topping
1 cup sour cream
1 pound red grapes (seedless)
1 pound green grapes
1 small package slivered almonds

Mix sugar, whipped topping, and sour cream. Add grapes and slivered almonds.

Frozen Fruit Salad

2 ripe bananas
1 (16 ounce) can pineapple juice
2 tablespoons lemon juice
1 cup orange juice
½ cup mayonnaise or salad dressing
1 (10 ounce) can mandarin oranges, undrained
¼ cup sugar
Iceburg lettuce

Combine in blender: bananas, pineapple juice, and lemon juice. Blend 1 minute on low speed until smooth. Add and whirl 30 seconds on low: orange juice, mayonnaise or salad dressing, oranges, and sugar. Pour into six 6-ounce molds, or 9x9x2-inch pan. Freeze 4 hours or until firm. Cut. Serve on lettuce leaf. Serve as a dessert or as a salad.

Fruit Whip

1 (8 ounce) package cream cheese
1 (14 ounce) can sweetened condensed milk
1 (8 ounce) container whipped topping
1 (20 ounce) can fruit cocktail, drained
1 (20 ounce) can mandarin oranges, drained
1 (20 ounce) can chunk pineapple, drained
Any fruit or nuts desired

Beat cream cheese and milk until smooth. Add whipped topping and fold in drained fruits and nuts if desired. Chill and serve.

Honey Fruit Salad

⅓ cup honey
½ cup mayonnaise (can be light)
½ cup chopped English walnuts
3 cored, unpeeled apples, chopped
2 bananas, peeled and sliced
1 (11 ounce) can mandarin oranges, drained
1 cup seedless grapes
1 tablespoon lemon juice
1 cup shredded lettuce

Blend honey and mayonnaise until smooth. Toss remaining ingredients (except lettuce) with lemon juice. Stir in honey mixture; refrigerate. Just before serving, toss in lettuce.

Makes about 7 cups.

Watermelon Salad

1 (6 ounce) package raspberry gelatin
2 cups boiling water
1 cup miniature marshmallows
1 cup crushed pineapple, drained
1 cup diced cantaloupe
1 cup seedless white grapes
1½ cups cubed watermelon

Dissolve gelatin in water; add marshmallows, stirring until dissolved. Chill until slightly thickened; fold in remaining ingredients. Spoon into 8-cup mold; chill until firm.

Yield: 6 to 8 servings

Minty Mixed Melon

2 cups chopped cantaloupe, about 1 large
2 cups chopped honeydew melon, about 1 medium
2 cups chopped watermelon, about ½ small
1 cup sliced strawberries
1 teaspoon grated lime peel
2 tablespoons chopped fresh, or 2 teaspoons dried mint leaves
2 tablespoons honey

Mix all thoroughly in bowl. Cover and refrigerate at least 2 hours or until chilled.

Serves 6.

Cranberry Salad Supreme

1 (3 ounce) package raspberry gelatin
1 cup boiling water
1 (16 ounce) can whole cranberry sauce
1 (3 ounce) package lemon gelatin
1 cup boiling water
1 (3 ounce) package cream cheese
⅓ cup mayonnaise
1 (8 ounce) can crushed pineapple, undrained
½ cup whipping cream
1 cup miniature marshmallows
2 tablespoons chopped nuts

Dissolve raspberry gelatin in 1 cup boiling water. Stir in whole cranberry sauce. Turn into 9x9x2-inch baking dish. Chill until partially set. Dissolve lemon gelatin in 1 cup boiling water. Beat together cream cheese and mayonnaise, then gradually add lemon gelatin. Stir in undrained pineapple. Chill until partially set. Whip cream; fold in lemon mixture and marshmallows. Spread on top cranberry layer. Top with chopped nuts. Chill until firmly set.

Clara's Best Fresh Cranberry Salad

1 (6 ounce) box any flavor red gelatin
1 package plain gelatin
½ cup cold water
1 pound fresh cranberries
1 large package cream cheese
1½ cups sugar
Rind of 1 orange, grated
1 small can crushed pineapple, drained
1 cup crushed pecans (optional)
1 cup boiling water

Dissolve red gelatin. Dissolve plain gelatin in ½ cup cold water. Put all in blender or food processor. Add fresh cranberries until well crushed. Add cream cheese and sugar. Pour into large bowl and add all remaining ingredients. Let chill and serve.

Serves 8 or more.

Spiced Cranberry Ring

2 (3 ounce) packages raspberry gelatin
⅛ teaspoon salt
2 cups boiling water
¼ teaspoon cinnamon
Dash ground cloves
2 (16 ounce) cans whole cranberry sauce
1 cup diced apples
½ cup diced celery
½ cup chopped walnuts

Dissolve gelatin and salt in boiling water. Stir in cinnamon and cloves. Add cranberry sauce; fold in apples, celery, and walnuts. Pour into 6-cup mold and chill until firm, about 4 hours. Unmold. Garnish as desired. Peach, pear, and apricot halves work well.

Serves 12.

Frozen Cranberry Salad

2 (3 ounce) packages cream cheese, softened (can use low-fat or fat-free)
2 tablespoons mayonnaise or salad dressing (can use low-fat or fat-free)
2 cups whipped topping
1 (8 ounce) can crushed pineapple, drained
½ cup chopped pecans or walnuts
2 cups flaked coconut (optional)
1 (14 ounce) can jellied cranberry sauce (or whole cranberry sauce)

In medium bowl, blend cream cheese and salad dressing. Fold in whipped topping; set aside. In large mixing bowl, combine pineapple, nuts, coconut, and cranberry sauce. Gently combine with cream cheese mixture. Spread into 9x13-inch pan. Cover and freeze. Thaw 10 to 15 minutes before serving. Cut into squares.

Strawberry Pretzel Salad

2½ cups crushed pretzels
1½ sticks margarine, melted
1 cup sugar
8 ounces cream cheese, softened
1 (8 ounce) container whipped topping
2 (3 ounce) packages strawberry gelatin
2 cups boiling water
20 ounces frozen strawberries

Mix pretzels and margarine. Spread in 9x13-inch pan. Bake 10 minutes. Stir once; let cool. Cream together sugar, cream cheese, and whipped topping. Spread over pretzels. Mix gelatin with boiling water. Add strawberries. Pour over cream cheese mixture when it starts to set up. Place in refrigerator until gelatin sets up.

Cranberry Salad

1 pound fresh cranberries
1 cup sugar
¾ pound marshmallows
1 pint whipping cream
1 cup crushed pineapple, drained

Grind cranberries; stir in sugar and mix well. Grind marshmallows and add to mixture. Whip cream and mix all ingredients together. Pour into pan or dishes. Place in freezing part of refrigerator. Let stand overnight.

Serves 12.

Striped Cookie Salad

2 cups buttermilk
8 to 16 ounces whipped topping
2 packages vanilla instant pudding
2 small cans mandarin oranges
Fudge-striped cookies, frozen and broken into pieces

Mix everything together except cookies. Put in refrigerator until ready to serve. Stir in cookies before serving.

Homestead Salad

1 large package frozen mixed vegetables
½ cup chopped onion
3 stalks celery
½ chopped green pepper
1 can red kidney beans

Marinated dressing:
¾ cup sugar
½ cup vinegar
½ cup water
1 teaspoon salt
1 tablespoon prepared mustard

Cook frozen vegetables; drain and cool. Mix onion, celery, and green pepper; add beans. Combine dressing ingredients; cook, stirring constantly, until thickened. Add cool dressing and refrigerate 8 to 10 hours. Keeps well several days.

Watergate Salad

1 (15 ounce) can crushed pineapple, with juice
1 (3 ounce) package pistachio instant pudding, or any flavor you like
1 cup miniature marshmallows
8 ounces whipped topping
½ cup chopped pecans

In large mixing bowl place crushed pineapple with juice. Sprinkle pudding mix over pineapple and add rest of ingredients; mix together. Put in serving bowl; chill until firm and ready to serve.

Overnight Layered Salad

1 head lettuce, cut into wedges
2 stalks celery, cut in 4-inch pieces
1 small onion, chopped
2 carrots, shredded
1 (10 ounce) package frozen peas, thawed
3 hard-boiled eggs, sliced
1½ cups mayonnaise
2 tablespoons sugar
4 slices bacon, fried and crumbled
½ cup grated cheese

Layer first six ingredients in 9x13-inch dish. Mix mayonnaise and sugar and spread over entire top of salad. Cover and chill overnight. Before serving top with bacon and cheese.

Yum Yum Salad

1 (6 ounce) package strawberry gelatin
1 small can crushed pineapple
¼ cup sugar
1 cup grated Velveeta cheese
½ pint whipping cream, whipped
2 cups miniature marshmallows

Prepare gelatin according to directions on package. Let cool. Combine pineapple with sugar in saucepan. Heat until sugar is dissolved. Combine gelatin, pineapple mixture, and cheese. Let cool second time. When slightly thickened, fold in whipped cream and marshmallows. Chill until set.

Layered Salad Medley

1 large head lettuce, shredded
⅓ cup chopped green onion
⅓ cup sliced celery
1 (6 ounce) can water chestnuts, sliced
10 ounces frozen peas, not thawed
2 cups mayonnaise
1½ tablespoons sugar
¾ pound bacon, fried and crumbled
3 to 4 hard-boiled eggs
3 tomatoes, sliced
Parmesan and Romano cheeses

Place lettuce in 9x13-inch casserole; sprinkle next three ingredients on top in layers. Break peas apart and sprinkle on top while frozen. Spread mayonnaise over top like frosting. Sprinkle with sugar. Cover and refrigerate overnight. Before serving add layers of bacon, egg, and tomato slices. Sprinkle with cheese. Do not toss salad; cut into squares.

Heavenly Broccoli Salad

1 bunch broccoli
1 small red onion, chopped (optional)
½ cup finely chopped celery
½ cup raisins, rinsed and drained
½ jar bacon bits
⅓ cup unsalted sunflower seeds
Seedless red grapes (optional)

Dressing:
½ cup mayonnaise
¼ cup sugar
1 or 2 tablespoons cider vinegar

Cut broccoli into small florets. Make sure onion and celery are in small pieces. Mix all salad ingredients together. Mix all dressing ingredients together. Mix salad ingredients and dressing. Cover and refrigerate until ready to serve.

Layered Salad

1 head lettuce, cut small
2 cucumbers, diced
2 tomatoes, diced
1 medium onion, diced
6 radishes, sliced thin
1 medium green pepper, diced
1 pound bacon, fried and crumbled
Salt and pepper to taste
1 (3 ounce) can English peas, drained
1 (3 ounce) can whole kernel corn, drained
1 pint mayonnaise
1 pound grated cheddar cheese

Layer salad ingredients one at a time in 9x13-inch dish. Spread mayonnaise over salad ingredients and sprinkle cheddar cheese on top. Serve with egg turner.

Seven-Layer Salad

1 head lettuce, cut into bite-size pieces
2 (16 ounce) cans sweet peas, drained
2 green peppers, chopped
1 large onion, chopped
Miracle Whip
1 package shredded cheddar cheese
Bacon bits

Layer lettuce on bottom of salad bowl. Cover lettuce with layers of peas, green pepper, onion, Miracle Whip, cheese, then bacon bits. Cover and refrigerate overnight.

Twelve-Layer Salad

1 each of five different 3-ounce packages gelatin: cherry, lemon, orange, lime, and strawberry
16 ounces sour cream

Add 1 cup boiling water to cherry gelatin. Take out ½ cup and add ⅓ cup sour cream, slowly. Pour into 9x13-inch pan. Chill 20 minutes or until firm. Add 3 tablespoons cold water to remaining gelatin and pour on top of first layer. Chill this until firm. Repeat these steps with each flavor of gelatin, fixing in order given. May add whipped topping on top.

Frosted Peach Gelatin

2 packages peach gelatin
2 cups boiling water
2 cups 7UP, or other lemon-lime soda
1 cup peaches, drained, juice reserved
2 large bananas

Frosting:
½ cup sugar
3 tablespoons flour
1 egg
2 tablespoons butter
1 cup whipped topping

Make gelatin and add remaining ingredients; let set. To make frosting, combine sugar and flour. Add reserved juice and egg. Heat over medium heat until thick; cool, then add whipped topping. Spread over gelatin mixture.

Church Dinner Salad

¼ cup water
1 tablespoon unflavored gelatin
¼ cup water
1½ cups sugar
1 teaspoon salt
1 cup vinegar
1 teaspoon celery salt, or celery seed
1 cup salad oil
1 bell pepper
6 to 8 cups chopped cabbage (about 1 medium head)
2 large carrots
1 onion, chopped

Mix ¼ cup water and gelatin; set aside. Bring to boil ¼ cup water, sugar, salt, vinegar, and celery salt. Mix with gelatin while still hot. Cool completely. When cool, add salad oil. Mix with electric mixer about 2 minutes. Prepare vegetables. Pour dressing over vegetables and mix well. Refrigerate 24 hours before serving.

Ginger Ale Salad

1 small can mandarin oranges
1 (16 ounce) can pineapple chunks
1 (15 ounce) can grapefruit sections
1 small jar maraschino cherries
½ to 1 cup seedless grapes (if in season, and if desired)
2 envelopes unflavored gelatin
4 tablespoons cold water
½ cup sugar
⅛ teaspoon salt
1 pint ginger ale
Juice of 1 lemon

Drain first three fruits and reserve juice. Mix juices together. Drain, seed, and slice cherries in half. If you use grapes, wash and quarter. Peel and seed red grapes. Soak gelatin in cold water. Bring ½ cup reserved juice to boil. Dissolve gelatin mixture in juice. Stir in sugar, salt, ginger ale, and lemon juice; mix well. Refrigerate until partially set then fold in chilled fruits. Pour into wet salad mold and chill until set. Unmold onto plate of lettuce. Serve plain or with a mixture of mayonnaise and whipped cream.

Serves 10.

Quickie Cool Salad

24 ounces cottage cheese
1 (8 ounce) container whipped topping
1 can crushed pineapple, drained
1 package red or green gelatin (for holiday)

Mix all together. Serve.

Chow Mein Noodle Salad

1 package frozen peas, cooked and cooled
4 hard-boiled eggs, chopped
1 (7 ounce) can Spam, cubed
½ cup diced green pepper
1 tablespoon chopped green onion
1 cup mayonnaise
1 (3 ounce) can chow mein noodles

Combine all ingredients except noodles; chill overnight. Just before serving add chow mein noodles.

Roman Pasta Salad

1 pound thin spaghetti, or other pasta
2 large tomatoes
1 large onion
1 large cucumber
1 large green pepper
16 ounces Italian dressing
1 envelope Italian dressing mix

Cook and cool pasta; set aside. Cut and dice vegetables. Mix vegetables with Italian dressing and dressing mix. Add to cool pasta; refrigerate overnight.

Napa Salad

1 head Napa cabbage, shredded
2 bunches green onions, chopped
½ cup butter
2 packages Ramen noodles, broken (discard seasoning packet)
2 tablespoons sesame seeds
½ to 1 cup sliced almonds
¾ cup peanut oil
½ cup sugar
¼ cup rice vinegar
2 tablespoons soy sauce, more to taste
Garlic salt (optional)
Croutons (optional)

Combine cabbage and green onion in large serving bowl. In fry pan melt butter and add Ramen noodles, sesame seeds, and almonds; brown these together. In another pan boil peanut oil, sugar, rice vinegar, and soy sauce to make dressing. Pour dressing over combined cabbage and noodles, toss, and serve.

BLT Pasta Salad

1 cup mayonnaise
⅓ cup chili sauce
¼ cup lemon juice
2 teaspoons chicken-flavored instant bouillon
2 teaspoons sugar or sweetener
1 large tomato, chopped
¼ cup sliced green onions
4 cups sliced lettuce
8 slices bacon, cooked and crumbled
1 (7 ounce) package elbow macaroni, cooked and drained

Combine mayonnaise, chili sauce, lemon juice, bouillon, and sugar. Stir in tomato and onions. Add macaroni, cover, and chill. Just before serving stir in lettuce and bacon. Refrigerate leftovers.

Makes about 8 cups.

Shell Mac Salad

1 (1 pound) box small shell macaroni
2 large green peppers, diced
2 large purple onions, diced
3 cups grated carrots

Dressing:
1 (14 ounce) can condensed milk
½ cup white vinegar
½ cup vegetable oil
½ cup sugar
2 cups mayonnaise

Boil macaroni until tender; drain and rinse under cold water. Toss together with veggies. Mix dressing ingredients and add to macaroni mixture.

Taco Salad Toss

2 cups chopped lettuce
1 (1 pound) can kidney beans, drained
2 medium tomatoes, chopped, drained
1 tablespoon canned green chilies, chopped
2 tablespoons Italian dressing
1 teaspoon chili powder
1 teaspoon dried minced onions
¼ teaspoon salt
Dash pepper
1 medium avocado, mashed
½ cup sour cream
½ cup cubed cheddar cheese
½ cup corn chips
Ripe olives (optional)

Combine lettuce, kidney beans, and tomatoes and chill. Add next four ingredients. Mix well. Season with salt and pepper. Blend avocado and sour cream. Toss salad with avocado/sour cream dressing; top with cheese and corn chips. Garnish with ripe olives if desired.

Taco Salad

1 (1¼ ounce) package taco seasoning
1 pound hamburger, browned and drained
1 small head lettuce, broken up
1 medium onion, diced
1 green pepper, diced
3 small tomatoes, chopped
1 cup shredded cheddar cheese
1 can kidney beans
1 (14 ounce) package Tostitos chips, broken
1 bottle ranch dressing with bacon

Mix taco seasoning into hamburger. Cool in refrigerator. Just before serving mix in remaining ingredients and toss with dressing.

Three-Bean Salad

1 can yellow beans, drained
1 can green beans, drained
1 can red beans, drained
1 small onion, chopped
½ cup chopped red or green peppers
¾ cup (or less) sugar
⅔ cup vinegar
⅓ cup salad or olive oil
Salt and pepper

Stir all ingredients together. Put in covered dish and refrigerate. Use slotted spoon to serve.

Carrot Ambrosia Salad

1 pound carrots, scraped and shredded
1 (8 ounce) carton sour cream
1 (20 ounce) can crushed pineapple, drained
¾ cup golden raisins
¾ cup flaked coconut
¾ cup mini marshmallows
2 tablespoons honey

Combine all ingredients, tossing well. Cover and chill at least 2 hours.

Makes 6 to 8 servings.

Fresh Broccoli Salad

1 package fresh broccoli
3 stalks celery (or 1 large Vidalia onion)
1 cup raisins
½ cup bacon bits (or 6 bacon slices, cooked and crumbled)
1 tablespoon vinegar
1 teaspoon sugar
3 tablespoons mayonnaise

Chop florets of broccoli and celery. Add other ingredients. Chill 1 hour or more.

Marinated Salad

1 package dry Italian dressing mix
1 head cauliflower
1 head broccoli
1 can black olives
1 can mushrooms
1 can water chestnuts
Cherry tomatoes
Carrots
Celery
Other raw vegetables of your choice

Pour Italian dressing mix and bottled dressing (more or less to taste) over all; mix well. Refrigerate 24 hours before serving.

Tree Salad

1 head broccoli
1 head cauliflower
1 (8 ounce) package shredded mild cheddar cheese
1 pound bacon, cooked until crisp
¼ cup salad dressing (Miracle Whip)
¼ cup sugar
2 teaspoons vinegar

Cut up broccoli and cauliflower into bowl. Add cheese. Crumble bacon into bowl. Mix Miracle Whip, sugar, and vinegar (if you like a lot of dressing, make a double batch). Pour over broccoli and cauliflower; mix well.

Broccoli-Cauliflower Salad

1 head broccoli, cut into bite-size pieces
1 head cauliflower, cut into bite-size pieces

Dressing:
¾ cup Green Goddess dressing
1 tablespoon sugar
1 tablespoon apple cider vinegar
¾ cup mayonnaise
½ cup bacon bits
Onion if desired

*Green Goddess dressing is hard to find, so use the following recipe if you need to:

1½ cups mayonnaise
¼ cup chopped chives
2 tablespoons tarragon vinegar
2 tablespoons diced parsley
1 tablespoon tarragon, crushed
1 green onion, chopped

Mix broccoli and cauliflower together with dressing. Cover and let set overnight.

Corn Salad

2 cans whole kernel corn
1 onion, diced
1 bell pepper, diced
1 large cucumber, peeled and diced
Pinch salt
¼ to ½ teaspoon pepper
3 to 4 large tablespoons mayonnaise

Mix all ingredients together and chill.

Corn Bread Salad

1 small box corn bread mix
¼ cup chopped onion
¼ cup chopped celery
¼ cup chopped green pepper
½ cup chopped ripe tomato
Mayonnaise or salad dressing

Bake corn bread according to directions; cool. Crumble bread into mixing bowl. Mix vegetables with crumbs. Moisten with mayonnaise or salad dressing. Chill about 3 to 4 hours.

Cauliflower-Pea Salad

1 large head cauliflower
¼ cup chopped onion
1 (10 ounce) package frozen peas
1 pint, or less, mayonnaise
1 jar bacon bits
2 tablespoons Salad Supreme or Salad Delight
4 ounces shredded cheese

Cut cauliflower into bite-size pieces and spread in 9x13-inch pan or dish. Sprinkle onion over cauliflower. Slightly thaw frozen peas; spread over cauliflower and onion. Spread mayonnaise over vegetables. Spread bacon bits over mayonnaise. Add Salad Supreme. Over all, sprinkle shredded cheese and let stand for at least 24 hours in refrigerator. Lightly toss when ready to serve.

Ranch Crunchy Pea Salad

1 (10 ounce) package frozen baby peas, thawed
1 cup diced celery
1 cup chopped cauliflower
¼ cup diced green onions
1 cup cashew halves
½ cup sour cream*
1 cup prepared ranch dressing*
Bacon, cooked and crumbled (for garnish)

Combine all ingredients; garnish with cooked, crumbled bacon. Chill before serving.

*Use fat-free sour cream and lite ranch dressing to lower fat content.

Black-Eyed Pea Salad

3 tablespoons chopped onion
½ teaspoon red pepper
2 tablespoons white vinegar
3 tablespoons oil
¼ teaspoon salt
1 tablespoon sugar
4 (15 ounce) cans black-eyed peas, drained

Mix all ingredients together, except peas, until sugar is dissolved. Pour over black-eyed peas and refrigerate. Will keep in refrigerator for several days.

Apple Cabbage Coleslaw

½ large cabbage, shredded
1 red apple, unpeeled and chopped
½ cup fat-free salad dressing
Pinch salt
½ tablespoon white vinegar
6 packages artificial sweetener
2 tablespoons skim milk

Place shredded cabbage and chopped apples in large bowl. Mix together salad dressing, salt, vinegar, artificial sweetener, and milk. Pour over cabbage and apples. Mix well. Chill before serving. Keeps several days in refrigerator.

Colleen's "Tastes-Like-More" Potato Salad

4 medium potatoes, cooked and cooled to handling temperature (best to use White Rose potatoes)
1 medium onion (better yet, several green onions with tops), chopped
4 hard-boiled eggs, cooled and chopped
4 dill pickles, finely chopped

Toss all ingredients lightly with pre-stirred blend of mayonnaise, prepared mustard, a little dill pickle juice, and pepper. Good served right away or chilled. Refrigerate.

Variation: black or ripe olives, cherry tomatoes, and/or fresh parsley can be used for garnish.

Lettuce Slaw

1 head lettuce
1 head cauliflower, cut up
1 tomato, diced
1 can sliced black olives
1 purple or red onion, sliced, broken into rings
Mayonnaise
⅓ cup Parmesan cheese
1 cup crumbled bacon
1 tablespoon sugar

Mix lettuce, cauliflower, tomato, olives, and onion with enough mayonnaise to lightly coat. Refrigerate for about 2 hours. Mix well Parmesan cheese, bacon, and sugar. Add just before serving.

Sauerkraut Salad

1 pound sauerkraut
1 cup chopped celery
1 medium onion, chopped
1 small (1 ounce) can chopped pimientos
½ cup vinegar
½ cup salad oil
1 cup sugar

Place kraut in strainer and scald. Let cool; add all ingredients. Chill overnight. Stir once or twice.

Picnic Potato Salad Spud

2 baked potatoes
2 tablespoons chopped onion
2 tablespoons chopped pickle
1 celery stalk, chopped
2 tablespoons chopped pimientos
1 hard-boiled egg, chopped
⅓ cup mayonnaise
1 teaspoon mustard
1 teaspoon vinegar or juice from sour pickle
¼ teaspoon salt
2 shakes black pepper
Powdered paprika to garnish

Cool potatoes, cut thin slice from top, remove pulp, and dice. Combine potato, onion, pickle, celery, pimientos, and egg; stir lightly. Combine mayonnaise, mustard, vinegar, salt, and pepper; mix thoroughly. Combine potato mixture and mayonnaise mixture; mix well. Heap into potato shells. Sprinkle with paprika; chill.

Hong Kong Chicken Salad

6 ounces cooked and shredded chicken
3 cups shredded Romaine lettuce
1 cup fresh bean sprouts
3 to 4 green onions, slivered lengthwise and cut into 1-inch pieces
1 cucumber, chopped into ½- to 1-inch pieces

Dressing:
1½ teaspoons rice vinegar
4 teaspoons salad oil
1 teaspoon sugar
⅛ teaspoon pepper
¼ teaspoon salt
2 teaspoons dark sesame oil

Make dressing ahead of time and chill. Just before serving add dressing to chilled salad.

Flying Farmer Chicken Salad

5 cups cooked and cubed chicken
2 tablespoons salad oil
1 teaspoon salt
2 tablespoons orange juice
2 tablespoons vinegar
Mayonnaise

Mix and pour over chicken. Let stand in refrigerator overnight.

Buffet Chicken Salad

2 whole fryers
1 cup chopped celery
1 (20 ounce) can white grapes, drained
1 (20 ounce) can pineapple chunks, drained
1 (11 ounce) can mandarin oranges, drained
2 tablespoons soy sauce
1 cup mayonnaise
1 cup slivered almonds, toasted

Boil chicken in lightly salted water until very tender. Chill and remove all skin and bones. Cut in bite-size pieces. Add celery and fruit. Mix soy sauce and mayonnaise and blend with chicken mixture. Sprinkle toasted almonds over the top.

Serves 8.

Low-Cal Italian Dressing

½ cup water
½ cup vinegar
2 teaspoons cornstarch
1 tablespoon vinegar
¼ teaspoon dry mustard
¼ teaspoon paprika
1 teaspoon salt (or No Salt salt substitute)
Sugar
½ teaspoon sweet basil
⅛ teaspoon instant minced garlic
Pepper to taste

Bring water and ½ cup vinegar to boil. Remove from heat and stir in cornstarch dissolved in 1 tablespoon vinegar. Return to low heat and stir until just boiling. Remove from heat and beat in other ingredients—OR—Beat all ingredients in microwave-safe pint container. Microwave on high about 3 minutes, stirring twice during cooking.

Makes 1 cup.

Vegetables

Asparagus Casserole

4 slices of bread, toasted
1 can asparagus, juice drained and reserved
1 (10¾ ounce) can cream of chicken soup
Shredded cheddar cheese

OVEN 400°

Break toasted bread in bottom of dish. Put drained asparagus on top of bread. Mix asparagus juice with cream of chicken soup. Pour over mixture. Top with cheese. Bake at 400° for 45 minutes to 1 hour.

Asparagus Delight

1 (10¾ ounce) can cream of asparagus soup
1 (10¾ ounce) can cream of celery soup
1½ cans milk
1 stick margarine or butter

Mix together and simmer over low heat until creamy. Serve with snack crackers.

Baked Sweet Potatoes

6 to 8 large sweet potatoes

OVEN 425°

Wash potatoes; cut ends and scars off. Preheat oven to 425°. Wrap each potato in aluminum foil. Place loosely on cookie sheet; bake on center oven rack for 45 minutes or until fork passes easily through. Unwrap potatoes, butter generously, and enjoy! Refrigerate any leftovers and reheat when needed.

Option: Add cinnamon with butter.

Grandma's Sweet Potato Casserole

3 to 6 cups mashed sweet potatoes
½ cup margarine, melted
2 eggs
1 cup sugar
1 tablespoon vanilla
1 cup brown sugar
⅓ cup flour
1 cup chopped nuts

OVEN 350°

Mix sweet potatoes, ½ cup melted margarine, eggs, sugar, and vanilla together in bowl. Pour into buttered casserole. Mix remaining ingredients with ⅓ cup margarine. Sprinkle over potato mixture. Bake at 350° for 20 minutes.

Sweet Potato Casserole

1 large can sweet potatoes
¾ cup sugar
2 eggs
1 teaspoon vanilla
1 stick margarine, melted
½ cup evaporated milk

Topping:
1 cup brown sugar
⅓ cup flour
1 cup chopped nuts
⅓ cup margarine

OVEN 350°

Mash potatoes with juice. Mix all ingredients with potatoes and pour into greased 9x13-inch pan. Mix topping ingredients together until crumbly and sprinkle on top of mixture. Do not stir. Bake at 350° for about 40 minutes.

Pecan Sweet Potatoes

6 medium sweet potatoes, baked, cooled, and peeled
½ cup brown sugar
½ cup chopped pecans
1 tablespoon orange peel
1 cup orange juice
1½ tablespoons butter, cut up
½ teaspoon salt

OVEN 350°

Lightly spray 9x13-inch baking pan with vegetable spray. Slice potatoes in ¼-inch slices and layer in pan; set aside. In small bowl, combine brown sugar, pecans, and orange peel. Pour mixture over sweet potatoes. Pour orange juice over all. Dot with butter. Season with salt to taste. Cover and refrigerate until ready to use. Bake at 350° for 45 minutes; uncover and bake 15 to 20 minutes longer.

Sweet Potato Soufflé

5 fresh sweet potatoes
½ cup sugar
3 tablespoons butter
2 eggs
¼ teaspoon cinnamon
½ teaspoon vanilla
½ cup milk or to desired consistency

Topping:
Chopped pecans
Brown sugar
Marshmallows

OVEN 350°

Cook potatoes until tender, then puree. Add remaining ingredients with milk to desired consistency. Bake at 350° for 1 hour. Top with chopped pecans and brown sugar during last 10 minutes of baking time. Or top with marshmallows during last 5 minutes of baking time.

Sweet Potato Casserole

2 large or 4 small cans sweet potatoes, drained
1 cup sugar
2 eggs
1 teaspoon vanilla
½ cup butter or margarine, melted

Topping:
2 cups brown sugar
⅔ cup flour
1 cup chopped pecans or almonds
⅔ cup margarine or butter, softened

OVEN 350°

Mix all ingredients and pour into 9x13-inch casserole dish. Combine topping ingredients and sprinkle on top. Bake at 350° for 30 to 35 minutes.

Hominy Casserole

3 small cans yellow hominy, drained
1 (10¾ ounce) can cream of mushroom soup
1 (8 ounce) jar jalapeño processed cheese
3 green onions, finely chopped
1 cup corn chips, crushed

OVEN 300°

Mix all ingredients except chips and spread in casserole dish. Sprinkle crushed corn chips on top. Bake for 20 minutes at 300°.

Creamy Scalloped Potatoes

8 medium potatoes
12 slices American cheese
1 (10¾ ounce) can cream of chicken soup
1 can water

OVEN 350°

Peel potatoes and slice into thin slices (crosswise). Use 4 for first layer in oblong dish. Salt and pepper to taste. Put 6 slices of cheese on top of potato layer; spread half of soup over cheese. Repeat. Pour 1 can water over top slowly. Cover with foil and bake 45 minutes to 1 hour at 350° until done.

Grilled Parmesan Taters

1 pound small red potatoes, cut into ½-inch cubes
¼ cup chopped onion
2 teaspoons oil
1 tablespoon Parmesan cheese
1 teaspoon oregano
½ teaspoon garlic salt
¼ teaspoon pepper
Heavy-duty foil

Place taters in bowl, add onion and oil; toss. Put in center of foil. Combine dry ingredients and sprinkle over taters. Fold foil into pouch; put on grill for 18 to 20 minutes or until taters are tender.

Serves 4.

Make-Ahead Mashed Potato Casserole

12 large potatoes, peeled and boiled in salted water, drained
8 ounces sour cream
1 (8 ounce) package cream cheese
1 teaspoon onion powder
¼ cup margarine or butter, melted
Paprika

OVEN 350°

Mix together all ingredients except butter and paprika. Mash or whip until fluffy, adding milk if necessary. Spread in buttered 9x13-inch casserole and top with melted butter and paprika. Bake at 350° for 1 hour. May be kept in refrigerator or frozen for future use.

Hash Brown Potato Casserole

1 (2 pound) bag frozen hash browns
1 stick margarine or butter
½ to 1 teaspoon salt
½ teaspoon pepper
1 (10¾ ounce) can cream of chicken soup (can use reduced fat/sodium)
1 pint sour cream (can use low-fat)
¼ cup chopped onion
8 to 10 ounces shredded cheddar cheese
1 cup cornflakes
3 tablespoons melted butter
2 cups diced ham (optional)

Mix all ingredients except cornflakes and melted butter. Pour in large baking dish. Sprinkle top with cornflakes and butter. Bake at 350° for 1½ hours.

Variation: Add 1 can potato soup (can use reduced fat or low-sodium type).

Potato Casserole

8 ounces cream cheese
1 onion, chopped
2 eggs
2 cups mashed potatoes, whipped smooth
1 can French fried onions

OVEN 350°

Add cream cheese, onion, and eggs to potatoes; beat all until smooth. Pour into casserole dish; sprinkle with French fried onions. Bake about 20 minutes at 350°.

Scalloped Potatoes

6 medium potatoes, thinly sliced
6 tablespoons butter or margarine
2 tablespoon flour
Salt and pepper to taste
2 cups milk (½% or 1%)
¾ cup grated cheddar cheese

OVEN 375°

Place sliced potatoes in casserole dish sprayed with cooking spray. Melt butter over low heat. Add flour; stir until smooth. Add salt and pepper to taste, milk, and cheese, stirring constantly until thickened. Pour over potatoes and bake uncovered at 375° for 1 hour.

Serves 6.

Quick and Easy Scalloped Potatoes

4 cups peeled and sliced potatoes
½ medium green pepper, cut in strips
1 (10¾ ounce) can cream of mushroom soup

In 2-quart casserole dish combine potatoes and green pepper; cover with glass lid. Microwave on high 10 to 12 minutes, stirring once. Stir in soup and re-cover. Cook on high 5 to 6 minutes or until tender, stirring once. Sprinkle with paprika or cheese if desired. Let stand covered 2 minutes.

Makes 4 to 6 servings.

Roasted Potato Bites

6 to 8 potatoes
¼ cup cooking oil
2 tablespoons Parmesan cheese
¼ teaspoon pepper
1 teaspoon garlic salt
½ teaspoon paprika

OVEN 375°

Cut potatoes into 4 to 6 wedges, depending on size. Mix potatoes and cooking oil. Mix remaining ingredients, put just a little of mixture at a time in plastic bag, shake 4 to 5 pieces of wedges, and place on sprayed baking sheet. Repeat until all potatoes are coated. Bake at 375° for 45 minutes or until tender.

Potato and Apple What?

2 medium red delicious apples
2 red potatoes
½ cup water
2 medium onions
1 teaspoon garlic powder
1 teaspoon cinnamon
Dash mace
½ cup raisins
1 tablespoon molasses

Cut apples into bite-size chunks. Clean and cut potatoes into bite-size chunks; put into pan with water. Turn heat on low. Cut onions and add to pot. Add garlic powder, cinnamon, and mace; bring to boil. Boil uncovered until tender. Add raisins and molasses and let stand about 2 minutes. Eat it hot or cold. Will look grayish but tastes great!

Party Potatoes

6 medium potatoes, peeled
3 ounces cream cheese
1 small container sour cream
Salt to taste
Butter or margarine
Paprika

OVEN 375°

Boil and mash potatoes. Add cream cheese and sour cream; beat. If not thin enough, add some milk. Salt to taste. Pour in baking dish. Dot with butter; sprinkle top with paprika. Bake in 375° oven 30 minutes or until brown on top. Can be made early and baked later.

Party Potatoes

6 large potatoes
½ stick margarine
1 (10¾ ounce) can cream of chicken soup
1 pint sour cream
¾ cup chopped green onions, with tops
1½ cups grated cheddar cheese
½ cup bread crumbs

OVEN 375°

Boil potatoes in jackets, cool, and grate with large grater. Melt margarine and remove from heat. Add to undiluted soup, sour cream, onions, and cheese. Fold this mixture into potatoes. Put in greased casserole. Top with crumbs and bake at 375° for 45 minutes.

Cheesy Potatoes

32 ounces frozen hash brown potatoes, baked
1 (10¾ ounce) can creamy chicken mushroom soup or cream of mushroom soup
½ pint sour cream
½ cup milk
1 stick butter or margarine, melted
1 cup cheddar cheese, grated

OVEN 350°

In bowl, mix together hash brown potatoes with soup, sour cream, and milk. When mixed well, add melted butter and about half the grated cheese. Spread into greased 9x13-inch pan and top with remaining cheese. Bake uncovered at 350° for about 45 minutes.

Serves 6 to 8.

Colcannon

3 pounds potatoes
1 small head cabbage or 1 bunch kale (called curly kale in Ireland)
½ to 1 cup chopped onion (chopped green onions can be substituted)
Salt and black pepper
½ stick margarine or butter
1 cup milk (more or less as needed)
½ to 1 cup shredded cheddar cheese

OVEN 350°

Boil spuds and mash. Chop cabbage or kale very fine and steam with onions (or boil in potato water). Onions could also be sautéed, if you have the time. Chopped green onions could be left raw but should be chopped very fine. Mix mashed potatoes, cabbage/kale, onions, salt and pepper, margarine/butter, and milk together. Mix well. Transfer to greased dish and bake in 350° oven for 20 to 30 minutes. If you do not want crusty top, cover with foil. During last 5 minutes, sprinkle with shredded cheese. Good as side dish or as a whole lunch served with vegetable soup.

Louisianna Fried Taters

4 large potatoes, unpeeled and diced
1 large onion, diced
Salt and pepper to taste
1 small yellow squash
1 large tomato, diced

Fry potatoes and onion until half done. Salt and pepper to taste. Add squash and fry until all done. Add tomato; cook until tomato is just warm. Serve hot.

$20 Potatoes

6 to 7 potatoes, peeled and boiled
¼ cup butter
1 (10¾ ounce) can cream of mushroom soup
3 tablespoons minced onion
2 cups sour cream
1½ cups shredded cheddar cheese
1 teaspoon salt
½ teaspoon pepper
½ cup cornflakes

OVEN 350°

Grate potatoes in bowl. Heat butter and soup in pan, stirring until smooth. Stir in onion, sour cream, cheese, and salt and pepper. Add to potatoes, mix well, and spoon into baking dish. Top with cornflakes. Bake at 350° for 1 hour.

Lefse

5 cups white potatoes, peeled
½ cup sour cream
1 teaspoon salt
¼ cup butter, melted
2¾ cups flour

Cook potatoes until done. Drain. Put through ricer and cool completely. Mix sour cream, salt, and butter in bowl. Alternately add potatoes and flour, mixing well. (You may wish to use your hands to mix.) If mixture is too moist, add more flour. Divide dough in half. Make 2 long rolls. Place in refrigerator at least 30 minutes. Preheat electric griddle to 410°. Slice dough into 1- to 2-inch pieces. Roll into very thin rounds (about 8 inches in diameter) on floured board. (Use only enough flour on board to keep dough from sticking. Too much flour will toughen the lefse.) Bake until little brown spots appear. Turn and bake on other side. Rounds should be soft when done. Cover baked rounds immediately to prevent them from drying out. Store in tight containers in refrigerator.

Makes 16 rounds.

In the past, lefse was often wrapped around a piece of meat. Today it is commonly eaten as a sweet. The rounds are cut into four pie-shaped pieces. Each piece is then spread with butter and either white or brown sugar. The pieces are rolled to make them easier to eat.

Corn Casserole

1 (1 pound) can whole kernel corn
1 (1 pound) can cream-style corn
8 ounces sour cream (or 1 cup milk)
1 egg, beaten
3 tablespoons chopped onion
1 small box corn muffin mix
½ stick margarine
½ teaspoon parsley
½ teaspoon salt
½ teaspoon pepper

OVEN 350°

Combine all ingredients. Bake in greased 7x11-inch casserole dish in 350° oven for 45 minutes.

Serves 10.

Corn Fritters

1¼ cups flour
1 teaspoon baking powder
1½ teaspoons salt
2 eggs
2 cups chopped fresh corn
Milk

Combine ingredients; batter should be thick. Add more flour to batter if needed. Drop into hot oil, using small tablespoon.

Corn Soufflé

1 stick margarine, melted
1 can creamed corn
1 can whole kernel corn, drained
1 box corn muffin mix
8 ounces sour cream

OVEN 375°

Mix ingredients together and pour into greased dish. Bake covered at 375° for 45 minutes.

Mock Fresh Fried Corn

4 tablespoons flour
3 cans shoe peg corn (white); juice and all, Green Giant brand
Salt and pepper to taste
½ pint whipping cream, do not whip
½ stick margarine

OVEN 350°

Mix flour with corn; add salt and pepper and whipping cream. Cut margarine and put in corn. Bake at 350° for 30 to 40 minutes.

Quick Corn Casserole

3 tablespoons butter or margarine
1 cup baking mix
2 cups whole kernel corn
2 tablespoons flour
1 cup evaporated milk
1 tablespoon sugar
2 eggs
⅛ teaspoon pepper
¼ teaspoon salt

OVEN 350°

Cut butter into baking mix. Set aside for topping. Run frozen corn under warm water to thaw, or drain canned corn. Place all ingredients except corn and topping into blender. Blend 5 seconds, until egg is incorporated. Add corn and blend 2 seconds. Some large pieces of corn should remain. Do not overblend! Pour corn mixture into buttered 9x9-inch casserole dish. Sprinkle with topping. Bake at 350° for 30 minutes, until knife inserted in center comes out clean.

Green Bean Casserole

2 quarts green beans, drained
2 (10¾ ounce) cans cream of mushroom soup
Salt and pepper
Milk
1 large can French fried onion rings

OVEN 350°

Mix beans, soup, and salt and pepper to taste with enough milk to slightly dilute soup. Spread in cake pan and sprinkle with onion rings. Bake at 350° until bubbly and onion rings are slightly brown.

Pinto Beans

2 cups pinto beans, washed
4 cups water
1 pound ground beef
1 medium onion, chopped
1 cup diced tomato
Salt and pepper to taste
Chili powder to taste

Put beans in pan with 4 cups water. Bring to boil and cook 5 minutes. Turn off heat and let stand for 1 hour. Drain and put in 2 cups water; cook beans until they start to get tender. Brown ground beef and onion; add to beans. Add tomatoes to beans. You can now season with salt, pepper, and chili powder if you like. (It is good with chili powder.) Let simmer until beans are done and flavors are well mixed. Serve with corn bread or over rice.

Cheesy Green Beans

1 pound bacon
3 cans of sliced green beans
1 (16 ounce) jar processed cheese

OVEN 325°

Cook bacon until crisp and set aside. Drain green beans and put into baking dish. Microwave processed cheese and pour onto green beans. Crumble bacon and add to mixture. Mix well. Bake in 325° oven until bubbly and hot. Serve immediately.

Lentil-Rice Casserole

3 cups chicken broth
¾ cup uncooked lentils
½ cup uncooked brown rice
1 small onion, chopped
½ teaspoon basil
¼ teaspoon oregano
¼ teaspoon thyme
¼ teaspoon garlic powder
¾ cup grated mozzarella, cheddar, or Colby cheese

OVEN 300°

Mix all ingredients together in large casserole dish. Cover and bake at 300° for 2 to 2½ hours. Top with cheese 20 minutes before baking is over.

Pinto Bean Casserole

1 to 1½ pounds hamburger
1 medium onion, chopped
1 (10¾ ounce) can tomato soup
1 can pinto beans
1 can chili beans
½ package Mexican corn bread mix

OVEN 350°

Cook hamburger and onions, then drain grease. Press into bottom of 9x13-inch baking dish. Spread tomato soup over meat mixture, then pour beans over soup. Mix corn bread as directed on package and spread over beans. Bake at 350° about 1 hour or until bread is cooked and light brown.

Cheese Squash Casserole

1 medium onion
1 bell pepper
1 tablespoon butter
3 cups cooked squash, drained
1 pound ground beef, browned and drained
8 ounces processed cheese spread
1 roll Ritz crackers, crushed
2 eggs, beaten
1 can Rotel tomatoes
1 (10¾ ounce) can cream of mushroom soup
Salt and pepper
1 can French fried onions

OVEN 350°

Sauté onion and bell pepper in butter. Combine all ingredients except fried onions, adding salt and pepper to taste. Put in 9x13-inch casserole dish; top with fried onions. Bake at 350° for 30 minutes.

Squash Dressing

1 cup diced onion
1 stick margarine
2 cups corn bread
2 cups yellow squash, cooked and mashed
2 cups diced cooked chicken
Salt and pepper to taste
1 (10¾ ounce) can cream of chicken soup (do not dilute)
1 can sliced mushrooms
1 teaspoon sage
½ cup egg substitute, beaten, or 2 eggs

OVEN 350°

Sauté onion in margarine. Mix all ingredients and bake at 350° for 30 to 40 minutes, until golden brown on top.

Crescent Roll Zucchini Pie

4 cups thinly sliced zucchini
1 cup chopped onion
¼ to ½ cup margarine
1 teaspoon salt
½ teaspoon pepper
¼ teaspoon oregano
2 eggs, beaten
8 ounces mozzarella cheese
1 tube refrigerated crescent rolls
2 teaspoons mustard

OVEN 375°

Cook and stir zucchini, onion, and margarine for 10 minutes. Stir in salt, pepper, and oregano. Combine eggs and mozzarella cheese; stir into zucchini mixture. Spread crescent rolls into 10-inch greased pan and spread crust with mustard. Top with zucchini mixture. Bake at 375° for 18 to 20 minutes or until set. Let stand for 10 minutes before serving.

Summer Zucchini Casserole

3 or 4 tomatoes, sliced
1 medium zucchini, chopped
2 white potatoes, chopped
2 green peppers, chopped
2 carrots, chopped
1 celery stalk, chopped
⅓ cup raw rice (not instant)
1¾ cups shredded cheddar cheese

Combine the following and let stand while chopping the vegetables:
⅓ cup olive oil
2 tablespoons wine vinegar
2 tablespoons parsley
3 teaspoons salt
¾ teaspoon pepper
1 teaspoon Tabasco, to taste

OVEN 350°

Spray large casserole dish with cooking spray. Cover bottom of dish with layer of tomatoes followed by half of chopped vegetables. Then add another layer of tomatoes. Sprinkle rice over top and add rest of vegetables topped by final layer of tomatoes. Pour oil mixture over all and bake at 350° for 1½ hours. Sprinkle cheese on top at end of baking time and let it melt.

Zucchini Squash Casserole

2 pounds zucchini squash, chopped
1 onion, chopped
1 bell pepper, chopped
1 carrot, grated
1 (10¾ ounce) can cream of chicken soup
½ pint yogurt
1 stick margarine
1 (8 ounce) package herb dressing mix

OVEN 350°

Cook squash and onions until tender, then mash. Add pepper, carrot, soup, and yogurt; mix well. Melt margarine and add to dressing mix. Put two-thirds of dressing mix with squash. Pour into greased casserole dish and put remaining one-third of dressing on top. Bake at 350° for 35 minutes.

Takes a large casserole dish. Can be prepared ahead of time and frozen.

Zucchini Half Shells

¼ cup butter, melted
1 tablespoon grated onion
1 beef bouillon cube, crushed
6 small zucchini, ends cut off and cut in half lengthwise
2 tablespoons water

Melt butter in large skillet; add grated onion and bouillon cube. Add zucchini, cut side down; cook until golden. Turn; add 2 tablespoons water. Cover and cook over low heat about 10 minutes.

Serves 5 to 6.

Buttered Squash

Take fresh crookneck squash, wash and cut it. Use plenty of cut-up onions, butter, salt, and pepper. Add water and bake in microwave oven until done; serve.

Cabbage Casserole

1½ pounds ground meat
1 head cabbage, shredded
1 cup rice
1 small bag carrots, sliced
1 (16 ounce) can tomato sauce
½ cup sugar
Salt and pepper to taste

OVEN 350°

Brown and drain ground meat. Boil cabbage for 10 minutes. Cook rice as package directs and set aside. Add carrots, tomato sauce, sugar, rice, and cabbage to meat in 9x13-inch casserole dish. Bake at 350° for 1 to 1½ hours.

Serves 6.

Broccoli and Cauliflower Casserole

16 ounces frozen broccoli
8 ounces frozen cauliflower
½ cup chopped onion
½ cup sliced celery
Slivered almonds
1 tablespoon butter
1 (10¾ ounce) can cream of mushroom soup
1 (8 ounce) jar processed cheese spread
1 (8 ounce) can sliced chestnuts, drained
1½ cups quick-cook rice (dry)
1 cup milk
½ cup butter

OVEN 350°

Cook broccoli and cauliflower until tender and crisp; drain. Sauté onions, celery, and almonds in 1 tablespoon butter. Combine all ingredients and pour into greased 2½-quart (9x13-inch) pan. Bake at 350° for 40 minutes.

Broccoli and Rice Casserole

1 (10¾ ounce) can cream of mushroom soup
1 small jar processed cheese spread
1 stick margarine
1 cup diced celery
1 cup chopped onion
1½ cups quick-cooking rice, uncooked
20 ounces frozen chopped broccoli, thawed

OVEN 350°

Heat soup, cheese, margarine, celery, and onion just enough to melt cheese and margarine. Add uncooked rice and broccoli. Stir well. Pour into greased 9x13-inch casserole dish. Bake at 350° for 35 minutes.

Broccoli Soufflé

2 packages frozen broccoli
1 egg, beaten foamy
¾ cup mayonnaise
1 small onion, chopped
2 (10¾ ounce) cans cream of mushroom soup
1 (1 pound) package grated yellow cheese
1 package croutons

OVEN 350°

Cook broccoli as instructions direct. Drain. Mix egg and mayonnaise with broccoli. Put in buttered casserole in layers: broccoli, onions, soup, cheese, croutons. Repeat until all ingredients are used. Bake 1 hour at 350°.

Barbecued Beans

1 pound hamburger
1 onion, chopped
4 (1 pound) cans pork and beans in tomato sauce
1 tablespoon Worcestershire sauce
Salt and pepper to taste
2 tablespoons vinegar
2 tablespoons brown sugar
½ cup ketchup
Dash chili powder

OVEN 350°

Brown hamburger and onion; drain off fat. Add remaining ingredients. Bake at 350° for 35 minutes. Or make in large frying pan; cook on low heat stirring often, until boiling. Simmer about 10 to 15 minutes.

Barbecued Green Beans

4 slices bacon, cut up
¼ cup chopped onion
½ cup ketchup
¼ cup brown sugar
1 tablespoon Worcestershire sauce
2 (16 ounce) cans green beans, drained

OVEN 350°

Brown bacon and onions, then add ketchup, brown sugar, and Worcestershire sauce. Simmer 2 minutes. Place beans in 2-quart casserole dish. Pour sauce over beans. Don't stir. Bake at 350° for 20 to 30 minutes.

Sharon's Scrumptious Beans

1 pound ground beef
3 (16 ounce) cans pinto beans
2 (16 ounce) cans chili beans
1 (16 ounce) can diced tomatoes
1 medium onion, chopped
Salt and pepper to taste

Cook ground beef and drain. In slow cooker, combine all ingredients and cook for 2 to 3 hours.

Mom's Best Baked Beans

1 pound ground whole hog or venison sausage
1 large green bell pepper, chopped
1 large onion, chopped
1 (32 ounce) can pork and beans
1 small bottle barbecue sauce
Garlic powder
Cajun seasoning
Salt and pepper

OVEN 350°

Cook sausage (we prefer venison), drain, and crumble. Sauté pepper and onion together. Mix all ingredients in large casserole. Season to taste with garlic powder, Cajun seasoning, salt, and pepper. Bake at 350° for 1½ hours.

Roger's Baked Beans

6 slices bacon, chopped
1 medium onion, chopped
1 can kidney beans
1 can baked beans
1 can butter beans
¼ pound processed cheese spread
½ cup sugar
⅓ cup brown sugar
2 tablespoons Worcestershire sauce

OVEN 350°

Cook bacon and onion; drain. Mix remaining ingredients then stir in the bacon and onions. Bake 1 hour at 350° or place in slow cooker and simmer all day.

Western Beans

¾ cup brown sugar
½ cup vinegar
½ teaspoon dry mustard
½ teaspoon salt and pepper
8 slices bacon
3 medium onions, chopped
1 (16 ounce) can green beans
1 (16 ounce) can butter beans
1 cup sliced carrots
1 (29 ounce) can pork and beans or kidney beans

OVEN 350°

Combine brown sugar, vinegar, dry mustard, salt, and pepper for sweet and sour sauce. Fry bacon and sauté onion in 3 tablespoons bacon grease. Discard remaining grease. Combine all ingredients and bake at 350° until cooked down. (You may want to double sweet and sour sauce.)

Spicy Apple Bean Bake

1 (40 ounce) can baked beans (or pork and beans)
1 (16 ounce) can kidney beans
2 large apples, chopped
½ cup raisins
1½ cups chopped onion
1 cup chopped green pepper
1 pound lean ground beef, browned (or 3 cups leftover meat)
1 cup ketchup
½ cup sweet pickle relish
½ cup brown sugar
1 teaspoon dry mustard
½ cup molasses
4 slices crisp bacon (optional)

OVEN 275°

Mix ingredients in 3-quart casserole. Cover and bake at 275° for 2½ hours.

Better Than Baked Beans

1 can pork and beans
1 teaspoon parsley flakes
1 tablespoon blackstrap molasses (the best!), or brown sugar
Dash minced onion (optional)
½ teaspoon celery seed
¼ to ½ cup barbecue sauce

Combine ingredients and cook 5 minutes on stove over medium heat.

Onion Pie

4 tablespoons plus 2 teaspoons margarine, divided
1 cup crushed Ritz crackers
2 cups thinly sliced sweet onion
2 eggs
¾ cup milk
¾ teaspoon salt
¾ teaspoon pepper
¼ cup grated cheddar cheese
Paprika
Fresh parsley

OVEN 350°

Preheat oven to 350°. Melt 4 tablespoons margarine; mix in cracker crumbs. Press crumbs into pie plate to make crust. In large skillet, melt 2 teaspoons margarine. Sauté onions until clear but not brown. Spoon onion mixture into crust. In small bowl beat eggs with milk, salt, and pepper. Pour over onions. Top with cheese and paprika. Bake for 30 minutes. After baking, sprinkle parsley on top.

Green Chili Pie

1 onion, chopped
1 tablespoon butter
1 (4 ounce) can chopped green chilies
1 (10¾ ounce) can cream of chicken soup
1 (14 ounce) can evaporated milk
1 package corn tortillas
2 cups grated cheddar cheese

OVEN 325°

Sauté onions in butter. Add chilies; then add soup and evaporated milk. Warm thoroughly. In 2-quart casserole dish tear up and layer 3 tortillas; add layer of chili mixture then cheese. Repeat 2 more times; top with cheese. Bake in 325° oven for 20 minutes. Serve with tacos.

Barbecued Kraut

2 cans sauerkraut, juice reserved
2 cans tomatoes
1 cup firmly packed brown sugar
½ pound bacon

OVEN 350°

To juice of 1 can kraut, add 1 can tomatoes. Stir in brown sugar. Fry bacon until crisp and sprinkle over top. Bake 1 to 1½ hours at 350° (or until juice is gone).

Vegetable Medley

1 potato
1 squash
1 cup sliced okra
1 onion, sliced and separated (less if desired)

Peel potato, quarter, and slice thinly. Slice squash, quartering if large. Place all vegetables together. Add salt and pepper to taste; lightly coat with cornmeal. Fry in ¼-inch oil, turning as necessary to cook thoroughly. Cover.

(Either squash or okra may be omitted.)

Homemade Beets

5 or 6 raw red beets
1 cup red beet juice
1 cup vinegar
1 teaspoon salt
½ cup brown sugar

Wash beets; cut tops off only (do not peel). Cook with skin on until beets are done. Reserve 1 cup juice. Scrape shell off; cut into slices or cubes. Mix vinegar, salt, reserved juice, and sugar together; pour over beets.

Baked Garden Vegetables

1 cup carrots, julienned
2 cups potatoes, peeled, sliced
1 (16 ounce) package frozen baby lima beans
2 medium zucchini, quartered and sliced
2 cups bok choy, coarsely chopped (may use cabbage)
¼ cup butter (not margarine)
3 tablespoons fresh parsley, minced
¼ teaspoon Spike (salt-free seasoning)
½ teaspoon sea salt
Fresh ground black pepper

OVEN 325°

Preheat oven to 325°. Layer all vegetables in heavy casserole. Dot with butter; sprinkle with parsley and seasonings. Cover casserole and bake 45 to 60 minutes or until tender. Toss with additional butter if desired. Serve with fresh diced tomatoes.

Serves 4, generously.

Eggplant Soufflé

1 eggplant, cooked, drained, and mashed
½ (10¾ ounce) can cream of mushroom soup
1 cup soft bread crumbs
½ cup grated cheese
2 teaspoons grated onion
1 tablespoon ketchup
1 teaspoon salt
2 eggs, separated

OVEN 375°

Combine all ingredients except egg whites. Beat whites stiff and fold in. Pour into 2-quart casserole. Bake at 375° for 45 minutes or until knife inserted in center comes out clean.

Easy Eggplant Parmesan

2 medium eggplants
2 large eggs
2 tablespoons butter
1¼ cups dry bread crumbs
1½ to 2 cans spaghetti sauce
1 (8 ounce) package mozzarella cheese, shredded
2 tablespoons Parmesan cheese

OVEN 375°

Cut eggplants lengthwise into ½-inch thick slices. Beat eggs with butter until blended. Dip eggplant slices into egg mixture, then bread crumbs. Arrange on cookie sheet and broil 10 to 12 minutes until tender, turning once. Repeat with remaining slices. In 9x13-inch pan, spoon 1 cup sauce, top with eggplant, then with more sauce and half the mozzarella cheese. Repeat layering. Sprinkle Parmesan cheese on top. Bake 40 minutes, covered. Garnish with parsley.

Stuffed Peppers

1 pound ground beef
⅓ cup chopped onion
1 (16 ounce) can diced tomatoes
½ cup uncooked long-grain rice
½ cup water
1 teaspoon Worcestershire sauce
½ teaspoon salt
Dash pepper
6 green peppers, tops cut off, insides cleaned

OVEN 350°

Sauté beef and onion until brown. Add tomatoes, rice, water, Worcestershire sauce, salt, and pepper, and simmer covered for 15 minutes. While this is cooking, cut tops off peppers, clean insides out and cook 5 minutes in salted water. Stuff cooked peppers. Bake in dish 20 to 25 minutes at 350°.

Serves 6.

Carrot Hash Browns

2 tablespoons butter
1 teaspoon safflower oil
3 medium carrots, finely grated
3 medium potatoes, finely grated
½ small onion, finely grated
½ teaspoon salt

In large skillet melt butter and oil. Add carrots, potatoes, and onion. Add salt. Sauté until browned on one side. Flip over and sauté other side until browned. Break apart into small chunks or serve in wedges.

Serves 3.

Carrot Soufflé

2 pounds cooked carrots
2 cups sugar
6 eggs
2 sticks margarine
6 tablespoons flour
2 teaspoons baking powder
2 teaspoons vanilla

OVEN 350°

Blend or mash carrots; gradually add other ingredients; add baking powder and vanilla last. Beat or whip until smooth. Place in casserole. Bake 30 to 45 minutes at 350°, until firm.

Soups

Busy Day Soup

1 pound hamburger
2¼ cups tomato juice
1½ cups diced potatoes
1 cup diced celery
1 cup diced carrots
½ cup diced onion
¼ cup uncooked rice
1 can corn
1 can diced tomatoes
2 teaspoons salt
¼ teaspoon pepper
2 teaspoons Worcestershire sauce
¼ teaspoon chili powder
5 cups water

Brown hamburger. Place all ingredients in large soup pot. Cover and simmer 1 to 1½ hours until vegetables are done.

Grandma's Milk or Rivel Soup

2 quarts milk
2 to 3 tablespoons cream (or 1 to 2 tablespoons butter)
½ teaspoon salt
1 large egg
1 cup flour

Heat milk to boiling point in top of double boiler or heavy kettle. Add salt. Make rivels: cut together egg and flour to cherry-stone-size rivels. Drop rivels into hot milk. Keep milk at boiling point for 3 to 5 minutes.

Chicken and Cracker Ball Soup

Chicken (any parts)
3 cans chicken stock
1 box salted or unsalted crackers
6 eggs
2 cups milk
Salt and pepper to taste

Cover chicken with water. Add chicken stock, cover, and simmer until chicken is done. Remove and debone; set aside. Crush crackers in blender or use rolling pin until like sand. Put in bowl, add eggs, and mix slowly. Add milk until moist. Roll into balls, larger than marbles, smaller than Ping-Pong balls. Bring soup to boil. Add balls; cover for 15 minutes. Return chicken to pot.

Sopa de la Casa

8 slices bacon, diced
1¼ cups finely chopped onion
1¼ cups finely chopped celery
2 green peppers, finely chopped
2 cloves garlic, minced
2 (14½ ounce) cans broth
1 (31 ounce) can refried beans
½ teaspoon pepper
2 tablespoons chili powder
Tortilla chips
Shredded Monterey Jack cheese

In heavy pot cook bacon until crisp. Drain bacon drippings. Add onion, celery, green pepper, and garlic. Sauté until tender. Blend into broth, refried beans, and seasonings. Bring to boil; remove immediately. Garnish with chips and cheese.

Yields: 8 cups.

Granddaddy's Soup

2 chorizo (Spanish sausage), sliced
½ pound white bacon
1 pound ham, cut into bite-size pieces
1 pound stew beef, cut into bite-size pieces
1 large onion
*Small piece of sour pork (optional)
2 packages frozen turnip greens, with roots
2 large potatoes, cut up
2 large (gallon size) cans white beans
Salt and pepper to taste

In large pot put all ingredients except greens, potatoes, and beans. Cover with water and bring to boil. Reduce heat and simmer until meat is tender. Add greens, potatoes, and beans. Cook until tender. (Better the next day.)

*This is just a piece of salt pork that has been left out and turned yellow. It puts a tang in the soup. Can be bought in Tampa but you can put some in airtight container and store on shelf. Lasts years! Also, soup can be made with collard greens, but we like turnip greens best.

Lentil Soup

1 pound bacon
2 cups chopped onion
2 cups, or 1 (12 ounce) package, lentils
½ cup flour
8 cups beef stock
2 cups sliced celery
3 medium carrots, diced
2 cups diced potatoes

Sauté bacon with onion until golden; add lentils and flour. Mix well. Add broth and diced vegetables. Boil; simmer 2 hours. Salt and pepper to taste.

Hamburger Soup

1 pound ground beef
½ teaspoon salt
¼ teaspoon oregano
¼ teaspoon basil
1 tablespoon soy sauce
1 small onion, diced (or 1 package onion soup mix)
1 large or 2 small (10¾ ounce) cans tomato soup
6 cups water

Brown beef in skillet; drain off fat. In large pot put browned meat, salt, oregano, basil, soy sauce, onions or soup mix, tomato soup, and water. Add desired vegetables (carrots, potatoes, celery, etc.) and cook until tender. Bring to slow boil, then turn down to simmer. You can add a few egg noodles, macaroni, spaghetti, or beef bouillon cubes.

Hearty Hamburger Soup

2 pounds lean ground beef
1 medium onion, diced
1½ cups diced carrots
1 cup diced celery
2 cups tomato juice
2 quarts water
2 teaspoons salt
¼ teaspoon pepper
¼ cup rice or barley
2 cups diced potatoes

Brown meat lightly. Add all other ingredients except potatoes and simmer 1 hour in heavy kettle. Add potatoes and simmer 1 hour longer. Freezes well.

Cheeseburger Rice Soup

1 small onion, chopped
1 cup chopped carrots
1 cup chopped celery
2 pounds hamburger
4 cups cooked rice
4 cups milk
Small box processed cheese spread
4 tablespoons chicken seasoning cubes
16 ounces sour cream
Salt and pepper to taste

Cook onions, carrots, and celery until tender. Add fried hamburger, rice, milk, cheese, and seasoning cubes. Add sour cream last and do not boil. Season with salt and pepper.

Hodgepodge Crock-Pot Soup

1 pound ground beef
1 onion, chopped
Salt and pepper
1 (10¾ ounce) can tomato soup
1 can mixed vegetables
1 can kidney beans
1 can SpaghettiOs
½ to 1 soup can water

Optional:
1 can great northern or lima beans
1 (10¾ ounce) can minestrone soup

Brown meat and onion; drain. Add remaining ingredients. Cook in slow cooker for 2 to 3 hours.

Note: Lower salt and cholesterol by using ½ pound ground round. Use special packages (low salt and fat) of other ingredients.

Taco Soup

1 pound ground beef
1 (1¼ ounce) envelope taco seasoning
1 (14½ ounce) can stewed tomatoes
1 small can pinto beans
1 (15 ounce) can kidney beans, undrained
1 cup water
Shredded cheddar cheese (about 1¼ cups per serving)
Sliced onions
Sour cream, corn, or tortilla chips for garnish (optional)

Brown ground beef in large Dutch oven. Drain fat. Add taco seasoning, tomatoes, beans, and water; heat until soup comes to boil and is heated through. Ladle into individual bowls; top with cheese.

Yield: 5 cups.

Taco Soup

1 pound lean ground beef or turkey
1 small onion, chopped
1 large can diced tomatoes
1 package powdered ranch salad dressing
1 (1¼ ounce) package taco seasoning
1 can each kidney beans, black beans, pinto beans, white beans, and garbanzo beans, with liquid (may substitute other beans for garbanzo beans)

Brown ground beef or turkey and onion. Drain off fat. Add tomatoes, seasonings, and beans with liquid. Bring to boil and let cook until ready to serve. Serve with hot corn bread or chips. If you like it spicy, add 1 can Rotel tomatoes.

Cheddar Chowder

2 cups boiling water
2 cups diced potatoes
1 cup diced carrots
1 cup diced celery
½ cup chopped onion
1 cup cubed ham
1 small can whole kernel corn

White Sauce:
¼ cup margarine
¼ cup flour
2 cups milk
2 cups shredded cheddar cheese (Velveeta brand works well)

Combine ingredients and simmer until tender, not soft; do not drain. Make white sauce with margarine, flour, and milk in saucepan over low heat. Add cheese and blend until melted. Add to undrained vegetables slowly (can curdle), then simmer about 15 minutes. Add salt and pepper to taste. Great with corn bread!

Harvest Chowder

4 slices bacon
½ cup chopped onion, fresh or frozen
1 small clove garlic, minced
1 teaspoon basil, crumbled
1 can chicken broth
1 (10 ounce) package frozen corn
1 (10 ounce) package frozen peas and carrots
1 cup frozen hash browns
¾ teaspoon salt (optional)
¼ teaspoon pepper
1 tablespoon cornstarch
2 cups half-and-half
2 tablespoons chopped parsley (optional)

In large saucepan or Dutch oven, cook bacon until crisp. Remove bacon and add onion, garlic, and basil to drippings. Cook slowly until onion is tender. Add chicken broth, corn, peas and carrots, hash browns, salt, and pepper. Bring to boil; cover and reduce heat to simmer. Cook over moderate heat for 10 minutes or until vegetables are tender. Mix in cornstarch. Add half-and-half. Cook, stirring until soup comes to full boil. Crumble bacon and add as garnish to chowder. Also add parsley as garnish.

Makes 1½ quarts chowder, enough for 6 to 8 servings.

Potato Soup

2 medium potatoes, diced
1 large onion, diced
1 (10¾ ounce) can low-fat cream of chicken soup
Velveeta brand light cheese, cut into strips

Put ingredients in saucepan with lots of water. (Adjust to taste—lots of soup or mostly potatoes.) Salt and pepper to taste. Simmer until potatoes and onions are done. Add Velveeta and stir until cheese is melted. (Stirring is necessary to keep cheese from sticking to pan.) Remove from heat and serve.

Homemade Potato Soup

6 potatoes, peeled and cut into bite-size pieces
1 onion, chopped
1 carrot, pared and sliced
1 stalk celery, sliced
4 chicken bouillon cubes
1 teaspoon parsley flakes
Ham, cut into bite-size pieces
5 cups water
1 teaspoon salt
Pepper to taste
⅓ cup butter
1 (14 ounce) can evaporated milk

Put all ingredients except milk into pan. Cook until all vegetables are done. Stir in evaporated milk and heat to boiling point. If desired, mash potatoes with masher before serving.

Cream of Potato Soup

10 pounds of potatoes, pared and diced small
1 very small onion, diced
Parsley
2 teaspoons celery salt
1 teaspoon salt
1 stick butter
½ pint half-and-half
1 hard-boiled egg, diced

Put potatoes and onion in covered pot, in enough water to cover them. Add parsley, celery salt, and regular salt. Cook until potatoes are done and water is almost cooked off. Turn off burner and add butter and half-and-half; stir in. Then add diced egg.

Cheesy Potato Soup

4 chicken bouillon cubes
4 cups water
1 cup diced onions
1 cup diced carrots
3 cups diced potatoes
1 package California blend vegetables (optional)
2 cups broccoli florets (optional)
1 pound processed cheese, diced
3 cups milk

Combine first five ingredients plus optional choices and cook for 20 minutes. Add cheese during last 10 minutes, stirring until melted. Add milk. Continue to simmer until hot, being careful not to scorch. Reheat in double boiler. Can be frozen.

Serves 8.

Potato-Cheese Soup

3 medium potatoes, diced
1 small onion, finely chopped
Milk
3 tablespoons butter or margarine, melted
2 tablespoons flour
2 tablespoons parsley, snipped
¾ teaspoon salt
Dash pepper
1 cup shredded cheddar cheese

In 2-quart saucepan, add potatoes and onion to 1 cup salted boiling water. Cover and cook about 20 minutes or until potatoes are tender. Mash potatoes slightly; do not drain. Measure mixture and add enough milk to make 5 cups. Blend melted butter, flour, parsley, salt, and pepper. Stir into potato mixture in saucepan; cook and stir until thickened and bubbly. Add cheese. Cook and stir until cheese is partially melted. Serve immediately.

Potato Cheese Chowder

6 slices bacon
2 cups chopped onion
1 cup chopped green pepper
4 to 5 cups diced potatoes
1 cup picante sauce
3 cups water
Salt, pepper, and garlic powder to taste
1 pound processed cheese cut into 1-inch cubes

Fry bacon in large soup kettle. Set bacon aside and reserve 2 tablespoons bacon drippings. Discard remaining drippings. Add onions and pepper to drippings in kettle and cook over medium heat until soft. Add all remaining ingredients except cheese and cook until potatoes are done. Remove from heat. Add cheese and stir until melted. Serve topped with crumbled bacon.

Fifteen Bean Soup

15-beans package
2 ham hocks, or ham bone
4 small onions, chopped
⅔ cup ketchup
⅓ cup molasses
¼ cup sugar
¼ teaspoon dry mustard
1 teaspoon soy sauce

Soften beans overnight or bring to boil and let stand for 1 hour. In fresh water, simmer beans, ham, and onions for 2 hours. Combine remaining ingredients in separate bowl. Add to beans and cook for another 30 minutes.

Carrot and Ginger Soup

1 medium onion, diced
2 tablespoons ginger
½ stick butter or margarine
2 packages sliced carrots
6 medium potatoes, cubed
1 can chicken broth
1 cup water
1 tablespoon parsley
1 teaspoon grated orange peel
1 cup sour cream
½ cup skim milk
Salt and pepper to taste

Sauté onions and ginger in butter. Add carrots, potatoes, broth, and water. Simmer until vegetables are soft. Add spices. Puree. Return to pot. Add sour cream, milk, salt, and pepper to taste.

Serves 6 to 8.

Main Dishes

Easy Chicken Pot Pie

Filling:

2 cups chicken, cooked and diced
1 medium onion, chopped
4 hard-boiled eggs, sliced
2 cans mixed vegetables, drained
1 (10¾ ounce) can cream of chicken soup
1 (10¾ ounce) can cream of celery soup
½ cup chicken broth

Crust:

1 cup sweet milk
1 cup mayonnaise
1 cup self-rising flour

OVEN 350°

Preheat oven to 350°. Layer chicken, onion, and egg in greased 9x13-inch casserole dish or pan. Mix remaining ingredients and pour over layers of chicken, onion, and egg. Mix crust ingredients and spread evenly over soup and vegetable layers. Bake 1 to 1½ hours or until crust is golden brown.

Chicken Pot Pie

3 cups chicken, cooked and deboned
1 can peas
1 can sliced carrots
1¼ cups chicken broth
1 (10¾ ounce) can cream of celery soup

Topping:

1 teaspoon salt
¼ teaspoon pepper
2 teaspoons baking powder
1 cup flour
1 stick butter or margarine
1 cup milk

OVEN 375°

Place chicken in large casserole dish. Top with peas and carrots. Mix broth and soup. Pour over vegetables. Salt and pepper to taste. To make topping, mix dry ingredients. Cut butter into flour mixture. Add milk. Blend well. Pour over chicken. Bake at 375° for about 30 minutes.

Chicken Dish

3 cups chicken breast, cooked and cut up
1 package quick-cooking rice, combination long grain and wild rice with herbs and seasoning
1 (10¾ ounce) can cream of celery soup
1 small onion, chopped
1 can French-style beans, drained
1 cup mayonnaise
1 can water chestnuts, drained
Salt and pepper to taste

OVEN 350°

Mix ingredients together. Put in 2½- to 3-quart casserole dish. Bake at 350° for 30 minutes.

Overnight Chicken

2 cups cooked and diced chicken
2 cups uncooked macaroni
2 cups milk
1 (10¾ ounce) can mushroom soup
1 (10¾ ounce) can cream of chicken soup
1 cup shredded cheese
1 onion, chopped

OVEN 350°

Mix all ingredients using your own seasoning. Refrigerate overnight or for 4 hours. Bake at 350° for 60 minutes.

Oven Barbecued Chicken

6 chicken breasts, deboned and skinned
¼ cup brown sugar
⅛ teaspoon garlic powder
1 teaspoon onion powder
1 cup ketchup
½ cup water
½ cup apple cider vinegar
2 teaspoons Worcestershire sauce

Topping:
¼ cup fat-free Parmesan cheese
1 teaspoon oregano

OVEN 375°

Wash chicken and set aside. Mix together remaining ingredients in saucepan and heat to boiling. Pour over chicken. Bake 20 minutes at 375°. Turn over chicken; cover with sauce. Sprinkle with topping; bake another 15 to 20 minutes.

Creamy Baked Chicken

4 boneless chicken breasts
4 slices Swiss cheese
1 (10¾ ounce) can cream of chicken soup (thinned with water)
2 cups herb-seasoned stuffing crumbs
½ cup butter (optional)

OVEN 350°

Lay chicken in baking dish. Add cheese slice on each. Pour soup over all. Sprinkle with crumbs on top. Drizzle butter on top. Bake uncovered at 350° for 50 to 55 minutes.

Hawaiian Haystacks

2 (10¾ ounce) cans cream of chicken soup
1 cup chicken broth
2 cups cooked chicken, diced
2 cups cooked rice

Combine soup and broth to make gravy. Stir to blend. Add chicken and simmer 8 to 10 minutes. Serve gravy over rice.

Guests may add any or all of the following to their haystack. Place each in separate bowls:

1 (9 ounce) can chow mein noodles
3 tomatoes, chopped
1 cup chopped celery
½ cup chopped green pepper
½ cup chopped green onion, or may use red sweet onion
1 (20 ounce) can pineapple chunks
1 cup grated cheese
½ cup coconut
½ cup halved maraschino cherries
1 cup mandarin oranges

Phoney Abalone

5 boneless, skinless chicken breasts
2 teaspoons garlic salt
1½ teaspoons parsley
1 bottle clam juice
2 tablespoons grated Romano cheese
2½ cups cracker crumbs

Pound chicken until thin. Mix garlic salt, parsley, and clam juice in medium bowl. Add chicken and cover with tight lid. Shake to cover all chicken. Refrigerate 24 hours. Mix Romano cheese and cracker crumbs. Coat chicken with cracker mixture and brown in frying pan with small amount of oil.

Chicken and Peppers

2 chicken breasts, deboned, cut into 1-inch squares
1 envelope onion soup mix
3 tablespoons cooking oil, divided
3 tablespoons soy sauce, divided
1 clove garlic, minced
3 teaspoons cornstarch, divided
2 sweet peppers (1 green, 1 red), cut into 1-inch squares
3 stalks celery, cut into ½-inch slices
8 green onions, cut into ½-inch strips
¾ cup cold water
½ teaspoon sugar

In medium bowl combine chicken, onion soup mix, 1 tablespoon oil, 1 tablespoon soy sauce, garlic, and 1 teaspoon cornstarch; marinate 20 to 30 minutes. In large skillet heat remaining oil; cook peppers and celery over high heat for 3 minutes, stirring frequently. Add green onions and cook 2 minutes; remove from pan. Add chicken to skillet and cook 3 minutes. In small bowl, mix remaining soy sauce and cornstarch with water and sugar. Add to skillet with vegetables; simmer 3 minutes.

Makes 4 servings.

Chicken-etti

- 1 (8 ounce) package spaghetti, cooked and broken into 2 inch pieces equaling 2 cups
- 3 or 4 cups cooked and diced chicken
- ¼ cup diced green peppers
- 2 (10¾ ounce) cans cream of mushroom soup
- 1 cup chicken broth
- ¼ teaspoon celery salt
- ¼ teaspoon pepper
- 1 onion, grated
- ¾ pound processed cheese, grated (makes 2 cups)

OVEN 350°

Keep about 1 cup grated cheese for top of casserole. Combine ingredients and bake 1 hour at 350°.

Savory Poppy Seed Chicken

- 1 (10¾ ounce) can cream of chicken soup
- 8 ounces sour cream
- 1 sleeve Ritz-type crackers, crumbled
- 1 stick butter or margarine, melted
- 2 tablespoons ground poppy seeds
- 2 cups chicken, cooked and diced

OVEN 350°

Combine soup and sour cream, then set aside. Mix crumbled crackers with melted butter and poppy seeds; stir well. Place chicken in 2- or 3-quart casserole dish and pour soup mixture over all. Sprinkle with cracker crumbs. Bake at 350° for 25 minutes or until bubbly and browned on top. Great with rice!

Smoked Chicken

- 1 cup Morton Tender Quick curing salt (or slightly less)
- 8 to 10 cups water
- 1 chicken (12 pieces)
- 3 tablespoons liquid smoke

OVEN 350°

Dissolve Tender Quick in water, pour over chicken, and let stand 2 days in brine. Drain, rub on liquid smoke, and let stand overnight. Bake at 350° for 18 to 20 minutes per pound. (Bake covered.)

Classic Chicken Divan

2 (10 ounce) packages frozen broccoli spears
¼ cup butter
6 tablespoons flour
½ teaspoon each salt and pepper
2 cups chicken broth
½ cup whipping cream
3 tablespoons dry white wine
3 chicken breasts, halved and cooked
¼ cup grated Parmesan cheese

OVEN 350°

Cook broccoli using package directions; drain. Melt butter. Blend in flour, salt, and pepper. Add chicken broth; cook and stir until mixture thickens and bubbles. Stir in cream and wine. Place broccoli crosswise in 8x12-inch baking dish. Pour half the sauce over broccoli. Top with chicken. To remaining sauce add cheese; pour over chicken. Sprinkle with additional Parmesan cheese. Bake for 20 minutes or until heated through. Broil just until sauce is golden, about 5 minutes.

Crunchy Chicken Bake

1 envelope Lipton Cream of Chicken flavor Cup-a-Soup
⅓ cup hot water
1 whole chicken breast (skinless and boneless), about 1 pound
¾ cup crushed herb seasoning mix
1 tablespoon butter or margarine, melted

OVEN 375°

Preheat oven to 375°. In bowl, blend Cup-a-Soup with hot water. Dip chicken in soup mixture, then in seasoning mix; place in shallow baking dish and drizzle with butter. Bake 45 minutes or until tender.

Makes about 2 servings.

Better 'n' Fried Chicken

1½ pounds fryer chicken
½ cup powdered milk
2½ teaspoons paprika
½ teaspoon garlic salt
1 teaspoon poultry seasoning
¼ teaspoon pepper

OVEN 350°

Remove all skin and all visible fat from chicken. Put all ingredients in plastic bag with chicken pieces and shake. Bake at 350° for 1 hour.

Lemon-Pepper Chicken

1 stick margarine
5 boneless chicken breasts
Lemon pepper seasoning
1 (10¾ ounce) can cream of mushroom soup
Cooked rice

Melt margarine over medium heat. Place chicken breasts in skillet of melted margarine, sprinkle liberally with lemon pepper seasoning. Cover with lid and cook about 5 minutes. Turn breasts over and sprinkle with seasoning again. Turn breasts over again, in 5 to 7 minutes, to keep from burning. Cook approximately 20 to 25 minutes if frozen. When they are brown and done, remove from skillet. Open soup and stir into butter and drippings left. Stir well; brown. (Everything will be loosened from bottom of skillet.) Add 2½ to 3 cups water to mixture until it looks like gravy. Serve over cooked rice.

Oven-Baked Chicken

1 chicken
1 stick margarine, melted
½ cup mayonnaise
2 teaspoons dry mustard
Pepperidge Farm brand corn bread mix

OVEN 350°

Dip chicken in mixture of melted margarine, mayonnaise, and mustard. Roll in corn bread mix and put on aluminum foil on baking sheet. Bake at 350° for 30 minutes or until fork inserts easily in meat.

Chicken Reuben

4 chicken breasts, split and deboned (8 pieces)
¼ teaspoon salt
⅛ teaspoon pepper
1 (16 ounce) can sauerkraut, drained and pressed
4 slices Swiss cheese
1½ cups bottled Thousand Island dressing
1 tablespoon chopped parsley

OVEN 325°

Place chicken in greased baking dish. Sprinkle with salt and pepper. Place sauerkraut on top of chicken. Top with Swiss cheese. Spread dressing over mixture and cover with foil. Bake at 325° for 1½ hours. Sprinkle with chopped parsley.

Serves 6 to 8.

Vineyard Chicken

4 boneless, skinless chicken breasts, halved
2 tablespoons flour
¼ teaspoon dried basil
¼ teaspoon dried tarragon
¼ teaspoon paprika
Salt and freshly ground pepper
1 tablespoon butter
1 tablespoon safflower oil
2 garlic cloves, minced
1 can chicken broth
½ cup cooking wine or lemon juice
1 cup halved red grapes

Mix flour, basil, tarragon, paprika, salt, and pepper in plastic bag; toss chicken pieces in bag, one at a time. Add butter, oil, and garlic to fry pan. Brown chicken over medium-high heat for several minutes. Turn, heat, and simmer; add broth and cooking wine. Cook until reduced liquid. Add grapes. Serve over rice.

Serves 4.

Cheesy Chicken

5 (or more) pieces of chicken
1 (10¾ ounce) can cream of chicken or cream of mushroom soup
Cheese slices (regular or sharp, your choice)
Butter
Garlic salt

OVEN 350°

Place chicken in shallow pan and pour soup over top; place cheese slices on top of soup. Put butter on each piece and then sprinkle with garlic salt. Bake in 350° oven for 1 hour. Tastes great over rice or noodles.

Hot Chicken Supreme

3 whole chicken breasts, cooked and diced
1½ cups chopped celery
1 cup shredded sharp cheddar cheese
½ cup mayonnaise
¼ cup slivered almonds, toasted
¼ cup chopped pimientos
2 teaspoons chopped onion
½ teaspoon poultry seasoning
½ teaspoon grated lemon rind
1 (3 ounce) can chow mein noodles

OVEN 350°

Combine all ingredients except noodles; stir well. Spoon chicken mixture into greased 1½-quart casserole and top with noodles. Bake at 350° for 30 minutes.

Teriyaki Chicken

½ cup white sugar
½ cup soy sauce
1 teaspoon garlic powder
½ teaspoon salt
½ teaspoon ginger
1 cut-up chicken

OVEN 350°

Mix together sugar, soy sauce, garlic, salt, and ginger; dip chicken into mixture. Bake at 350° for 30 minutes each side, totaling 1 hour.

Crescent Roll Chicken

½ cup grated cheddar cheese
1 (10¾ ounce) can cream of chicken soup
½ cup milk
1 tube refrigerated crescent rolls
3 chicken breasts, cooked, boned, and cut into small pieces

OVEN 350°

Combine cheese, soup, and milk. Pour half in 9x13-inch pan. Separate rolls; place as much cut-up chicken in each roll as will fit; roll up, tucking in edges. Place in pan. Spoon other half of sauce over rolls. Sprinkle grated cheese over all (optional). Bake at 350° for 25 to 30 minutes or until lightly browned.

Note: If using 29-ounce can of chicken soup, use more cheese and 2 packages of crescent rolls.

Chicken Roll-Ups

1 package flour tortillas
4 cups leftover chicken, cut in bite-size pieces
1 (10¾ ounce) can cream of chicken soup
1 can Rotel tomatoes with chilies
8 ounces sour cream
1 cup shredded cheddar cheese

OVEN 350°

Warm tortillas in microwave for easier handling. Spoon chicken in center of tortilla and roll up tightly. Place seam side down in baking dish. Continue until all chicken is used. Mix together soup, tomatoes, and sour cream until well blended. Spoon over roll-ups, allowing to cover completely and run down sides. Spread cheddar on top. Bake at 350° for 30 minutes until cheese is melted.

Makes 10.

Chicken Bar-B-Que Sauce

12 chicken halves
1 cup oil
1½ cups vinegar
¼ cup salt
½ teaspoon pepper
3 teaspoons poultry seasoning
1 egg

Mix sauce ingredients together and shake or beat well. You can cook your chicken in pit, on grill, or in oven. If you choose to skin chicken, keep basting with sauce occasionally. It is delicious. And if you're not cooking for a crowd, keep sauce in refrigerator for later use.

Baked Steak

3-pound round steak
2 teaspoons butter
1 small onion, cut into rings
1 cup ketchup
1 tablespoon Worcestershire sauce
¼ cup water

OVEN 350°

Place meat in shallow baking pan. Spread butter over meat and top with onion rings. Mix remaining ingredients and pour over meat. Cover pan with foil and bake at 350° for 2½ to 3 hours.

Steak and Squash

2 pounds round steak, cut into cubes
6 to 8 large yellow squash, sliced
1 onion, chopped (optional)
Salt and pepper to taste

Add a little oil to skillet. Put steak cubes in skillet and let brown. Add sliced squash and onions. Add 1 cup water to skillet and let simmer, covered, over medium heat. Stir occasionally until done and juice is cooked down. Cooking time: 30 minutes. Remove lid and let brown 2 minutes.

Poor Man Steak

2 pounds lean ground beef
1 chopped onion
2 cups crushed crackers
1 (14 ounce) can evaporated milk
2 teaspoons salt
1 teaspoon pepper
2 (10¾ ounce) cans mushroom soup

OVEN 350°

Mix all except soup in loaf pan; press and let stand in refrigerator over night. Cut into slices and fry on each side, then put in baking dish and put some soup on each slice. Rinse cans with a little water and add to meat mixture. Bake at 350° for 1 hour. Use more soup if needed and use as gravy.

Deer Steak and Gravy

1 medium onion
1 bell pepper
½ cup oil
1 cup flour
2 teaspoons salt
1 teaspoon pepper
3 pounds deer steak
1 (10¾ ounce) can cream of mushroom soup

Slice onion and pepper in rings. Brown onion and pepper lightly in oil. Remove and drain. Mix flour, salt, and pepper. Pound into trimmed deer steaks. Brown on both sides. Drain off oil. Place onion and pepper rings on top of steak and spread soup on top of all. Add water to almost cover meat. Simmer, adding water as needed, until tender.

Foolproof Roast

1 roast
Favorite vegetables

Wrap roast with all of your favorite vegetables—carrots, celery, onion, etc.—in heavy-duty foil, sealing tightly. Place in Dutch oven or pan. Place pan in cold oven then turn it on to highest temperature setting for 1 hour, not to broil. Do not open oven! After 1 hour, turn oven off and leave roast inside for 3 to 4 hours. Again, it is very important that you *do not open oven*. You should serve up a perfectly cooked roast every time without worry of the house burning down while you are away.

Round Steak Stuff

1 (10¾ ounce) can cream of mushroom soup
2 (10¾ ounce) cans cream of chicken soup
2 soup cans water
1 stick margarine
1 cup uncooked rice
1½ pounds round steak

OVEN 325°

Mix soups, water, and margarine and put half of mixture in pan. Stir in rice. Cut steak into serving portions and layer on top of rice. Cover with remaining soup mixture. Cover with foil and bake at 325° for 2 to 2½ hours.

Deluxe Roast Beef

3 or more pounds roast beef
1 or 2 onions
1 (10¾ ounce) can cream of celery soup
1 (10¾ ounce) can cream of mushroom soup
½ soup can water

OVEN 325°

Heat oven to 325°. Generously line 9x13-inch pan with aluminum foil, leaving enough foil on sides to cover and seal meat. Cut off as much visible fat from meat as you can. Place meat in center of foil-lined pan. Slice onion. Place pieces on top and sides of meat.

In medium bowl, combine soups. Add water. Stir soup mixture well. Spoon over beef, moistening all visible meat. Seal meat in aluminum foil. Cook at 325° for about 45 minutes a pound so that it comes out fork tender.

If you prefer super simple gravies, don't add seasoning. Most soups on the market should have enough salt on their own. However, there's no reason why you cannot add thyme, sage, or other herbs and spices to your gravy, suited to your taste.

Creamed potatoes are perfect with this entrée since you'll have gravy. You may also serve either green peas or a medley of fresh cauliflower, broccoli, and carrots boiled together as your second vegetable. And don't forget the bread if company's coming!

Brisket

½ cup Coca-Cola brand soda pop
½ cup ketchup
4 to 6 pounds brisket
1 package dry onion soup mix
Salt and pepper

OVEN 325°

Pour Coke and ketchup over brisket; then add onion soup mix and salt and pepper. Seal well. Bake 6 hours at 325°. Serve with rice.

Creamy Ham and Broccoli Bake

1½ pounds fresh broccoli, cooked to almost tender
½ cup ham, cut into small pieces
1 (10¾ ounce) can cream soup (any kind)
¼ cup milk
½ cup shredded cheese
1 cup baking mix
¼ cup firm margarine

OVEN 400°

Place cooked broccoli and ham in 1½-quart baking dish. Heat oven to 400°. Beat soup and milk until smooth. Pour over broccoli and ham. Sprinkle with cheese. Mix baking mix with margarine until crumbly; sprinkle over top. Bake until crumbs are light brown, about 20 minutes.

Makes about 6 servings.

Family Delight Ham Loaf

2 pounds ground ham, or more according to taste
½ to 1 pound lean ground chuck
1 to 1½ cups dry bread crumbs
2 eggs, not beaten
½ to 1 cup brown sugar
1 (15 to 16 ounce) can crushed pineapple, with juice
1 to 2 tablespoons mustard

OVEN 350°

Use hand grinder or blender to grind ham. Mix all ingredients together and press into glass or metal oblong baking dish. Bake at 350° (lower if hot oven) for 45 minutes to 1 hour. Cut into cubes. If for holiday treat, put piece of maraschino or candied cherry on top.

Pineapple-Ham Corn Bread Bake

1 can crushed pineapple, drained, juice reserved
Ham, chopped
Favorite corn bread recipe
⅓ cup water
Dash salt
Sugar to taste
1 tablespoon cornstarch
1 tablespoon butter

OVEN 350°

Butter an 8x8- or 9x13-inch baking dish. Add layer of drained pineapple, then ham; top with favorite corn bread. (Add ¾ cup, per 8x8-inch pan, of cream-style corn to recipe for buttermilk corn bread. It makes it moist.) Bake at 350° for 30 to 40 minutes (until corn bread is done). Add about ⅓ cup water to reserved pineapple juice, along with dash of salt and sugar to taste; thicken with 1 tablespoon cornstarch. Add 1 tablespoon butter. May need extra juice to make enough sauce. Cut casserole into squares. Turn over on plate and pour a little sauce over top.

Crustless Grits and Ham Pie

⅓ cup quick-cooking grits, uncooked
1 cup water
1 cup evaporated skim milk
¾ cup (3 ounces) shredded cheddar cheese
¾ cup chopped lean ham
3 eggs, beaten
1 tablespoon chopped fresh parsley
½ teaspoon dry mustard
½ teaspoon hot sauce
¼ teaspoon salt
Vegetable oil cooking spray

OVEN 350°

Cook grits in water according to package directions, omitting salt. Combine cooked grits, milk, cheese, ham, eggs, parsley, mustard, hot sauce, and salt; mix well. Pour grits mixture into 9-inch pie plate coated with cooking spray. Bake at 350° for 30 to 35 minutes or until set. Let stand 5 to 10 minutes before serving.

Cranberry Pork Roast

1 lean, boneless pork roast (size can vary)
1 can jellied cranberry sauce
½ cup cranberry juice
½ cup sugar
1 teaspoon dry mustard
⅛ teaspoon cloves

Place roast in slow cooker. Combine and pour remaining ingredients over roast. Cook on low 6 to 8 hours. Thicken juice with cornstarch. Makes terrific gravy for mashed potatoes.

Candied Pork Chops

4 to 6 pork chops
2 to 3 apples, sliced with cores removed
Brown sugar
1 stick butter or margarine

OVEN 350°

Brown pork chops on both sides in skillet in small amount of oil. Heat oven to 350°. Line 9x13-inch pan with apple slices. Sprinkle apple slices generously with brown sugar. Dot with thin pats of butter or margarine. Add pork chops. Bake at 350° for 1 hour, turning chops halfway through. Baste chops often with juice from apples and brown sugar.

This dish is good with cheesy scalloped potatoes, pork-flavored stuffing, and fresh or frozen green peas.

Barbecued Pork and Beef Sandwiches

1½ pounds stew beef
1½ pounds pork cubes
2 cups chopped onion
3 green peppers, chopped
1 (6 ounce) can tomato paste
½ cup brown sugar
¼ cup cider vinegar
¼ cup chili powder
2 teaspoons salt
1 teaspoon dry mustard
2 teaspoons Worcestershire sauce

In 3½- to 5-quart slow cooker, combine all ingredients. Cover and cook on high (300°) for 8 hours. With wire whisk, stir mixture until meat is shredded. Begin 8½ hours before serving.

Makes 12 sandwiches.

Country Pork 'n' Kraut

2 pounds country-style pork ribs
1 medium onion, chopped
1 tablespoon cooking oil
1 (14 ounce) can sauerkraut, undrained
1 cup applesauce
1 teaspoon garlic powder
2 tablespoons brown sugar

Cook ribs and onion in oil until ribs are browned and onion is tender. Place in slow cooker. Combine remaining ingredients and pour over ribs. Cook on high 4 to 6 hours (or until ribs are tender). May also be cooked in Dutch oven and baked at 350° for 1½ to 2 hours.

Sausage Gumbo

½ stick margarine
1 cup diced carrots
1 cup diced onion
1 cup diced celery
1 cup diced green pepper
1 cup sliced fresh mushrooms
¼ cup soy sauce
1 quart tomato juice
1 can diced tomatoes
1 to 1½ pounds sausage, browned and drained well

In large skillet sauté in margarine carrots, onion, celery, green pepper, and mushrooms. When vegetables start to get tender, add soy sauce. Keep vegetables crunchy. In big pot put tomato juice, diced tomatoes, sausage, vegetables, and cooked rice. Heat until hot; do not boil. (Add more juice if necessary.) Good with corn bread.

African Chow Mein

1 pound lean ground beef
1 onion, chopped
2 cups water
2 cups chopped fresh celery
½ cup uncooked rice
1 (10¾ ounce) can cream of mushroom soup
1 (10¾ ounce) can chicken rice soup
¼ cup soy sauce
2 tablespoons Worcestershire sauce

OVEN 350°

Brown beef and onions. Drain grease. Boil 2 cups water and pour over other ingredients. Combine ingredients and bake 1 hour at 350°.

Serves 8.

American Stir-Fry

4 potatoes, peeled and cubed
1 pound kielbasa or Polish sausage, sliced into bite-size pieces
1 large green pepper, diced
1 can whole kernel corn, drained
Salt and pepper to taste

In skillet place enough oil to fry potatoes on high heat. Once potatoes brown and begin to soften, add sausage and brown. Stir often to keep from scorching and for even cooking. After sausage has browned, reduce heat to medium and add green pepper. Stir thoroughly then add corn; stir again and leave on heat just long enough for peppers and corn to be heated through.

S.T.T.T. (Something I Threw Together)

1 pound leftover meat
2 cups leftover vegetables
1 (10¾ ounce) can tomato soup (for spicy dish, try salsa or spaghetti sauce)
1 (10¾ ounce) can cheddar cheese soup (for spicy dish, use nacho cheese soup)
1 pound cooked macaroni

OVEN 350°

Mix meat, vegetables, and tomato soup; put in casserole dish. Mix cheddar cheese soup and macaroni; spread on top of meat mixture. Bake at 350° for 20 minutes. Vary soups to make different flavors. Also works with canned meats, mixed meats, and canned vegetables.

Mousaka

1½ pounds ground meat (soy may be used instead or a combination of the two)
2 tablespoons chopped onion
4 tablespoons butter or margarine, divided
½ cup water, or wine
1½ pounds ripe tomatoes (canned tomatoes may be substituted)
2 tablespoons chopped parsley
Salt and pepper to taste
2½ pounds eggplant
Oil for frying
1 cup dry bread crumbs
½ cup grated Parmesan cheese

White Sauce:
2 tablespoons butter
2 tablespoons flour
1 cup milk
Salt and pepper to taste

OVEN 375°

Brown ground meat and onion in 2 tablespoons butter. Stir to avoid lumping and pour in water. Add strained tomatoes, parsley, salt, and pepper and let simmer until all liquid is absorbed. Meanwhile, wash, dry, and clean eggplant. Cut lengthwise, one by one, into thin slices (a little bit less than ½-inch thick) and fry both sides in hot oil. Remove, drain, and sprinkle with salt and pepper.

Prepare white sauce: In small saucepan melt butter. Over low heat add flour and stir until flour vanishes. Slowly stir in milk and stir until sauce thickens. Season with salt and pepper.

Lay half of eggplant slices in rows on bottom of large baking dish. Add half the bread crumbs and half the cheese to ground meat. Mix and spread mixture on top of eggplant. Layer rest of eggplant over meat sauce and cover it all with white sauce. Sprinkle with remainder of cheese and bread crumbs. Pour 2 tablespoons melted butter over top and bake for 1 hour, or until top turns golden brown.

Hamburger Rice and Cheese

1½ pounds hamburger
1 medium onion, diced
2 cups brown rice
1 cup grated cheddar cheese

In large fry pan, fry hamburger and onion. In separate saucepan, boil rice; drain. Add rice to hamburger and onion; stir. Sprinkle cheese over top and cover with lid until cheese melts.

Hot Dog/Sloppy Joe Sauce

4 pounds ground beef
2 cups chopped onion
1 green pepper, chopped
4 cups ketchup
4 teaspoons salt
4 teaspoons pepper
4 tablespoons chili powder
2 teaspoons mustard
1 cup vinegar
1 cup sugar
1 cup water

Brown ground beef, onion, and green pepper together; then drain. Add remaining ingredients and bring just to boiling stage. Reduce to simmer. Cook on low, stirring intermittently, for 1 hour. Can be stored in refrigerator for up to a week.

Makes approximately 1 gallon.

Hamburger Summer Sausage

¾ cup water
2 pounds lean hamburger
¼ teaspoon onion powder
1 tablespoon liquid hickory smoke
1 tablespoon mustard seed
¼ teaspoon pepper
¼ teaspoon salt
¼ teaspoon garlic powder
2 tablespoons Morton Tender Quick curing salt

OVEN 350°

Mix all ingredients together. Form two long rolls; wrap in foil. Refrigerate 24 hours. Poke fork hole on bottom of rolls. Place on rack over pan to catch liquid. Bake at 350° for 1 hour 15 minutes.

Heavenly Hamburger

1½ pounds ground beef
1 clove garlic
Salt to taste
Dash pepper
1 teaspoon sugar
2 tablespoons butter
2 small cans tomato sauce
1 (8 ounce) package lasagna noodles
1 (3 ounce) package cream cheese
1 cup sour cream
8 green onions, tops cut off
½ pound grated cheddar cheese

OVEN 350°

Brown meat, garlic, salt, pepper, and sugar in butter. Drain excess grease. Add tomato sauce and simmer 20 minutes. Cook noodles in salted water and drain. Soften cream cheese. Add to sour cream and onions. Layer noodles with sauce and cheese in 9x13-inch pan. Bake at 350° for 20 minutes.

Dad's Favorite Six-Layer Baked Dinner

2 medium white potatoes, sliced
1 onion, sliced
½ cup white rice, uncooked
1 pound lean ground beef, uncooked
2 medium carrots, thinly sliced
1 large can tomatoes, or 1 quart canned

OVEN 350°

Layer potatoes, onions, rice, ground beef, and carrots in large oven-safe dish and top with tomatoes. Sprinkle salt and pepper on each layer. Cover and bake in 350° oven for 3 hours.

Optional: After baked, sprinkle with grated cheddar cheese.

Pizza Burgers

1 pound ground beef
1 (10¾ ounce) can tomato soup
1 (15 ounce) can pizza sauce
12 sandwich buns
8 ounces mozzarella cheese

Brown ground beef in skillet; add tomato soup and pizza sauce; mix well. Cover and simmer 10 minutes. Separate buns, place on cookie sheet, put sauce on buns, and add mozzarella cheese on top. Place under broiler in oven for 3 minutes or until brown.

Pizza/Hamburger Crust

1 pound ground beef
½ cup dry bread crumbs
1 teaspoon salt
½ teaspoon oregano
1 cup tomato sauce
1 can kidney beans
Shredded cheddar or mozzarella cheese

OVEN 425°

Mix in large bowl, with spoon, ground beef, bread crumbs, salt, and oregano. Stir in tomato sauce. Spread meat mixture in ungreased 10-inch pizza pan. Pour ½ cup tomato sauce on top. Add kidney beans. Sprinkle with cheddar or mozzarella cheese. Bake uncovered for 20 minutes.

Serves 4.

Sattler Family Goop

1 pound ground beef
1 onion
1 package macaroni and cheese dinner
1 (10¾ ounce) can tomato soup
1 (10¾ ounce) can cream of mushroom soup
Grated Parmesan cheese (optional)

Brown ground beef with onion; drain fat. Cook macaroni and drain. When meat is cooked, add soups and cheese sauce package mix (no milk or butter, Just powder), and stir well. Heat until bubbly. Add macaroni and serve. Sprinkle with grated Parmesan cheese if desired.

Italian Delight

1 pound ground beef
1 small onion, chopped
1 package egg noodles, cooked and drained
1 can Italian stewed tomatoes
1 (4 ounce) can tomato sauce
1 (4 ounce) can mushroom pieces, drained (optional)
1 cup grated mozzarella cheese
1 cup grated cheddar cheese

OVEN 350°

Cook beef and onion together, while boiling noodles. Combine beef/onion mixture with noodles, tomatoes, sauce, and mushrooms. Toss until mixed well. Pour into 2½-quart baking dish. Top with cheeses. Bake at 350° for 30 minutes or until heated through and cheese melts.

Gloop, Glop, and Gleep

1 pound ground beef
Lawry's seasoned salt
Pepper
Worcestershire sauce
1 large onion, thinly sliced
3 medium potatoes, thinly sliced
1 (15 ounce) can creamed corn
1 (10 ounce) can condensed tomato soup

OVEN 350°

Brown beef, making into small chunks. Season to taste with Lawry's salt, pepper, and Worcestershire sauce. Pour off excess grease. Layer onions, then potatoes, then onions, then potatoes, about 3 layers of each, and season each layer. Spread can of creamed corn over potatoes, then tomato soup (undiluted) over all. Cover and bake in 350° oven for 1 hour or until potatoes are done.

Haystack Dinner

1 pound ground beef
Sloppy joe seasoning mix
Brown sugar
Mustard
1 small can tomato sauce
1 cup cooked rice
1 (10¾ ounce) can nacho cheese soup
1 soup can milk
1 tablespoon flour
12 club-style crackers, crumbled
2 cups chopped/shredded of each:
  lettuce, tomato, green pepper,
  cheddar cheese, mozzarella cheese

Brown ground beef; add sloppy joe seasoning mix (with onion if you like), brown sugar, mustard, and tomato sauce (like sloppy joe mixture). Set aside. Prepare rice following package instructions. (Either cooked or minute kind will work.) To prepare cheese sauce, heat cheese soup and milk. Thicken slightly with white sauce (flour and milk).

Each person then "builds his or her own "stack." Layer as follows: crumbled club crackers, rice, sloppy joe mixture, lettuce, tomato, green pepper, grated cheeses, and hot cheese sauce.

This amount serves approximately 6.

Shepherd's Pie

2 cups chopped cooked roast beef
1 can corn
1½ cups brown gravy
3 cups mashed potatoes

OVEN 350°

In casserole dish, layer beef, corn, gravy, then top with potatoes. Bake for 30 minutes at 350°. Hot rolls are a great addition to this meal.

Shepherd's Pie

1½ pounds hamburger
1 medium onion, chopped
1 (10¾ ounce) can tomato soup
1 (15 ounce) can tomato sauce
1 can whole kernel corn
1 can green beans
Grated cheddar cheese
7 or 8 potatoes, cooked and sliced
Salt to taste
Garlic powder to taste
Cheese spread

Brown hamburger with onion; drain. Add other ingredients. Season with salt and garlic powder. Pour into 9x13-inch baking dish. Sprinkle with cheese spread.

Super Supper Pie

1 pound hamburger
½ cup chopped celery
¼ cup chopped green pepper
1 small onion, chopped
2 medium carrots, grated
¼ teaspoon chili powder
½ cup uncooked rice
1 cup water
¼ cup ketchup
Favorite biscuit dough
1 (10¾ ounce) can cream soup
(chicken, mushroom, or celery)
½ soup can milk
½ cup grated cheese

OVEN 375°

Brown hamburger, celery, green pepper, and onion. Add carrots, chili powder, uncooked rice, and water. Simmer until rice is tender. Add ketchup. Mix favorite biscuit dough and divide in half. Pat half into pie pan. Spread meat mixture on dough. Dilute soup with milk. Pour over meat. Sprinkle with grated cheese. Roll out remaining dough and cover pie. Bake at 375° for 25 to 30 minutes.

Note: Meat mixture alone makes a skillet meal. It can be varied to taste.

German Skillet Dinner

2 tablespoons margarine
1 (1 pound) can sauerkraut, with juice
¾ cup quick-cooking rice, uncooked
1 medium onion, diced
1 to 1½ pounds ground beef
8 ounces tomato sauce

In 10-inch skillet with lid, melt margarine and add sauerkraut (with juice). Spread kraut evenly and add uncooked rice. Sprinkle diced onion over rice and kraut. Distribute uncooked ground beef over mixture. Pour tomato sauce over all. Cover and cook over medium heat for 20 minutes.

Shipswreck

2 pounds hamburger
1 small onion, chopped
3 to 4 large potatoes, sliced
2 (15 ounce) cans pork and beans
2 (10¾ ounce) cans tomato soup
8 ounces grated cheese

OVEN 350°

Cook hamburger and onion together. Layer potatoes, hamburger mixture, pork and beans, and then soup in 9x13-inch baking dish. Bake at 350° until potatoes are done, about 1½ hours. Put cheese on top and resume cooking until cheese is melted.

Oven Meatballs

2 pounds lean ground beef
1 cup cornflake crumbs
¼ cup chopped parsley
2 eggs
2 tablespoons soy sauce
¼ teaspoon pepper
½ teaspoon garlic powder
⅓ cup ketchup
2 tablespoons dried minced onion

Sauce:
1 can jellied cranberry sauce
1 (12 ounce) bottle chili sauce
2 tablespoons brown sugar
1 tablespoon lemon juice

OVEN 350°

Combine meatball ingredients; shape into 20 small balls. Place in 9x13-inch pan. Combine sauce ingredients. Cook over medium heat, stirring until smooth. Pour over meatballs. Bake uncovered 35 to 45 minutes.

Barbecued Meatballs

3 pounds ground chuck
2 cups oats
2 eggs
1 (14 ounce) can evaporated milk
1 cup chopped onions
2 teaspoons salt
½ tablespoon garlic powder
2 teaspoons chili powder
½ teaspoon pepper

Sauce:
2 cups ketchup
1½ cups brown sugar
½ teaspoon garlic powder
½ cup chopped onion

OVEN 350°

Mix meatball ingredients and make into balls. Place in flat pan, one layer to each pan. Bake 20 minutes at 350°. Remove from oven and drain grease. Mix sauce ingredients together until sugar dissolves. Pour over balls and bake uncovered about 40 minutes.

Meatballs with Sauce

3 pounds hamburger
1 (12 ounce) can evaporated milk
2 eggs
2 cups quick-cooking oats
2 teaspoons salt
½ teaspoon pepper
1 onion, chopped
½ teaspoon garlic powder
2 teaspoons chili powder
2 to 3 tablespoons Worcestershire sauce

Sauce:
2 cups ketchup
2 teaspoons liquid smoke
1½ cups brown sugar
¾ cup chopped onion
½ teaspoon garlic powder

OVEN 350°

Mix meatball ingredients together and shape into balls about 1½ inches in diameter. Place in single layer in pan. Pour sauce over top and bake for 1 hour.

Grandma Lucy's Meatballs

2 pounds ground beef
2 eggs
2½ cups bread crumbs
1 medium onion, finely chopped
1 tablespoon salt
1 teaspoon chili powder

Sauce:
2 cups water
1 teaspoon chili powder
1 teaspoon salt
1 (10¾ ounce) can tomato soup
1 onion, finely chopped
1 green pepper, finely chopped

Mix all meatball ingredients together and form into balls the size of an egg. Set aside. To make sauce, mix all ingredients together in Dutch oven or electric fry pan. Heat to boiling. Drop in meatballs. Bake 1 hour in moderate oven or cook on top of stove or in electric fry pan. Stir occasionally. Serve with rice, pasta, or potatoes.

Mexican Sandwiches

3 pounds ground beef
1 medium onion, chopped
1 (10 to 12 ounce) package grated Colby cheese
1 (15 ounce) can tomato sauce
1 (4 ounce) can chopped ripe olives
1 (4 ounce) can salsa
2 dozen hard rolls

OVEN 350°

Brown beef and onions; drain. Add remaining ingredients except rolls. Pinch bread out of center of rolls; fill with beef mixture. Wrap each roll in foil. Bake at 350° for 30 minutes.

Cheesy Barbecued Meatballs

2 cups cornflakes
2 eggs
⅓ cup milk
½ teaspoon salt
⅛ teaspoon pepper
½ pound ground beef
1 cup shredded cheddar or mozzarella cheese

Sauce:
1 cup ketchup
¾ cup water
2 tablespoons vinegar
3 tablespoons brown sugar
1 tablespoon minced onion
1 teaspoon salt

OVEN 350°

Crush cornflakes in medium bowl. Add eggs, milk, salt, and pepper. Mix well. Let stand 5 minutes. Add ground beef and cheese; mix well. Shape into 1-inch balls. Place in baking dish. Mix all ingredients for sauce together. Pour over meatballs. Bake at 350° for 40 to 50 minutes.

Swedish Meatballs

1 pound ground beef
½ cup cracker crumbs
1 egg
1 envelope dry onion soup mix
1 (10¾ ounce) can cream of chicken soup
½ soup can water

OVEN 350°

Mix ground beef, cracker crumbs, egg, and half of onion soup mix. Shape into balls and place in casserole dish. Combine chicken soup, water, and other half of onion soup mix. Pour over meatballs. Bake at 375° for 35 minutes.

Swedish Meatballs

2 pounds ground chuck
1 cup bread crumbs
½ cup milk
Salt and pepper to taste

Sauce:
2 tablespoons Worcestershire sauce
1 cup ketchup
2 tablespoons vinegar
Dash Tabasco sauce
Dash nutmeg
1 onion, finely chopped
2 tablespoons horseradish

OVEN 350°

Mix meatball ingredients together and shape into small balls. Place in ungreased casserole dish. Mix sauce ingredients together and pour over meatballs. Bake at 350° for 1 hour.

Swedish Meatballs

½ cup chopped onion
2 tablespoons butter or margarine
1 egg, slightly beaten
1½ cups bread crumbs
½ cup evaporated milk
¼ cup chopped fresh parsley
¼ teaspoon nutmeg
¼ teaspoon ginger
1¼ teaspoons salt
½ teaspoon pepper
1½ pounds ground beef or turkey

Sauce:
3 tablespoons butter
1 teaspoon beef bouillon
1 tablespoon soy sauce
2 tablespoons flour
1¼ cups water

OVEN 350°

Cook onion in butter until tender; drain (save butter). Combine beaten egg, bread crumbs, milk, spices, meat, and onion. Mix well, cover, and chill for at least 1 hour. Shape into balls. Spray pan with cooking spray. Bake at 350° for 10 to 12 minutes. While baking, in saucepan combine butter drippings with remaining sauce ingredients. Mix well. Cook, stirring until thick and bubbly. Drain excess grease off meatballs; then pour sauce over meatballs and bake about 20 minutes longer. Serve with mashed potatoes.

Saucy Meatballs

2 pounds ground beef (or turkey)
¼ teaspoon pepper
Dash salt
⅓ cup ketchup
1 cup crushed cornflakes
2 tablespoons finely chopped onion
½ teaspoon garlic powder
2 tablespoons low-salt soy sauce
2 eggs

Sauce:
½ bottle chili sauce
1 can jellied cranberry sauce
2 tablespoons brown sugar
1 teaspoon lemon juice

OVEN 350°

Mix all meatball ingredients well. Form into small balls, 1½ to 2 inches. Mix sauce ingredients together and pour over meatballs. Bake at 350° for about 45 minutes in foil-lined pan. These freeze well. Serve over noodles or mashed potatoes if desired.

Mushroom Meat Loaf

2 pounds very lean ground beef
1 cup coarse oats
3 large eggs
2 (10¾ ounce) cans mushroom soup
Heavy sprinkle garlic powder
Black pepper to taste
Chopped onion to taste (2 to 4 tablespoons)
No salt (salt in soup)

OVEN 350°

Measure all, reserving 1 can mushroom soup for topping, into baking dish; mix well. Smooth out and put second can of mushroom soup over top. Cut through mixture, once, end to end. Cut across 3 times. Bake at 350° until well done, about 1 hour. Freezes well.

Veggie Meat Loaf

1 pound ground beef
1 onion
1 egg
Salt and pepper to taste
1 (10¾ ounce) can vegetable soup
Enough cracker crumbs to hold loaf together

OVEN 350°

Mix all ingredients; put into baking dish. Bake at 350° for about 1 hour.

Meat Loaf Using Tapioca

2½ to 3 pounds ground beef
1 large onion, chopped
4 tablespoons quick-cooking tapioca
1 teaspoon salt
2 eggs, beaten
1½ cups canned diced tomatoes, drained
4 tablespoons ketchup
½ teaspoon pepper
1 teaspoon Worcestershire sauce

OVEN 375°

Mix together all ingredients thoroughly. Put into loaf pan. Bake at 375° for 45 minutes.

Meat Loaf with Oatmeal

1 pound lean ground beef or ground chuck
1 tablespoon diced minced onion or 2 ounces chopped onion
2 tablespoons chopped parsley
1 teaspoon seasoned salt
½ teaspoon oregano
2 tablespoons ketchup
¾ cup oats
1 cup milk
1 tablespoon Worcestershire sauce
1 tablespoon brown sugar

OVEN 350°

Combine all ingredients. Place in loaf pan and press into meat loaf form. Bake uncovered at 350° for at least 1 hour until meat is no longer pink.

Optional: After pressing into pan, cover with ketchup. May also cover with cornflake crumbs.

Meat Loaf with Carrots

1½ pounds ground beef
1 tablespoon diced onion
1 cup crushed crackers
Salt and pepper to taste
½ cup grated carrots
2 eggs
¼ cup milk

Topping:
¼ cup brown sugar
1 tablespoon mustard
¼ cup ketchup

OVEN 350°

Combine meat loaf ingredients. Put into loaf pan. Combine topping ingredients and pour over top of meat. Bake at 350° for 45 minutes.

Meat Loaf with Sauce

2 pounds ground beef
½ cup oats
½ cup bread crumbs
4 eggs
1 medium onion, diced
¼ cup dill pickle juice

Sauce:
½ cup ketchup
¼ cup water
2 teaspoons sugar
1 teaspoon Worcestershire sauce
½ cup diced dill pickles

OVEN 350°

Mix meat loaf ingredients together thoroughly and put into greased pan. Mix sauce and pour over shaped loaf. Bake at 350° for 1 to 1½ hours.

Fluffy Meat Loaf

1 pound ground beef
½ pound ground pork
2 cups bread crumbs
1 egg, beaten
1½ cups milk
4 tablespoons minced onion
2 teaspoons salt
¼ teaspoon pepper
¼ teaspoon mustard
⅛ teaspoon sage

OVEN 350°

Mix all ingredients thoroughly; pack into greased baking dish. Bake 1½ hours at 350°.

Tamale Loaf

1 large onion, minced
Cooking oil
1 large can creamed corn
1 large can tomatoes with puree
Salt and pepper to taste
¾ cup cornmeal
1 egg, beaten
Olives
1 cup raw ground meat

OVEN 350°

Fry onion in oil until tender. Add corn, tomatoes, salt, and pepper (break up tomatoes). Bring to boil and add cornmeal gradually. Cook about 10 minutes. Remove from heat; add egg, olives, and raw ground meat. Bake about 45 minutes at 350°.

Mexican Meat Loaf

1½ pounds hamburger
½ onion, chopped
1 (6 ounce) can tomato paste
1 (4 ounce) can chopped green chilies
1 (10¾ ounce) can chicken rice soup
Tortilla chips
Grated cheese

OVEN 350°

Brown hamburger and onion together. Add tomato paste, chilies, and soup to meat mixture. Put half of mixture into casserole. Layer tortilla chips on top. Add rest of meat mixture. Sprinkle cheese on top. Bake at 350° for 30 minutes.

Black Bean Burritos

2 medium carrots, chopped
2 cloves garlic, chopped
1 medium onion, chopped
2 teaspoons vegetable oil
1 can black beans, drained
1 cup corn
¾ teaspoon cumin
¼ teaspoon salt
¼ teaspoon pepper
8 flour tortillas
1 cup shredded Monterey Jack cheese

OVEN 350°

Preheat oven to 350°. In large skillet, sauté carrots, garlic, and onion in oil for 5 minutes, until tender. Partially mash beans. Add to skillet with corn, cumin, salt, and pepper. Cook 2 minutes. Lay tortillas on flat work surface; place ¼ cup bean mixture in center of each tortilla. Roll up and place seam side down in 9x13-inch pan. Sprinkle with cheese; bake 10 minutes. Serve immediately.

Festive Fajitas

3 to 4 boneless chicken breasts
1 tablespoon oil
¼ teaspoon garlic powder
1 cup green pepper, cut into strips
¾ cup sliced onions
1 (10 ounce) package Mexican-style processed cheese
8-inch tortillas
Chopped tomatoes

Cut chicken breasts and stir-fry in oil and garlic powder. Add green pepper strips and onions. Continue to stir-fry for 5 minutes. Cut cheese into cubes and add to chicken. Stir until cheese is melted; do not allow to boil. Place desired amount of chicken/cheese mixture in center of 8-inch tortilla. Top with chopped tomatoes. Fold.

Mexican Roll-Ups

2½ cups cubed chicken or turkey (leftovers work great!)
½ cup sour cream
1 cup shredded cheese
1½ teaspoons taco seasoning
½ (10¾ ounce) can mushroom soup
1 small onion, chopped
½ cup salsa
¼ cup sliced ripe olives
10 (7-inch) flour tortillas

Sauce:
1 cup sour cream
1½ teaspoons taco seasoning
½ (10¾ ounce) can mushroom soup

OVEN 350°

Combine roll-up ingredients and place ⅓ cup on each of 10 flour tortillas; roll up and place in greased 9x13-inch baking dish. Combine sauce ingredients and pour over tortillas; bake at 350°

for 30 minutes. Sprinkle with more shredded cheese. Serve with shredded lettuce, chopped tomatoes, and salsa.

Black Bean and Cheese Tortilla Pie

1 deep-dish piecrust
3 tablespoons vegetable oil
½ cup chopped onion
½ cup chopped green pepper
1 (15 ounce) can black beans, drained and rinsed
½ cup salsa
2 cups shredded cheddar cheese
3 flour tortillas
Sour cream (optional)

OVEN 350°

Prepare piecrust per package directions for unfilled crust. Heat oil in skillet; add onion and green pepper. Stir-fry until tender (about 5 minutes). Add beans and salsa; simmer 7 to 10 minutes. Spoon ½ cup bean mixture into piecrust. Layer with cheese then tortilla. Repeat layers twice. Bake at 350° until cheese is melted. Serve with sour cream if desired.

Mexican Bean Rolls

1½ pounds ground chuck (browned and drained)
1 (1¼ ounce) package taco seasoning mix
1 can Rotel tomatoes with chilies
1 can water
1 or 2 cans refried beans
Flour tortillas
Monterey Jack cheese for topping

Simmer down until thick. Put meat mix in flour tortillas and roll up. Sprinkle with Monterey Jack cheese. Microwave until cheese melts. Top with lettuce, tomatoes, olives, and sour cream.

Taco Pie

Taco chips
1 pound ground turkey or beef
1 (1¼ ounce) package taco seasoning mix
¾ cup water
1 large jar mild salsa
1 (8 ounce) can kidney beans
Shredded cheddar cheese

OVEN 350°

Crumble chips to cover bottom of 9x13-inch pan. Brown meat and spread on chips. Mix taco seasoning and water; pour over meat. In blender, mix salsa and beans; pour on top. Top with cheese. Bake at 350° for 20 minutes. Top each serving with favorite taco toppings.

Chicken Taco

4 boiled chicken breasts, torn in pieces
½ pound processed cheese, cubed
1 (10¾ ounce) can mushroom soup
1 can Rotel tomatoes, regular or hot
1 (8 ounce) bag tortilla chips

Mix all ingredients together, except tortilla chips, in baking dish. Top with chips. Heat in microwave until cheese is bubbly. Serve with more chips.

Chile Rellenos Casserole

1 cup half-and-half
2 eggs
⅓ cup flour
½ pound grated Monterey Jack cheese
½ pound grated longhorn Colby cheese
3 (4 ounce) cans whole green chilies or fresh chilies
1 can tomato sauce

OVEN 350°

In blender, mix together half-and-half, eggs, and flour until smooth. Toss together cheeses and reserve ½ cup. Split chilies and wash seeds out; drain on paper towels. Make layers of cheese, chilies, and egg mixture; repeat until done. Pour tomato sauce over top and sprinkle with cheese. Bake 45 minutes to 1 hour at 350°, until done.

Taco Casserole

1 bag tortilla chips
1 pound ground beef, browned and drained
1 can chili beans, drained
1 can Rotel tomatoes
1 (10¾ ounce) can cream of mushroom soup
1 (1¼ ounce) package taco seasoning mix
Lettuce
Chopped tomatoes
Shredded cheddar cheese

OVEN 350°

In casserole dish, crumble enough of tortilla chips to cover bottom of dish. In large bowl, mix together beef, chili beans, Rotel, and cream of mushroom soup. Add taco seasoning. Pour into casserole dish; top with crushed tortilla chips. Bake at 350° for 30 minutes. Top with lettuce, chopped tomatoes, and shredded cheddar cheese.

Pop-Over Taco

1 pound ground beef
1 large onion, diced
1 (1¼ ounce) package taco seasoning mix
1 (15 ounce) can tomato sauce
½ cup water
1 (16 ounce) can refried beans
4 ounces chopped green chilies, divided
1 cup grated Monterey Jack cheese
1 cup milk
2 eggs
1 tablespoon oil
1 cup flour

OVEN 400°

Brown beef and onion. Stir in taco seasoning, tomato sauce, and water. Simmer 10 minutes. Spread refried beans in greased 9x13-inch baking pan. Layer half of chilies over beans, pour meat mixture evenly over chilies, layer remaining chilies over meat. Top with grated cheese.

Blend milk, eggs, oil, and flour. Pour evenly over pan. Bake at 400° for 30 minutes or until golden brown. Cut into squares.

Navajo Taco

1 rounded tablespoon shortening
¾ cup water
¼ cup milk
2 cups flour
1 teaspoon baking powder
1 teaspoon salt

Cut shortening into water and milk. Mix with dry ingredients and knead until elastic. If top is sticky, add flour sparingly. Let stand 15 minutes or let rest in refrigerator up to a few hours. Divide dough into 8 equal parts. Roll out as pie dough. Fry in ½ inch hot grease until medium light brown. Turn to other side and brown. Top with lettuce, tomatoes, and cheddar cheese.

Chicken Enchilada Casserole

1 medium onion, chopped
2 to 3 tablespoons margarine
4 cups chicken, cooked and cubed
1 cup chicken broth
1 cup cream of mushroom soup
1 cup cream of chicken soup
1 (4 ounce) can chopped green chilies
12 corn tortillas, torn into eighths
1 pound grated longhorn cheese

OVEN 350°

Sauté onion in margarine. Mix all ingredients except tortillas and cheese together in large bowl. Spray large casserole dish with cooking spray. Layer several times: chicken mixture, tortillas, and cheese. Bake at 350° for 30 minutes.

Serves 8.

Chicken Enchiladas

8 to 10 chicken breasts or turkey, boiled and chopped
2 (4 ounce) cans diced green chilies
1 medium onion, chopped
2 dozen corn tortillas
2 (10¾ ounce) cans cream of chicken soup
1 cup broth from boiled chicken
¼ teaspoon cumin
¼ teaspoon sage
½ teaspoon chili powder
½ teaspoon oregano
Grated cheese
Black olives (optional)

OVEN 300°

Mix chopped chicken with chilies and onion. Set aside. Dip tortillas in hot oil until soft. Place small amount of chicken mixture in each tortilla and roll. Place tortilla rolls in deep pan. Combine soup, broth, and spices. Pour over tortilla rolls and cover with cheese and olives. Bake at 300° for 30 minutes. Can be served with lettuce, tomatoes, and taco sauce. Reheats well.

Jean's Chicken Enchiladas

8 large flour tortillas
2 (10¾ ounce) cans cream of chicken soup
1 cup sour cream
½ teaspoon salt

Filling:
1 pound grated longhorn cheese
1 cup diced onion
1 whole chicken, cooked and diced

OVEN 350°

Heat soup, sour cream, and salt until smooth. Mix cheese, onion, and chicken together. Fill each tortilla with cheese mix. Add small amount of sauce to filling, then roll each tortilla. Place in greased 9x13-inch pan or dish. Pour sauce over top and bake 25 to 30 minutes in 350° oven. Freezes very well.

Chicken Enchiladas

1 medium onion, chopped
2 tablespoons margarine
½ cup shredded cooked chicken
12 ounces picante sauce, divided
3 ounces cream cheese, cubed
8 ounces shredded sharp cheese, divided
8 (6-inch) flour tortillas

OVEN 350°

Cook and stir onion in margarine in skillet until tender. Stir in chicken, ¼ cup picante, and cream cheese. Cook until thoroughly heated. Stir in 1 cup cheese. Spoon about ⅓ cup mixture in center of each tortilla; roll up. Place seam side down in 7x12-inch baking dish. Top with remaining picante and cheese. Bake for 15 minutes at 350°.

Chicken Enchiladas

1 medium onion, chopped
1 (4 ounce) can green chilies, drained
1 stick butter
2 (10¾ ounce) cans cream of chicken soup
1 (12 ounce) can evaporated milk
Shredded cooked chicken
Grated cheddar cheese
Tortilla shells

OVEN 300°

Cook onion and chilies in butter until onions are clear. Mix soup and milk and add onions/chilies mixture. Roll shredded chicken and cheese in tortilla shells and place in 9x13-inch pan. Pour sauce over top. Bake at 300° for 30 minutes. Add cheese on top, bake until melted.

Mexican Casserole

1 pound hamburger
½ onion, chopped
1 (10¾ ounce) can cream of chicken soup
8 ounces taco sauce
1 can enchilada sauce
Corn tortillas
Grated cheddar cheese
1 can sliced black olives (optional)

OVEN 350°

Brown meat and onion; drain. Add soup and sauces. In 9x13-inch casserole dish layer tortillas, half of meat mixture, and half of cheese; repeat. Bake at 350° for 20 to 30 minutes.

Enchilada Casserole

1 (10¾ ounce) can mushroom soup
1 (10¾ ounce) can cheddar cheese soup
1 can enchilada sauce
1 (16 ounce) can refried beans
1 package corn tortillas, frozen
1 pound hamburger, browned
1 (4 ounce) can green chilies (optional)
1 onion, chopped
1 pound grated cheese

OVEN 350°

Mix soups, sauce, and beans together to make pudding. Layer ingredients starting with pudding, then tortillas, pudding, meat, chilies, onion, and cheese. Repeat until all ingredients are used. Bake at 350° for 30 minutes to 1 hour.

Chicken Enchiladas Texas Style

3 slices bacon
3 pounds skinless, boneless chicken breasts, cut in short thin strips
2 cloves garlic, minced
1 (16 ounce) can black beans, undrained
1 teaspoon ground cumin
¼ teaspoon salt
1½ cups picante sauce, divided
½ cup sliced green onions
12 (6 to 7 inch) flour tortillas
1½ cups shredded Monterey Jack cheese, divided

OVEN 350°

Cook bacon in 10-inch skillet until crisp; crumble. Pour off all but 2 tablespoons drippings. Cook and stir chicken and garlic in drippings until chicken is done. Stir in beans, cumin, salt, and ½ cup picante sauce. Simmer until thickened, 7 to 9 minutes, stirring occasionally. Stir in onions and bacon. Spoon heaping ¼ cup bean mixture down center of each tortilla; top with 1 tablespoon cheese. Roll up and place seam side down in lightly greased 9x13-inch dish. Spoon remaining picante sauce evenly over enchiladas. Bake at 350° for 15 minutes. Top with remaining cheese; return to oven for about 3 minutes. If desired, serve with additional picante sauce and top with lettuce, tomatoes, sour cream, and avocado slices.

Makes 6 servings.

Mexican Chicken Casserole

3 pounds chicken, cooked, deboned, and cut up
1 bag tortilla chips, crushed
1 large onion, chopped
2 (10¾ ounce) cans cream of mushroom soup
1 large can Rotel tomatoes, or regular diced tomatoes, undrained
1 pound grated cheddar or American cheese

OVEN 350°

Butter 4-quart dish. Add layers of chicken, chips, onions, soup, tomatoes with juice, and cheese in that order. Repeat layers. Top generously with cheese. Bake at 350° for 1 hour.

Mexican Chicken Casserole

1 onion, chopped
¼ pound butter
3 (10¾ ounce) cans cream of chicken soup
1 large bag Doritos
1 chicken, boiled, deboned, and cut up
8 ounces shredded cheese

OVEN 350°

Sauté onion in butter. Mix soups and add to onion mixture. Cook until hot and bubbly. Layer 9x13-inch dish with Doritos. Next layer, chicken pieces. Next layer, soup mixture. Next layer, Doritos. Next layer, shredded cheese. Bake at 350° for 30 minutes.

Easy Enchilada Pie

1½ pounds lean ground beef or turkey
½ cup chopped celery
½ cup chopped onion
1 small can mild enchilada sauce
2 or 3 (8 ounce) cans tomato sauce
1 package corn tortillas, torn up
Sliced black olives
8 ounces grated cheddar cheese

OVEN 350°

Brown meat, celery, and onion together. Add enchilada sauce and tomato sauce to meat (adding more tomato sauce will tone down the "heat" somewhat). In a 9x13-inch baking pan, put layer of meat sauce then layer of torn-up corn tortillas. Repeat, ending with sauce on top. Sprinkle olives and grated cheese on top. Bake at 350° for 30 minutes or until hot and bubbly.

This casserole is best served with cold side dish like tossed or fruit salad.

Easy Enchilada Casserole

1 pound ground beef, browned
2 cans enchilada sauce
Corn tortillas
Shredded cheddar cheese

OVEN 350°

Mix together beef and sauce; cook until bubbly. Place small amount (one-third) of mixture in bottom of 9x13-inch pan and spread. Place corn tortillas over mixture, then add cheese and repeat layers again. Bake at 350° for 45 minutes. Serve over rice with side dish of fresh or canned tomatoes.

Easy Casserole

1 pound ground beef
1 (10¾ ounce) can undiluted creamed soup (chicken, celery, or mushroom)
1 package frozen Tater Tots

OVEN 350°

Pat ground beef in bottom of square cake pan. Spread undiluted soup on top of meat. Sprinkle Tater Tots over top of soup. Bake at 350° for 45 minutes; drain off grease if necessary.

Quick Casserole

2 cups cooked elbow macaroni
2 cups hamburger, browned; or raw cubed chicken or ham
1 (10¾ ounce) can creamed soup (mushroom, chicken, or celery)
1 can milk, water, or broth
Parsley flakes
Onion flakes, or diced onion
Salt and pepper to taste
Shredded mozzarella cheese

OVEN 325°

Combine macaroni, meat, soup, and liquid. Stir together parsley, onion, salt, and pepper; add to meat mixture. Place in 9x13-inch pan. Sprinkle mozzarella cheese on top. Bake at 325° for 40 minutes.

Beef Enchiladas

2 cups hamburger
1 tablespoon vinegar
1 teaspoon salt
1 teaspoon chili powder
Tortillas

Sauce:
½ onion
¼ teaspoon cumin
¼ teaspoon oregano
1 teaspoon salt
2 cups tomato juice
2 tablespoons lard
1 tablespoon flour
2 tablespoons chili powder

Mix together meat, vinegar, salt, and chili powder; fry until brown. Blend onion and spices together. Put meat on fried tortillas. Combine sauce ingredients and pour over meat and tortillas. Top with shredded cheese if you wish.

Beef Enchiladas

1 pound ground beef
1 (16 ounce) can refried beans
1 cup shredded cheddar cheese
1 cup shredded mozzarella cheese
1 (10¾ ounce) can golden cream of mushroom soup
1 tablespoon salsa (optional)
10 flour tortillas

Brown meat and drain; mix in refried beans, half the cheese, half the soup, and the salsa. Heat on low until cheese melts. Spoon meat mixture onto tortillas, roll up, and place in casserole dish. Pour remaining soup and cheese over top and bake until cheese melts.

Note: This recipe can be easily altered for individual taste.

Casserole for a Busy Day

4 blade steaks or boneless pork chops
2 large onions
4 medium potatoes
Carrots
1 can low-salt tomato sauce

OVEN 350°

Sear meat on each side. Place in baking dish. Halve onions and place on each piece of meat. Place potatoes around meat and then add carrots. Dilute tomato sauce with half water. Pour over meat and vegetables. Place lid on dish and bake at 350° for about 2 to 2½ hours.

Serves 4.

Taco Casserole

1 pound ground meat
½ teaspoon garlic salt
1 (9½ ounce) package corn chips
1 cup grated cheese
Prepared salsa, or use recipe below

OVEN 350°

Cook meat until browned; drain. Stir in garlic salt. Coarsely crush corn chips and place in bottom of ungreased 8-inch square pan. Spoon hot meat over chips. Top with cheese. Bake at 350° for 10 to 12 minutes. Serve with salsa and lettuce.

Salsa:
1 (16 ounce) can stewed tomatoes
1 teaspoon sugar
¾ teaspoon oregano
½ teaspoon Worcestershire sauce
¼ teaspoon salt
⅛ teaspoon pepper
¼ teaspoon hot sauce
¼ cup chopped onion
¼ cup chopped green pepper

Casserole Ready in 45 Minutes

Ground beef
1 onion, chopped
1 (10¾ ounce) can cream of celery soup
1 small can sauerkraut
Tater Tots

OVEN 350°

Brown ground beef and onion, drain grease off, and put in casserole dish. Pour soup over top. Drain sauerkraut (usually rinse it to get rid of strong acid taste) and put over ground beef and soup. Cover top with Tater Tots. Bake at 350° for 45 minutes.

Hamburger Casserole

2 pounds ground beef
1 small package frozen chopped broccoli, thawed
2 medium onions, sliced (optional)
4 slices American cheese
1 (10¾ ounce) can cream of mushroom soup
1 (10¾ ounce) can cream of chicken soup
1 package frozen Tater Tots

OVEN 350°

Brown beef, drain, and place in square pan. Add broccoli after breaking it apart. Place separated onion rings over broccoli. Cover onions with cheese. Mix soups and pour over top. Place Tater Tots on top. Bake at 350° for 45 minutes.

Zucchini-Hamburger Casserole

1 pound hamburger
1 medium onion
¾ cup instant rice
2 medium yellow summer squash
1 to 2 large zucchini
1 or 2 cans stewed tomatoes
1 teaspoon basil leaves
¼ teaspoon dill weed
Mrs. Dash brand seasoning to taste
Salt and pepper to taste
Dry bread crumbs
Shredded cheese (optional)

OVEN 350°

Cook hamburger, onion, and rice in frying pan. In separate pan, in butter, cook squash and zucchini until tender. Combine all ingredients in glass dish, sprinkle bread crumbs on top (with cheese), and bake at 350° for ½ to 1 hour.

Zucchini-Beef Casserole

1 pound ground beef
1 zucchini, diced (medium or large)
1 medium onion, chopped
Buttered bread crumbs for topping

OVEN 350°

Brown ground beef; drain off fat. Cook zucchini and onion until tender. Drain water. Salt to taste. Grease 1½- to 2-quart casserole dish. Layer meat and zucchini mixture, starting with ground beef. Pour white sauce over mixture (recipe follows). Top with buttered bread crumbs. Bake at 350° for 25 minutes or until bubbly and bread crumbs have browned.

White Sauce:
4 tablespoons margarine
4 tablespoons flour
Dash pepper
½ teaspoon salt
2 cups milk

Melt margarine. Stir in flour and seasonings. Add cold milk and cook on medium heat until mixture thickens. Stir occasionally.

Note: Add shredded cheese if desired, and stir until cheese melts.

Lazy Linda's Casserole

3 cups dry macaroni, cooked and drained
1 (10¾ ounce) can cream of mushroom soup
1 (10¾ ounce) can cheddar cheese soup
½ cup milk
1½ pounds lean hamburger, browned
¼ cup dried minced onion, or fresh
Sprinkle parsley
1 cup green peas (optional to suit taste)
½ cup sour cream
1½ tablespoons Worcestershire sauce

OVEN 350°

Combine all ingredients; mix well. Pour into greased baking dish. Bake for 30 minutes at 350° (or put in heated slow cooker and slow cook).

Pork Chop and Rice Casserole

½ stick margarine
1 cup uncooked rice
Salt
4 to 5 pork chops
1 envelope dry onion soup mix
1 (10¾ ounce) can cream of mushroom soup
1½ cans water

OVEN 350°

Melt margarine in 9x13-inch baking dish; cool slightly. Pour rice over margarine; arrange salted pork chops over rice. Sprinkle with dry onion soup mix. Mix mushroom soup with water and pour over casserole. Cover tightly. Bake at 350° for 1 hour.

Yields 6 servings.

Chicken may be substituted, baking 1½ hours for medium fryer.

Broccoli and Rice Casserole

2 cups rice
4 cups water
1 pound frozen chopped broccoli
1 onion, chopped, sautéed
1 pound jalapeño processed cheese
2 cans water chestnuts, chopped
1 (10¾ ounce) can cream of mushroom soup
1 (10¾ ounce) can cream of celery soup

OVEN 350°

Cook rice in water. Add broccoli to onion and let soften over low heat. Melt cheese. Mix all ingredients together. Put in 9x13-inch pan. Bake uncovered at 350° for 45 minutes.

Broccoli and Rice Casserole

3 stalks fresh or 1 box frozen broccoli, steamed
1 cup short- or long-cook brown or white rice, cooked
1 (10¾ ounce) can cream of chicken soup (celery or mushroom is good, too)
½ cup mayonnaise
3 cups grated cheddar, Colby, or other favorite cheese

OVEN 350°

Mix steamed broccoli, cooked rice, soup, mayonnaise, and 1 cup cheese together. Salt and pepper to taste. Put remaining cheese on top of casserole. Bake at 375° for 20 to 30 minutes or until cheese on top is melted.

Pizza Casserole

- 1 to 2 pounds hamburger
- ½ cup chopped green pepper
- 1 (8 ounce) package noodles
- 1 (10¾ ounce) can cream of mushroom soup
- 1 small can pizza sauce
- 1 can mushrooms with liquid
- ¼ teaspoon garlic powder
- ½ teaspoon oregano
- ½ can Parmesan cheese
- Pepperoni (optional)
- Shredded mozzarella cheese

OVEN 350°

Fry hamburger; add green pepper. Cook noodles separately, then add remaining ingredients except pepperoni and cheese. Put in casserole dish and add pepperoni and cheese on top. Bake at 350° for 30 minutes.

Pizza Casserole

- 2 pounds hamburger
- ¼ cup chopped green pepper
- 1 small onion, chopped
- 12 ounces egg noodles
- 2 (10¾ ounce) cans cream of mushroom soup
- 2 (10¾ ounce) cans tomato soup
- ½ can water
- 1 can mushrooms, drained
- 1 teaspoon garlic salt
- ½ teaspoon oregano
- 12 ounces shredded mozzarella cheese
- 8 ounces pepperoni

OVEN 350°

Brown hamburger with green pepper and onion; drain excess grease. Boil noodles. In large mixing bowl mix soups, water, mushrooms, garlic salt, oregano, noodles, and browned meat. Preheat oven to 350°. Layer half in 9x13-inch pan and top with half the cheese, repeat and put pepperoni on top. Bake uncovered 1 hour or until done. Can cover toward end of baking if needed.

Chicken Delight Casserole

- 1½ cups diced potatoes
- 2 chicken breasts, cooked and cut into small pieces
- 1 can chicken broth; or 2 cups broth with grease removed; or 2 cups water and 2 cubes bouillon
- 1 (10¾ ounce) can cream of chicken soup
- 2 small cans mushroom pieces, drained
- 1 large bag bread cubes
- Shredded cheese (optional)

OVEN 350°

Cook potatoes. Mix all ingredients together very well until soup and broth are not lumpy. Put in casserole dish. Add bread cubes and cheese (optional). Cook in 350° oven for 30 to 40 minutes. Don't let top get too brown.

Biscuit-Topped Italian Casserole

1 pound ground beef
½ cup chopped onion
¾ cup water
¼ teaspoon pepper
1 (8 ounce) can tomato sauce
1 (6 ounce) can tomato paste
1 (9 ounce) package mixed vegetables, cooked thoroughly
2 cups shredded mozzarella cheese
1 tube refrigerated biscuits
½ teaspoon oregano

OVEN 375°

Grease 8x12-inch baking dish. Brown ground beef and onion; drain. Stir in water, pepper, tomato sauce, and tomato paste; simmer for 15 minutes, stirring occasionally. Remove from heat; stir in veggies and 1½ cups cheese. Spoon mixture into baking dish. Separate dough into 10 biscuits. Separate each biscuit into 2 layers. Place biscuits near outer edge of hot meat mixture, overlapping slightly. Sprinkle remaining cheese in center and around edge. Sprinkle with oregano. Bake at 375° for 22 to 27 minutes or until biscuits are golden brown.

Serves 6 to 8.

Tater Tot Casserole

1 pound ground turkey or beef
6 slices cheese
1 (10¾ ounce) can mushroom soup
1 (10¾ ounce) can cream of celery soup
1 package frozen Tater Tots

In 7x10-inch pan layer ingredients as listed. Put enough Tater Tots on top to cover casserole. You'll probably have some Tater Tots left. Bake at 350° for 1 hour.

Chicken-Broccoli Casserole

1 (10 ounce) package frozen broccoli
3 cups cooked and cubed chicken
1 cup reduced-fat cream of chicken soup
1 cup Hellmann's reduced-fat mayonnaise
1 (8 ounce) can water chestnuts, drained
1 onion, chopped
Reduced-fat Ritz brand crackers

OVEN 350°

Cook broccoli according to directions. Put chicken in large bowl. Add undiluted soup and mayonnaise and stir; add drained water chestnuts and broccoli. Place mixture in 3-quart casserole dish. Sprinkle crumbled Ritz crackers on top. Bake at 350° for 30 minutes.

May substitute green beans or 8 ounces artichoke hearts in place of broccoli.

Grace's Casserole Chicken

2 cups cooked, deboned chicken
1 (10¾ ounce) can cream of chicken soup
1 cup milk
Chopped celery
2 tablespoons chopped onion
1 small package stuffing mix
1 stick margarine
2 cups chicken broth

OVEN 350°

Place chicken in 2-quart baking dish. Combine soup and milk and pour over chicken. Top with layer of celery and onion and then cover with stuffing mix. Pour margarine and broth over all ingredients. Bake in 350° oven for 30 minutes.

Chicken Casserole

3 cups chicken, cooked and chopped
3 teaspoons chopped onion
2 cups chopped celery
1 (10¾ ounce) can cream of chicken soup
¾ cup Hellmann's mayonnaise
¼ cup margarine
1 small can water chestnuts, drained
1 cup croutons or cornflakes
1 cup sliced almonds (optional)

OVEN 350°

Mix all ingredients and put in casserole. Melt margarine and sprinkle over top. Over all this, sprinkle croutons or cornflakes and almonds. Bake at 350° for approximately 1 hour.

Serves 8.

Options: Add onions and garlic or mushrooms and pimientos. This recipe can be doubled or tripled for a crowd.

Chicken Casserole

3 to 4 pounds chicken, boiled and deboned (reserve 1½ cups liquid)
1 (12 ounce) can evaporated milk
1 (10¾ ounce) can cream of chicken soup
1 (10¾ ounce) can cream of mushroom soup
1 (8 ounce) package Pepperidge Farm dressing mix
⅓ cup butter, melted
1½ cups chicken broth

OVEN 350°

Mix first four ingredients and pour into greased 9x13-inch pan. Mix dressing mix, butter, and chicken broth. Mix well and spread on top of chicken mixture. Bake 45 minutes at 350°. Cover with foil to keep dressing moist.

Pecan Chicken Casserole

2 cups chopped cooked chicken
½ cup chopped pecans
2 teaspoons dried minced onion
2 cups sliced celery
1 cup mayonnaise
2 teaspoons lemon juice
1 cup crushed potato chips
½ cup shredded cheddar cheese

OVEN 350°

Mix first six ingredients together. Place in greased 1½-quart casserole. Mix chips and cheese and sprinkle on top. Bake uncovered at 350° for 30 minutes.

Nina's Chicken Casserole

1 whole chicken
1 (10¾ ounce) can mushroom soup
4 ounces sour cream
1 stick butter
8 ounces Ritz brand crackers

OVEN 350°

Boil chicken for 1 hour. Cool and debone. Mix chicken, mushroom soup, and sour cream together. Set aside. Melt butter slightly and mix with crackers. Put half of cracker mixture in pan then put chicken mixture next and remaining cracker mixture on top. Cook at 350° for 30 minutes until brown.

Ham and Macaroni Casserole

1 cup diced cooked ham
1 cup diced green onion, with tops
1 cup peeled, diced fresh tomatoes
1 cup elbow macaroni, cooked until half done
Salt and pepper to taste
2 cups diced American cheese
1¾ cups milk

OVEN 375°

Combine all except American cheese and milk; mix well. In saucepan put diced American cheese and milk; cook until cheese is dissolved; add to first mixture. Place in greased baking dish. Bake 1 hour at 375°.

Ham and Potato Casserole

3 (1 pound) bags frozen hash browns
3 (8 ounce) bags shredded cheddar cheese
2 pounds diced ham
2 (11 ounce) cans cheese soup
3 large onions, diced
1 quart skim milk

OVEN 400°

Mix all in large aluminum roaster pan. Bake at 400° for 1 hour. Stir occasionally (once or twice). Season to taste.

Turkey-Cheese Military Casserole

1 cup elbow macaroni, uncooked
¼ cup butter or margarine
¼ cup finely chopped onion
¼ cup flour
1 teaspoon salt
Dash thyme
¼ teaspoon pepper
2 cups milk
1¼ cups chopped cooked turkey
4 slices cheddar cheese
½ cup bread crumbs
2 tablespoons butter, melted
1 teaspoon minced parsley

OVEN 350°

Cook macaroni as directed. Drain. Melt butter, add onion, and cook over low heat 3 to 5 minutes. Stir in flour, salt, thyme, and pepper. Gradually add milk and cook, stirring constantly until thickened. Arrange half of macaroni in bottom of lightly greased 2-quart casserole. Put half of turkey over macaroni. Arrange half of cheese slices over turkey. Repeat. Pour sauce over all. Mix crumbs, butter, and parsley; sprinkle over top. Bake at 350° for 25 minutes.

Chicken, Rice, and Cheese Casserole

8 chicken breasts, cooked and cut up
8 cups cooked rice
2 (10¾ ounce) cans cream of mushroom soup
½ soup can milk
2 cups sliced processed cheese

OVEN 350°

Combine ingredients and bake at 350° for 20 to 30 minutes.

Can use cooked ham chopped up in place of chicken.

Bettie's Chicken and Rice Casserole

2 (10¾ ounce) cans cream of chicken soup, or substitute one can other cream soup
1 soup can water
1 cup rice, uncooked
6 to 8 large chicken breasts, skinned

OVEN 350°

Lightly spray 9x13-inch pan with nonstick cooking spray, or grease. Combine soup and water in bowl. Pour in pan and spread evenly. Sprinkle rice over soup. Place chicken on top. Cover tightly with foil. Bake at 350° for 1½ hours. Recipe can be halved.

Chicken-Rice Casserole

½ cup chopped onion
1 cup chopped celery
½ cup butter
2½ cups chicken, cooked and cubed
¼ teaspoon pepper
1 (10¾ ounce) can cream of chicken soup
1 cup milk
2½ cups chicken broth
1 cup rice, uncooked

OVEN 350°

Sauté onion and celery in butter, but do not brown. Mix everything together and bake 2 hours at 350°. Stir after 1 hour.

Spinach Quiche

1 package frozen chopped spinach, cooked and drained well
2 cups skim milk
4 eggs, beaten
¼ cup finely chopped onion
4 slices bacon, fried and broken into pieces
½ teaspoon salt
¼ teaspoon paprika
½ teaspoon dry mustard
1 cup shredded cheddar cheese
9-inch pie shell
¼ cup shredded cheese for topping

OVEN 400°

Add all ingredients and put in unbaked shell. Sprinkle ¼ cup cheese on top. Bake at 400° for 40 minutes or until set.

Serves 6.

Kathy's Kasserole

1 box chicken stuffing mix
1 (10¾ ounce) can cream of chicken soup
1 small can diced chicken, undrained
1 cup shredded cheddar cheese

OVEN 350°

Make stuffing according to box directions. Put soup and chicken in bottom of medium-size casserole dish and stir to mix. Sprinkle cheese over soup and chicken. Spoon cooked stuffing on top. Bake at 350° for 30 minutes.

Chicken Stuffing Casserole

8 ounces sour cream
1 (10¾ ounce) can cream of mushroom soup
1 chicken, boiled
1 box chicken stuffing mix

OVEN 350°

Mix sour cream and soup together in baking dish. Cut chicken in chunks. Mix stuffing according to directions on package. Spread stuffing over chicken. Bake at 350° for 45 minutes or until stuffing is crisp.

Hamburger Quiche

1 pound hamburger
1 onion, chopped
½ block sharp cheese, grated
2 tablespoons cornstarch
2 eggs
½ cup mayonnaise
½ cup milk
2 pie shells

OVEN 350°

Brown hamburger and onion. Drain. Combine remaining ingredients. Add hamburger. Pour into 2 unbaked pie shells. Bake at 350° for 30 minutes.

Asparagus Ham Quiche

1 (10 ounce) package frozen cut asparagus
½ pound chopped ham
1 cup shredded cheese
¼ cup chopped onion
3 eggs
1 cup milk
¾ cup baking mix
¼ teaspoon pepper

OVEN 375°

In greased 9-inch pie pan layer asparagus, ham, cheese, and onion. Beat eggs and milk. Add baking mix and pepper. Pour in pie pan. Bake at 375° 30 minutes or until done.

Vegetable Pizza

2 tubes refrigerated crescent rolls
1 cup mayonnaise
2 (8 ounce) packages cream cheese
1 package dry ranch dressing mix
Assorted vegetables, chopped
Shredded cheese

OVEN 375°

Spread rolls and press in 12x18-inch pan, joining seams for crust. Bake at 375° for 10 to 15 minutes or until golden brown. Mix mayonnaise, cream cheese, and dressing mix. Spread over cooled crust. Top with raw, chopped vegetables. Top with shredded cheese. After assembling, pizza can be covered with waxed paper and refrigerated overnight. Next day top with shredded cheese before serving. Cut with pizza cutter. Recipe can be halved.

Bubble-Up Pizza

3 (7 ounce) tubes refrigerated biscuits, quartered
8 ounces shredded mozzarella cheese, divided
1 (4 ounce) can mushrooms, drained
1 (15 ounce) can pizza sauce
Cooked sausage, ham, veggies, or anything else you like on your pizza

OVEN 350°

In medium bowl mix quartered biscuits, 1 cup mozzarella cheese, mushrooms, pizza sauce, and other items you've chosen. Pour into greased 9x13-inch baking dish. Sprinkle remaining cheese on top. Bake at 350° for 30 to 40 minutes or until biscuits are golden.

Vegetable Stir-Fry

¼ cup vegetable oil
2 cups chicken broth
1 teaspoon brown gravy sauce
1 tablespoon soy sauce
1 cup cooked cubed chicken (can be canned; optional)
¼ cup dry white wine (optional)
2 stalks celery, sliced
3 green onions or 1 medium onion, chopped
1 small bunch Chinese cabbage, or Chinese celery
1 cup sliced fresh mushrooms
16 ounces frozen pea pods, thawed
2 cloves garlic, crushed
1 can stir-fry vegetables (Hokan); contains small corn, water chestnuts, bean sprouts, bamboo shoots

Cook liquid and all ingredients, except vegetables, until thick and clear; add white wine if desired. Stir in vegetables. Serve over cooked rice.

Poor Man's Goulash

1 pound ground beef
1 tall can spaghetti
1 tall can pork and beans
1½ cups ketchup
¾ cup regular barbecue sauce
Shredded cheddar cheese

OVEN 350°

Brown beef and pour off fat. Add rest of ingredients and simmer. You can also pour into large casserole; top with shredded cheddar cheese and crumbs. Bake 1 hour at 350°.

Serve with tossed salad and garlic bread sticks.

Texas Hash

1 pound ground chuck
1 onion, chopped
½ cup chopped bell pepper
Hot pepper, chopped (to taste)
Salt and pepper to taste
¼ cup uncooked rice
1 (8 ounce) can tomato sauce
1 (16 ounce) can diced tomatoes
1 tablespoon sugar

Brown meat with onion, peppers, salt, and pepper. Drain off grease. Then add rice, sauce, tomatoes, and sugar. Add enough water to cook rice. Simmer until rice is done.

Red Flannel Hash

3 tablespoons cooking oil
1 (15 ounce) can sliced beets, drained and chopped
2 cups chopped cooked corned beef
2½ cups diced cooked potatoes
1 medium onion, chopped
¼ cup half-and-half
2 tablespoons butter or margarine, melted
2 teaspoons dried parsley flakes
1 teaspoon Worcestershire sauce
¼ teaspoon salt
⅛ teaspoon pepper

Heat oil in 12-inch skillet. Add remaining ingredients. Cook and stir over low heat for 20 minutes or until lightly browned and heated through.

Yield: 4 servings.

Barbecued Hamburger Muffins

1 pound hamburger
½ cup chopped onion
½ cup barbecue sauce
Garlic powder
1 (10 count) tube refrigerated biscuits
Grated cheese

OVEN 375°

Brown hamburger and onion. Add barbecue sauce and garlic powder. Put rolled-out biscuits in muffin pan. Put meat mixture on top of biscuits. Cook 15 to 20 minutes in 375° oven. Put grated cheese on top of each muffin and bake 5 minutes more.

Makes 10 muffins.

Bunsteaks

¼ pound processed cheese, 1 cup cubed
3 hard-boiled eggs, chopped
1 (7 ounce) can tuna fish or 2 cups diced cooked chicken
2 tablespoons chopped onion
2 tablespoons sweet pickle relish
½ cup mayonnaise or salad dressing
8 hot dog buns

OVEN 350°

Combine all except buns. Mix lightly. Fill sliced buns. Place, filling side up, in rectangular baking pan. Cover with aluminum foil tightly. Bake at 350° for 20 minutes until filling is heated and cheese melts. Serve hot.

Fills 8 buns.

Bunsteaks

¼ pound cheese, diced
3 hard-boiled eggs, chopped
1 small can tuna
2 tablespoons chopped onion
2 tablespoons chopped sweet pickle
½ cup margarine, melted
12 hot dog buns

OVEN 350°

Mix together and put into buns. Wrap each in foil. Bake at 350° for 20 minutes.

Makes 12.

Italian Subs

1 onion, diced
1 bell pepper, diced
1 teaspoon oregano
2 cans tomato sauce
3 pounds Italian link sausage
6 sub sandwich buns

Combine onion, bell pepper, oregano, and tomato sauce in slow cooker. Add Italian sausage links. Cook on medium heat about 4 hours. On each sub put one link sausage; add sauce to season.

Good served with tossed salad.

Crabmeat Casserole

1 (10¾ ounce) can cream of celery soup
⅓ cup milk
1 (4 ounce) can mushrooms, drained
1 can crabmeat, drained
Parsley to taste

OVEN 350°

Mix ingredients in casserole. Sprinkle with buttered bread crumbs. Bake in preheated 350° oven for 30 minutes.

"Seafood" Lunch

1 package hot dogs (octopus)
1 package goldfish crackers (fish)
1 package apple-biscuits (rocks)
Applesauce (sand)

Cut hot dogs in half. Cut each half lengthwise (do not cut completely) to make 8 legs for an octopus. Boil water, remove from heat, add hot dogs, and cover. Let sit for 10 minutes.

Mock Shrimp Casserole

1 pound sea legs
1 (10¾ ounce) can cream of shrimp soup
2 cups water
1 cup crushed Ritz brand crackers

OVEN 350°

Combine and bake at 350° for 30 to 45 minutes. Be sure it is thoroughly warmed.

Heavenly Broiled Fish

2 pounds fish fillets, fresh or frozen
½ cup grated Parmesan cheese
1 tablespoon margarine, softened
3 tablespoons reduced-calorie mayonnaise
3 tablespoons chopped green onions, with tops
Dash Tabasco sauce

Thaw fish if frozen. Place fillets in single layer on well-oiled baking pan. Combine remaining ingredients and spread evenly over fish. Broil 6 inches from source of heat for approximately 10 minutes, or until top is lightly browned and fish flakes easily when tested with fork.

Makes 6 to 8 servings.

Buttermilk Baked Cod

1½ pounds cod fillets
½ cup butter
1 teaspoon paprika
1 teaspoon garlic powder
1 teaspoon lemon juice
1 teaspoon salt
1 cup buttermilk
2 cups herb stuffing mix

OVEN 450°

Rinse and dry cod fillets; cut into serving pieces. Melt butter; add paprika, garlic powder, lemon juice, and salt. Dip fish in buttermilk; roll in stuffing. Place in foil-lined 9x13-inch baking pan. Drizzle butter mixture over fish. Bake at 450° for 10 to 15 minutes.

Tuna Surprise!

3½ cups wide egg noodles
13 ounces tuna (any type)
½ cup mayonnaise
1 cup chopped celery (optional)
⅓ cup chopped onion
¼ cup diced green pepper
1 teaspoon salt
1 (10¾ ounce) can cream of mushroom or celery soup (your preference)
½ cup milk
1 cup grated sharp or extra-sharp cheese

OVEN 425°

Prepare egg noodles; set aside. Chop tuna into small pieces in mixing bowl. Add and mix well all ingredients except soup, milk, and cheese. Mix milk into soup; add grated cheese and mix until blended. Heat until cheese is melted. Mix into tuna mixture and pour into casserole dish. Bake 20 minutes at 425°.

Rice and Tuna Pie

2 cups cooked rice
1 tablespoon chopped onion
2 tablespoons butter
¼ teaspoon dried marjoram, crushed
1 egg, slightly beaten
1 (9¼ ounce) can tuna, drained
3 eggs, beaten
4 ounces shredded Swiss cheese
1 cup milk
¼ teaspoon salt
Dash pepper
¼ teaspoon dried marjoram, crushed
1 tablespoon chopped onion

OVEN 350°

For rice shell, combine first five ingredients; press onto bottom and sides of lightly buttered 10-inch pie plate or 6x10-inch baking dish. Sprinkle tuna evenly over rice shell. Combine remaining ingredients; pour over tuna. Bake at 350° for 50 to 55 minutes or until knife inserted off center comes out clean.

Makes 6 servings.

Salmon Patties

1½ teaspoons baking powder
1 can salmon, drained; save liquid
1 egg
⅓ cup minced onion
½ cup flour

Combine baking powder with 2 tablespoons reserved salmon liquid. Mix all ingredients together and make into small balls. Deep fry until golden brown.

Variation:
1½ packages plain crackers, to taste
4 cans pink salmon
4 eggs (1 per can of salmon)

Crush crackers in plastic baggie. Drain salmon and put in bowl. Add eggs and crushed crackers. Mix together with hands. Form patties. Place in skillet with boiling grease. Fry until browned.

Crawfish Étouffée

1 cup chopped onion
1 cup chopped bell pepper
½ cup flour
1 stick butter, melted
¼ cup Worcestershire sauce
½ teaspoon chopped garlic
Pinch parsley
2 bay leaves
Salt and red pepper to taste
1 pound cooked crawfish tails

Sauté onion and bell pepper until tender; set aside. Add flour to melted butter, stirring until roux looks like peanut butter. Add Worcestershire sauce and enough hot water to make heavy gravy; add garlic, parsley, bay leaves, salt, and pepper (to taste). Should be on the hot side; add onion, bell pepper, and crawfish tails. Heat thoroughly. Serve over rice or corn bread. Top étouffée with fresh green onions.

Serves 4 to 6.

My Favorite Spaghetti

6 pork chops, trimmed of fat and cubed
½ cup brown sugar
1 (8 ounce) can crushed pineapple
1 (4 ounce) can mushroom pieces (optional)
30 ounces spaghetti sauce
Spaghetti

Fry pork chops until light brown on all sides. Add brown sugar, pineapple, and mushrooms (optional) to pork chops and simmer together until ready to serve over cooked spaghetti.

Mama Patton's Spaghetti

5 pounds hamburger
4 bell peppers, diced
4 large onions, diced
1 bunch celery, diced
10 large cans tomatoes
3 large cans tomato paste
3 large cans tomato sauce
4 tablespoons to ½ bottle Worcestershire sauce
1 tablespoon sugar
2 heaping tablespoons chili powder
Salt and pepper to taste
1 teaspoon celery salt
1 tablespoon garlic powder
Tabasco sauce, or 2 to 3 hot peppers

Fry meat; drain off grease. Sauté pepper, onion, and celery. Put tomatoes in large saucepan. Rinse cans with water, adding to tomatoes. Add sautéed veggies and meat to tomatoes. Add Worcestershire sauce, sugar, seasonings, and Tabasco sauce or hot peppers. Cook 6 hours. Serve over cooked spaghetti.

Spaghetti Pizza-Style

1 pound spaghetti
1 cup milk
2 eggs
½ teaspoon garlic powder
3 cups shredded mozzarella cheese, divided
1 (32 ounce) jar spaghetti sauce
½ pound ground beef
½ to 1 cup sliced pepperoni

OVEN 350°

Prepare spaghetti as directed; drain. Beat milk, eggs, garlic powder, and 1 cup cheese together and toss with noodles. Spread mixture in greased jelly roll pan, 11x18 inches. Pour spaghetti sauce over noodles. Crumble ground beef over sauce and then arrange pepperoni slices evenly over beef. Sprinkle with remaining cheese. Bake at 350° for 30 minutes. Let stand for 5 minutes before cutting into squares.

Dave's Spaghetti

1½ pounds ground beef
Seasonings to taste
1 (10¾ ounce) can cream of mushroom soup
1 (32 ounce) jar Ragu Old Style sauce
7 to 10 ounces spaghetti, cooked and drained
8 ounces grated mozzarella cheese

OVEN 350°

Brown meat and cook until done. Add seasonings to taste. Add soup and sauce to hamburger and cook slightly. In either baking dish or slow cooker, layer spaghetti, sauce, and cheese; repeat layers until all used up. Heat in oven until cheese is melted.

This is great to take to a friend's because after layering it is finished and can be kept covered in refrigerator overnight or for a day or two, then heated in oven at 350° until bubbly. Or it can sit overnight in slow cooker and be cooked in the morning and be ready for lunch!

Baked Spaghetti

1 (8 ounce) box spaghetti, cooked and drained
1 pound hamburger, browned and drained
1 cup grated cheese
1 jar Ragu sauce, traditional or original

OVEN 350°

Mix together spaghetti, hamburger, and cheese. Add sauce. Spray dish with cooking spray. Put mixture in dish and cover with grated cheese. Bake at 350° for 35 to 40 minutes.

Spaghetti Sauce

1 family-size can tomato sauce
2 (6 ounce) cans tomato paste (fill each can 3 times with water)
½ small onion, chopped
½ teaspoon garlic salt
½ teaspoon sugar
4 tablespoons grated cheese
½ teaspoon oregano
¼ teaspoon sweet basil
Salt and pepper to taste

Meatballs:
1½ pounds hamburger
3 slices bread (soak in water then squeeze out water)
½ small onion, chopped
Garlic salt to taste
Salt and pepper to taste

Put meatballs in sauce; cook over low heat for about 2 hours.

Night-Before Lasagna

2 pounds lean ground beef (ground turkey works well, too)
¼ teaspoon garlic powder
1 teaspoon salt
1 teaspoon basil
1 tablespoon parsley flakes
½ cup grated Parmesan cheese
2 (6 ounce) cans tomato paste
2 cups hot water
1 (1 pound) package oven-ready lasagna noodles
1 (12 ounce) carton low-fat cottage cheese
1½ cups grated low-fat mozzarella cheese

OVEN 350°

Brown meat and drain fat off. Mix in garlic powder, salt, basil, parsley, Parmesan cheese, and tomato paste, and blend with hot water. Simmer uncovered for 30 minutes. In 9x13-inch baking pan, layer half uncooked noodles, half cottage cheese, half meat sauce, and half mozzarella cheese. Repeat layers. Chill in refrigerator overnight. Bake for 55 minutes at 350°.

Not having to cook and drain the noodles makes this a super-simple recipe to make a day ahead of time.

Semi-Easy Lasagna

32 ounces spaghetti sauce, best homemade with 1 pound meat
9 strips ribbed lasagna noodles, cooked
15 ounces cottage cheese
12 ounces grated mozzarella cheese
¼ cup grated Parmesan cheese

OVEN 375°

Grease 9x13-inch pan. Cover bottom with small amount of spaghetti sauce. Place 3 strips cooked lasagna noodles lengthwise, spread ⅓ spaghetti sauce, ½ dry cottage cheese, and ⅓ cheese; repeat. Add last three strips, rest of sauce, mozzarella cheese, and sprinkle Parmesan cheese over dish. Cover; bake at 375° for 30 minutes; remove cover; cook 30 minutes more. Let stand 10 minutes before eating.

One-Dish Lasagna

32 ounces Prego spaghetti sauce
12 ounces lasagna noodles, uncooked
1 pound raw hamburger
¼ cup chopped onion
8 ounces cottage cheese
8 ounces American cheese
8 ounces mozzarella cheese
1½ cups hot water
Parmesan cheese

OVEN 375°

Cover bottom of pan with one-third of jar sauce; layer noodles, half of raw meat, onion, cottage cheese, one-third of sauce, noodles, American cheese, rest of raw meat, rest of sauce, mozzarella cheese. Press down with spoon; add hot water; press down again. Sprinkle with Parmesan cheese and cover with foil. Bake at 375° for 45 minutes or less, until thick or set.

Spaghetti-Pizza Lasagna

12 ounces spaghetti (can use up to 16 ounces)
1 cup milk
2 eggs
1 pound hamburger
Onion
32 ounces spaghetti sauce
Chopped green pepper (optional)
Pepperoni slices (optional)
2 to 3 cups shredded mozzarella cheese

OVEN 350°

Cook spaghetti according to package directions, drain, and pour into 9x13-inch pan. Mix spaghetti with milk; beat slightly; add eggs. Brown hamburger and onion; drain. Add sauce, and green pepper if desired. Pour sauce mixture over spaghetti in pan and mix all together. Top with pepperoni if you like. Top with mozzarella cheese. Bake at 350° for 35 minutes (cover with foil first 30 minutes then uncover for 5 minutes).

Pizza-Spaghetti Bake

1 pound spaghetti noodles, cooked and drained
½ cup milk
2 eggs
1 cup shredded mozzarella cheese
½ teaspoon salt
¾ teaspoon garlic powder
1½ teaspoons oregano
1 (32 ounce) jar spaghetti sauce
2 cups mozzarella cheese
12 ounces pepperoni slices

OVEN 400°

Combine first seven ingredients and put in greased 9x13-inch pan. Bake at 400° for 13 minutes. Take out and reduce heat to 350°. Add spaghetti sauce, mozzarella cheese, and pepperoni. Bake ½ hour.

Lasagna

1½ pounds ground beef
2 cloves garlic, minced
¼ cup chopped onion (optional)
1 (29 ounce or larger) can tomatoes
1 (6 ounce) can tomato paste
1 teaspoon salt
¾ teaspoon pepper
½ teaspoon oregano
¼ teaspoon marjoram
1 bay leaf
1 (8 ounce) package lasagna noodles
1 (12 ounce) carton cottage cheese
Enough grated Muenster and mozzarella cheese to equal 1½ cups
Parmesan cheese

OVEN 350°

Brown beef and garlic and onion if desired. Add tomatoes, tomato paste, salt, pepper, oregano, marjoram, and bay leaf. Cover and simmer 20 minutes. Cook noodles as directed on package. In 8x12-inch glass baking dish, alternate layers of meat sauce then noodles and cheeses. Sprinkle with Parmesan cheese. Bake at 350° for 20 to 30 minutes.

Felicia's Lasagna

1 to 2 pounds ground beef, browned and drained
1 (28 to 32 ounce) jar spaghetti sauce
12 to 16 oven-ready lasagna noodles
24 ounces shredded mozzarella cheese
Parmesan cheese

OVEN 350°

Brown ground beef; drain; mix with spaghetti sauce. Alternate noodles, sauce, and cheese to top of casserole dish. Sprinkle with Parmesan cheese until covered. Cover with aluminum foil. Bake at 350° for 50 minutes. Remove foil and bake for another 10 minutes to brown.

Fettuccini Alfredo

6 ounces (½ package) fettuccini, uncooked, or whole package fresh
¼ cup butter or margarine
¾ cup grated Parmesan cheese
½ cup heavy whipping cream
2 tablespoons chopped parsley (optional)

Cook fettuccini according to package directions; drain. Meanwhile in small saucepan, melt butter over medium heat; gradually stir in cheese then whipping cream until well blended. Continue heating sauce, stirring constantly, just to boiling point. Remove from heat; stir in parsley. Pour over noodles.

Can also add chicken, shrimp, bacon bits, or whatever you like.

Spinach and Mushroom Chicken Alfredo

1 (10 ounce) box frozen creamed spinach
1 to 2 tablespoons cornstarch
1½ cups milk, divided
4 boneless, skinless chicken breasts
1 to 2 tablespoons olive oil
1 small jar or can sliced mushrooms, drained
1 to 2 cloves garlic
2 tablespoons butter
½ cup grated Parmesan cheese
8 ounces spiral-shaped pasta, cooked

Prepare spinach according to package directions. Set aside. In small bowl, mix 1 tablespoon cornstarch with ½ cup milk to make paste. Set aside. Slice chicken into thin strips.

Heat olive oil in large frying pan over medium-high heat. Add mushrooms, garlic, and chicken to pan. Stir-fry until chicken browns. Remove chicken-mushroom mixture to separate plate and keep warm.

Alfredo sauce: In same frying pan, melt butter; stir bowl of cornstarch paste. Add to melted butter along with Parmesan cheese and remaining milk. Cook and stir until thick.

Return chicken-mushroom mixture to pan. Open bag of prepared spinach and add to pan. Heat and stir alfredo until bubbly. Serve over hot, cooked spiral pasta.

Western Macaroni

1 pound ground beef
½ cup chopped green pepper
¼ cup chopped onion
2 cups frozen whole kernel corn, thawed and drained
1 (8 ounce) can whole tomatoes, cut up (undrained)
1 teaspoon salt
Dash pepper
1 (7¼ ounce) package macaroni and cheese dinner

In small skillet, combine ground beef, green pepper, and onion. Cook until meat is browned; drain; add corn, tomatoes, salt, and pepper. Simmer 10 minutes. Prepare macaroni and cheese dinner as directed. Stir in meat mixture. Heat through. Refrigerate leftovers.

Serves 4 to 6.

Low-Cal Pasta

½ pound spaghetti
2 cups chicken, cut up
1 can chicken broth
Broccoli, cauliflower, celery, and carrots, cut up
Onion and green pepper, cut into strips
Mushrooms and water chestnuts
Cornstarch for thickening
1 (16 ounce) can peas
3 tablespoons soy sauce
2 tablespoons lemon juice
Salt and pepper to taste
2 packages Ramen seasoning

Cook and drain spaghetti; keep hot. In wok or chicken fryer, cook cut-up chicken until pink is gone. Put in chicken broth. Put in broccoli, cauliflower, carrots, and celery; cook about 10 minutes and then add onion, green pepper, mushrooms, and water chestnuts. Mix small amount of cornstarch with water; add to mixture to thicken (not too thick). Then add peas, soy sauce, lemon juice, salt, and pepper. Do not overcook vegetables. Put spaghetti in low flat dish; add vegetables and mix in Ramen seasoning.

Macaroni Bake

1½ cups dry elbow macaroni, cooked and drained
1 (10¾ ounce) can cream of mushroom soup, undiluted
1 small can mushrooms, undrained
¼ cup chopped green pepper
¼ cup chopped onion
1 (2 ounce) can pimientos
1 cup mayonnaise
1½ cups grated cheddar cheese
Bread crumbs

OVEN 350°

Mix all together; cover with buttered bread crumbs. Bake at 350° for 30 to 35 minutes.

Noodles and Glue

1 pound hamburger
1 box elbow macaroni
⅓ cup milk
8 ounces shredded mozzarella cheese

Cook hamburger in skillet. Prepare macaroni as directed on box. Combine macaroni, hamburger, and milk. Mix well. Mix a little cheese in and then let the rest melt on top.

Meatless Noodle Main Dish

8 ounces egg noodles
1 cup sour cream
2 eggs
8 ounces cottage cheese
⅓ cup buttermilk
1 teaspoon chives

OVEN 350°

Boil noodles in salted water until tender. Drain. Mix sour cream, eggs, cottage cheese, buttermilk, and chives in mixing bowl; blend thoroughly. Add noodles and mix again. Place in greased baking dish (9x13-inch or larger); dot with butter or grated cheese. If more moisture is needed, add more buttermilk. Bake at 350° for 1 hour until crusty brown.

Cavatini

1 pound ground beef
⅛ teaspoon garlic powder
1 onion, chopped
1 green pepper, chopped
1 package pepperoni slices
1 small can mushrooms, drained
32 ounces spaghetti sauce
½ pound curly noodles, cooked and drained
½ pound grated mozzarella cheese

OVEN 375°

Brown ground beef; add garlic powder, onion, and green pepper. Cook until tender and drain. Stir in pepperoni, mushrooms, and spaghetti sauce. Grease 9x13-inch pan. Layer cooked noodles and half the cheese. Add ground beef mixture. Top with remaining cheese. Bake at 375° for 35 to 40 minutes. Let stand 5 to 10 minutes before serving.

Mostaccioli

- 1 (1 pound) package Creamette brand mostaccioli
- 2 (26 ounce) jars Classico brand pasta sauce (tomato and basil)
- 1 pound lean ground beef, turkey, or pork
- 4 cups (1 pound) shredded mozzarella cheese, divided

OVEN 350°

Preheat oven to 350°. Prepare pasta as package directs. In large bowl, combine pasta, sauce, meat, and 2 cups cheese. Mix well. Turn into greased 9x13-inch baking dish; cover and bake 45 minutes or until hot and bubbly. Uncover; top with remaining 2 cups cheese. Bake 10 minutes or longer until cheese melts.

Makes 12 to 15 servings.

Chicken Wild Rice Casserole

- 3 cups diced cooked chicken or turkey
- 2½ cups cooked wild or regular rice
- 1 cup cream of chicken or celery soup
- 1 cup mushroom soup
- 1 soup can milk
- 1 (6 ounce) can sliced mushrooms, drained
- ½ cup chopped green pepper
- 1 (4 ounce) jar pimientos, drained and sliced
- ½ cup slivered almonds
- ½ cup minced onion

OVEN 350°

Combine ingredients and pour into 9x13-inch casserole dish. Bake at 350° for 40 to 45 minutes. Garnish with pimiento strips.

Wild Rice Hot Dish

- 1½ pounds hamburger
- 1 large onion, diced
- ½ cup raw wild rice (wash and pre-cook)
- ½ cup raw white rice (do not pre-cook)
- 2 cups celery, diced small
- ½ cup cashews
- 2 (10¾ ounce) cans cream of mushroom soup
- 2 (10¾ ounce) cans cream of chicken soup
- 1 can mushroom pieces, drained
- 1½ cups milk
- 2 tablespoons soy sauce
- 2 tablespoons brown sugar

OVEN 350°

Brown meat lightly. Add onion; do not brown. Combine all ingredients and put into greased 3-quart casserole. Bake at 350° for 2 hours or more until rice is done.

Serves 12.

Green Rice

2 boxes frozen chopped broccoli
1 onion, finely chopped
1 stick butter or margarine
1 (10¾ ounce) can cheddar cheese soup
1 (10¾ ounce) can cream of mushroom soup
¼ soup can water
½ cup milk
1 cup quick-cooking rice

OVEN 350°

Cook broccoli until tender; drain. In large skillet combine rest of ingredients, stirring until completely mixed. Pour into baking dish. Bake at 350° for 40 to 45 minutes until lightly browned.

Spanish Chicken and Rice

Olive oil, enough to cover bottom of skillet
4 green onions, diced
1 large Spanish yellow onion, chopped
2 cloves garlic, minced
1 cup Spanish green olives with pimientos, chopped
½ cup juice from green olives
1 teaspoon chili powder
1 teaspoon crushed red pepper
2 tablespoons Morton's seasoned salt
6 boneless, skinless chicken thighs, cubed
1 (16 ounce) package Spanish yellow rice
Water

Set electric skillet at 200° to 250°. Sauté in olive oil onions, garlic, olives, and juice. Sauté until onions are tender. Add seasonings and chicken. Continue to sauté until chicken is cooked through. Add rice with its seasonings and enough water to cover. Remember to stir in seasoning thoroughly. Cover and simmer until rice is desired texture, adding more water if needed.

Rice 'n' Mushrooms

1 cup rice (not instant)
1 can mushrooms, drained
1 (10¾ ounce) can French onion soup
1 can beef broth
¼ cup margarine
2 tablespoons Worcestershire sauce

OVEN 350°

Combine ingredients in 2-quart casserole dish. Bake uncovered 1 hour at 350°.

Dave's Texas Spanish Rice

2 tablespoons cooking oil
1 cup converted rice
1 large bell pepper, chopped
2 jalapeño peppers, chopped
1 large onion, or 2 bunches green onions, chopped
3 cans whole tomatoes, blended
¾ cup water
1 teaspoon cumin
1 teaspoon black pepper
Dash crushed red pepper
1 tablespoon salt
3 teaspoons chili powder

Heat oil in 9-inch nonstick skillet. Add raw rice and cook until lightly browned. Add peppers and onions; then sauté until translucent. Add tomatoes, water, and seasonings to rice mixture. Stir well and cook over low heat for about 20 to 25 minutes or until rice absorbs moisture. Stir frequently.

Frances's Stew

1 pound hamburger or ground chuck
1 large onion, chopped
2 cans tomato sauce
2 (16 ounce) cans mixed vegetables, or frozen vegetables
1 tablespoon curry, taco, or chili powder (any flavor you want)
Salt and pepper to taste

Brown meat with onion and drain. Add sauce and veggies to meat and simmer for 1 hour or less. Cook in Dutch oven or slow cooker. Serve with corn bread or over rice.

Serves 6.

Oven Stew

1½ pounds stew meat
1 envelope onion soup mix
1 (10¾ ounce) can cream of celery soup
1 (10¾ ounce) can cream of mushroom soup
2 stalks celery, cut up
6 carrots, cut up
5 potatoes, cut up
⅔ soup can water

OVEN 300°

Spread stew meat in large casserole dish. Sprinkle with onion soup mix. Add soups and sprinkle with celery. Add layer of veggies. Pour water over all. Cover with foil. Bake 4 hours in 300° oven. Don't peek!

Salsa Stew

1 to 2 pound steak
Salsa (amount used depends on your taste)
Kitchen Bouquet (optional)
1 or 2 (16 ounce) cans mixed vegetables

On trivet in pressure cooker place one steak. Cover with salsa (be sure there is water under the trivet); cook 15 minutes. Remove from heat; when pressure is down remove steak. Scrape any salsa from trivet, into liquid in cooker. Mix 1 heaping tablespoon with water and Kitchen Bouquet, if desired; stir into boiling liquid until mixed well. Add vegetables, depending on amount needed to feed your group. Add cut-up steak. Cook slowly for about 15 minutes.

Beef Stew

1 pound beef
1 medium onion, halved
1 rib celery, whole with leaves left on
2-inch wedge of cabbage
½ teaspoon seasoned salt
⅛ teaspoon pepper
1 beef bouillon cube
4 potatoes, peeled and quartered
1 carrot, peeled and cut into 1-inch lengths
1 tablespoon flour
¼ cup water

The night before, place beef (can be frozen), onion, celery, cabbage, seasoned salt, pepper, and bouillon cube in slow cooker with 1 quart water. Cook on low overnight. The next morning, remove onion, celery, and cabbage and discard them. Break beef into bite-size pieces, removing any fat or bone. Add potatoes and carrots to slow cooker. Cook until vegetables are tender but not mushy. Twenty minutes before serving, mix flour with water and stir into pot. Cover. Serve with hot bread.

Serves 4.

Hint: If slow cooker must simmer all day, cut potatoes in larger pieces to keep them from becoming overdone.

Oven Stew

2 pounds stew meat (do not brown)
8 potatoes, cubed
4 carrots, coined
2 (10¾ ounce) cans cream of mushroom soup, undiluted
1 (10¾ ounce) can tomato soup, undiluted
2 (10¾ ounce) cans onion soup, undiluted

OVEN 300°

Combine but do not stir. Bake at 300° for 3 hours.

Oven Beef Stew

1 pound stew meat, cut up
1 package dry onion soup mix
1 can beef broth
1 (10¾ ounce) can cream of mushroom soup
1 soup can water

Add desired amounts of:
Carrots, peeled and chopped
Potatoes, peeled and cut into chunks
Onions, peeled and cut into chunks

OVEN 300°

Cook 3 hours in 300° oven, or in 4- or 6-quart roaster oven.

Bologna Stew

1 ring bologna, cut in pieces
2 medium onions, cubed (optional)
¼ teaspoon meat tenderizer
8 to 10 potatoes, peeled and cubed
2 (16 ounce) cans pork and beans
½ cup ketchup (to taste)
1 (10¾ ounce) can tomato soup
1 can tomato juice
Salt and pepper to taste
Other seasonings to taste

Fry bologna and onions in fry pan to brown; then season with meat tenderizer. Boil potatoes until done. Add both to large pot. Add remaining ingredients. Simmer to hot. The longer you cook it the better it is. Stir often so beans do not stick to pot.

Skillet Chicken Stew

⅓ cup flour
½ teaspoon salt
Dash pepper
1½ pounds boneless chicken breasts, cut into 1-inch pieces
1 medium onion, sliced
3 ribs celery, sliced
3 tablespoons butter or margarine
2 medium potatoes, peeled and cut into ¾-inch cubes
3 medium carrots, sliced ¼-inch thick
1 cup chicken broth
½ teaspoon dried thyme
1 tablespoon ketchup
1 tablespoon cornstarch

Combine flour, salt, and pepper in shallow bowl; coat chicken. Place in skillet. Add onion, celery, and butter; cook for 3 minutes. Stir into skillet potatoes, carrots, broth, thyme, ketchup, and cornstarch. Bring to boil; reduce heat; cover and simmer for 15 to 20 minutes or until vegetables are tender.

Cabbage Patch Stew

2 pounds hamburger
3 tablespoons oil
1 large onion, chopped
1 large green pepper, chopped
½ large head cabbage
2 stems celery, chopped
5 or more cups water
1 can tomato sauce
2 cans chopped tomatoes
1 can chili beans
2 teaspoons garlic salt
2 teaspoons mustard seed
1 teaspoon crushed red pepper
½ teaspoon celery seed
4 teaspoons parsley flakes
1 tablespoon sugar
4 teaspoons salt
1 teaspoon oregano
½ teaspoon marjoram
1 teaspoon onion salt
1 teaspoon thyme

In large skillet cook hamburger in cooking oil until gray. Add onion, pepper, cabbage, and celery. Add water. Cover and simmer 15 minutes. Stir often. Transfer from skillet to Dutch oven or large pot. Add tomato sauce, chopped tomatoes, and all other seasonings. Cover and simmer over medium heat for 45 minutes, stirring often. May serve "as is" or over rice or creamed potatoes, or with Mexican or regular corn bread.

Crock-Pot Chili Con Carne

½ pound hamburger
1 medium onion, chopped
½ green pepper, chopped
1 clove garlic, minced
1 can Italian stewed tomatoes
1 can kidney beans, drained
1 teaspoon soy sauce
1 teaspoon parsley
1 teaspoon McCormick garlic and herb seasoning
2 to 3 partially cooked potatoes
1 teaspoon brown sugar (optional)

Sauté hamburger; add onion, green pepper, and garlic. Put in slow cooker; add tomatoes, beans, soy sauce, parsley, seasoning, and potatoes. Cook 4 to 8 hours on low.

Hot Dog Chili

1 pound hamburger
1 medium onion, finely chopped
1 (6 ounce) can tomato paste
3 cans water
½ cup ketchup
1 teaspoon vinegar
1½ teaspoons chili powder
1 teaspoon salt

Combine all ingredients, adding water 1 can at a time, mixing well after each can. Simmer 1½ hours. Freeze in small containers. Serve hot over hot dogs.

Sweet and Sour Venison Stew

¼ cup flour
2 teaspoons salt, divided
Dash pepper
2 pounds venison round steak, cut into 1-inch cubes
¼ cup cooking oil
1 cup water
½ cup ketchup
¼ cup brown sugar
¼ cup cider vinegar
1 tablespoon Worcestershire sauce
1 onion, chopped
3 carrots, cut into ¾-inch pieces

Combine flour, 1 teaspoon salt, and pepper; coat meat with flour mixture. In large skillet or Dutch oven, brown meat on all sides in hot oil. Combine water, ketchup, brown sugar, vinegar, Worcestershire sauce, and 1 teaspoon salt. Stir into browned meat; add onion. Cover and cook over low heat for 45 minutes to 1 hour, stirring once or twice. Add carrots and cook until meat and carrots are done (about 1 hour). Serve hot over cooked rice. You may substitute beef in this recipe.

Serves 4 to 6.

Chili

1 can Bush's chili beans
1 can Franco-American spaghetti with cheese
1 package Lipton onion soup
1 small jar mushrooms
½ (18 to 20 ounce) can Red Gold tomato juice
1 heaping tablespoon chili powder
1½ pounds hamburger, browned and drained

Add all together in 4-quart kettle. Simmer 30 minutes after start of boiling. Add 2 slices of sandwich cheese before serving.

White Chili

2 tablespoons vegetable oil
4 boneless chicken breasts, cooked and cut into small cubes
1 medium onion, finely chopped
1 (4 ounce) can chopped green chilies
2 teaspoons garlic powder
2 teaspoons salt
2 teaspoons ground cumin
2 teaspoons ground oregano
2 teaspoons ground coriander
½ teaspoon cayenne pepper
6 (15 or 16 ounce) cans great northern beans (do not drain)
2 (10¾ ounce) cans chicken broth

In large stock pot heat oil; cook chicken and onions. Add next seven ingredients; stir until well blended. Stir in remaining ingredients. Bring to boil; reduce heat to low. Simmer 15 to 20 minutes.

White Chicken Chili

1 (2- to 3-pound) chicken
½ pound great northern beans
1 large onion, chopped
1 cup chopped celery
1 can mushrooms, drained
1 cup chopped carrots
Dash cayenne pepper
Dash celery salt
Dash Season-All salt
Dash garlic
1 can chili-style tomatoes
1 (10¾ ounce) can cream of chicken soup
Sour cream and green onions, for topping

Boil, debone, and cut chicken into small pieces. Cook beans in broth until tender. Add onions, celery, mushrooms, and carrots. Simmer for a while. Add seasonings, tomatoes, and soup. Add chicken and cook until done. To serve, put chili in bowls; top with spoonful of sour cream and green onions.

Desserts

Emma's Ambrosia

12 large navel oranges
¾ cup sugar
Freshly grated coconut

Working over large bowl to save juice, peel oranges and cut across sections to form bite-size pieces. Remove any tough membranes. Stir in sugar (to taste) and coconut. Cover and refrigerate for 4 hours until very juicy. (Dessert will keep in refrigerator for 1 week. It may be made 3 to 4 weeks in advance and frozen.) Serve in compote dishes plain or garnished with whipped cream and cherry. Good alone or with cake and cookies. One serving per orange used.

Strawberry Delight

1 angel food cake
1 cup cold milk
2 (3 ounce) or 1 (6 ounce) packages vanilla instant pudding
1 quart vanilla ice cream, softened
1 (3 ounce) box strawberry gelatin
1 cup boiling water
2 (10 ounce) packages frozen strawberries

Slice angel food cake and arrange in 9x13-inch pan. Mix together milk and pudding until mixture starts to thicken. Add ice cream. Mix and pour over cake slices. Place in refrigerator. Mix together gelatin and boiling water until gelatin is dissolved. Add frozen strawberries and stir until berries are separated. Pour over ice cream mixture and chill.

Cherries in the Snow

2 cups powdered sugar
2 (8 ounce) packages cream cheese, softened
4 packages Dream Whip (powdered whipped topping)
1 angel food cake
2 (20 ounce) cans cherry pie filling

Combine sugar and softened cream cheese until smooth. Prepare Dream Whip according to package directions; add to creamed mixture. Butter 11x13-inch pan or large platter. Put half of mixture in pan with crumbled cake. Add remaining mixture. Cover top with cherry pie filling. Refrigerate before serving.

Variations: Blueberry or apple pie filling may be substituted. Sprinkle apple pie filling with cinnamon.

Any Fruit Cobbler

½ cup butter, softened
1 cup sugar
2 cups flour
4 teaspoons baking powder
4 teaspoons salt
1 cup milk
32 ounces canned fruit, juice drained and reserved
½ to ¾ cup sugar

OVEN 375°

Cream together butter and 1 cup sugar. Sift together flour, baking powder, and salt. Add to creamed mixture alternately with milk. Beat until smooth. Pour into greased 8x10-inch pan. Spoon drained fruit over batter; sprinkle sugar over top. Pour juice over this. Bake 45 to 50 minutes or until top springs back. Batter will rise to top.

Peach Cobbler

3 cups sliced fresh peaches
¾ cup sugar
3 tablespoons flour
2 tablespoons lemon juice
2 tablespoons butter

Topping:
2 cups flour
½ teaspoon salt
4 teaspoons baking powder
1 tablespoon sugar
⅓ cup butter
1 egg, well beaten
¾ cup milk

OVEN 425°

Put peaches in greased baking dish. Mix sugar and flour. Sprinkle over peaches. Sprinkle with lemon juice; dot with butter. Sift dry ingredients and mix in butter until mixture is like coarse crumbs. Add combined egg and milk; mix until just moistened. Drop dough in mounds over peaches. Bake for 30 minutes.

Quick Cobbler

½ cup margarine
1 cup flour
1 cup sugar
1 cup milk
1 teaspoon baking powder
2 (16 ounce) cans fruit

OVEN 375°

Melt margarine in 9x13-inch pan. Mix other ingredients, except fruit, together. Pour mixture over margarine. Pour fruit on top and bake 30 minutes.

Pumpkin Pie Dessert Squares

1 box yellow cake mix, divided
½ cup butter or margarine, melted
1 egg

Filling:
3 cups (1 pound 14 ounce can) pumpkin pie mix
2 eggs
⅔ cup milk

Topping:
1 cup reserved cake mix
¼ cup sugar
1 tablespoon cinnamon
¼ cup butter or margarine, room temperature

OVEN 350°

Grease bottom only of 9x13-inch pan. Reserve 1 cup cake mix for topping. Combine cake mix, melted butter or margarine, and egg. Press in bottom of pan. Mix filling ingredients until smooth and pour over bottom layer. Mix topping ingredients and sprinkle over top of filling. Bake for 40 to 45 minutes or until knife inserted in middle comes out clean. If desired, serve with whipped topping.

Variation: Increase sugar and cinnamon in topping for more cinnamon flavor.

Easy Cobbler Dessert

2 (20 ounce) cans cherry, apple, or peach pie filling
1 box white or yellow cake mix
1¼ sticks margarine, melted
1 cup pecans or walnuts

OVEN 350°

Place both cans of pie filling in 9x13-inch pan. Spread dry cake mix over fruit. Pour margarine evenly over cake mix. Top with nuts. Bake for 35 to 45 minutes. Serve hot with ice cream or top with whipped cream.

Fruit Cobbler

1 stick butter
1½ cups self-rising flour
1¼ cups milk
1 cup sugar
1 (20 ounce) can fruit pie filling

OVEN 350°

Melt butter in 9x9-inch baking pan. Mix flour, milk, and sugar well (should be soupy) and pour into baking pan. Divide pie filling into 6 to 8 globs that flour mixture comes around. Bake for about 1 hour and serve with vanilla ice cream.

Grandma's Candied Apples

Approximately 4 cups sugar
Approximately 4 cups water
Approximately ¾ cup cinnamon candies
10 to 12 Golden Delicious apples, peeled, halved, and cored

Combine equal parts sugar and water, enough to cover 2 inches in bottom of large pan. Cook over low heat, dissolving candies in sugar water. Cook one layer of apples at a time. Turn halfway through. Cook until soft but solid enough to use fork to lift out. Arrange on plate or platter. This dish makes very attractive addition to holiday table. Best served on same day they are cooked. After cooking apples, boil syrup until it is thick enough to cling to tines of fork. The syrup makes wonderful, tasty, and colorful jelly that keeps well in refrigerator.

Fluffy Ruffles

20 graham crackers or cookies, crushed
¼ cup butter
¼ cup sugar (optional)
3 (3 ounce) packages unflavored gelatin
1 (8 ounce) container whipped topping

OVEN 375°

Crust: In 9x13-inch pan combine graham crackers or cookies, butter, and sugar (optional). Mix well and pat into pan. Bake 8 minutes.

Filling: Dissolve gelatin according to quick-set instructions. When thickened add whipped topping. Mix well; pour over crust. Chill until set.

Light Danish Pastry

1 tablespoon cake yeast
½ cup milk
2¼ cups flour
⅔ cup shortening, melted
2 eggs, beaten
3 tablespoons sugar
1 teaspoon salt

OVEN 375°

Soften cake yeast in milk. Add flour to softened yeast mixture and refrigerate for 2 hours. Roll into 6x18-inch rectangle. Fold dough into thirds. Combine shortening, beaten eggs, sugar, and salt. After spreading with 1½ tablespoons shortening mixture, roll out after each fold. Make large coil. Let rise until doubled. Bake for 15 to 20 minutes.

Chocolate Peanut Butter Pizza

½ cup sugar
½ cup packed brown sugar
½ cup soft margarine
½ cup peanut butter
½ teaspoon vanilla
1 egg
1½ cups flour
2 cups miniature marshmallows
1 cup (6 ounces) semisweet chocolate chips

OVEN 375°

In large bowl, combine sugar, brown sugar, margarine, peanut butter, vanilla, and egg. Blend well. Stir in flour. Press dough evenly over bottom of 12- or 14-inch pizza pan, forming ridge along edge. Bake for 10 minutes. Sprinkle with marshmallows and chocolate chips. Bake 5 to 8 minutes more, or until marshmallows are lightly browned. Cool. Cut into wedges. Store tightly covered.

Makes 2 dozen wedges.

Banana Split Brownie Pizza

1 box brownie mix
1 (8 ounce) package cream cheese
⅓ cup sugar
3 bananas
1 pint fresh strawberries, sliced
1 (6 ounce) can crushed pineapple, drained
Caramel ice cream topping
Chopped nuts

Mix brownie mix according to directions and bake on round pizza pan. Cool. Blend cream cheese and sugar. Spread on cooled crust. Cut into bite-size squares. Layer sliced fruit and pineapple on cream cheese. Drizzle caramel topping over fruit and top with chopped nuts.

Lemon Dessert

1 package Jiffy yellow cake mix
1 (8 ounce) package cream cheese
½ cup milk
1 (3 ounce) package vanilla instant pudding
1½ cups milk
1 (20 ounce) can lemon pie filling
Whipped topping
Walnuts (optional)

OVEN 350°

Prepare cake mix according to package directions and pour into 9x13-inch pan. Bake for 10 to 15 minutes. Let cool. Beat cream cheese in ½ cup milk until smooth; then add vanilla pudding mix and 1½ cups milk. Spread on cooked cake. Top with lemon pie filling. Follow with layer of whipped topping; add chopped walnuts if desired.

Variation: For a chocolate-layered

dessert; use cherry or blueberry pie filling and chopped chocolate chips on top of whipped topping. Chocolate cake may be used instead of yellow cake.

Snickers Fruit Salad

1 (16 ounce) can fruit cocktail
3 bananas, cut up
3 apples, cut up
1 (8 ounce) container whipped topping
6 full-size Snickers candy bars, cut up
1½ cups miniature marshmallows

Mix all together and serve.

Ronzini

2 cans crushed pineapple
½ teaspoon salt
2 eggs
2 tablespoons flour
¾ cup sugar
1 pound orzo macaroni, cooked
1 large jar maraschino cherries, halved
1 (12 ounce) can mandarin oranges
1 bag miniature marshmallows
1 cup chopped nuts
1 (16 ounce) container whipped topping

Drain pineapple, save juice and pulp, and set pineapple aside in refrigerator. Bring juice, salt, eggs, flour, and sugar to boil. Cool and then add to cooked, well-drained macaroni. Let stand overnight in refrigerator. Next day fold in pineapple, cherries, oranges, marshmallows, nuts, and whipped topping.

Apple Cheese Casserole

2 cans sliced apples
1 stick margarine
1 cup sugar
¾ cup self-rising flour
8 ounces Velveeta cheese, cut up

OVEN 350°

Spray medium to large casserole dish with cooking spray. Place apples in casserole dish. In separate bowl combine margarine, sugar, flour, and Velveeta cheese. Put cheese mixture in microwave on high for 30 seconds at a time, stirring after each time until mixed well. (Usually takes less than 2 minutes.) Pour over apples and bake until golden. Delicious reheated in microwave.

Orange Fluff Jell-O

2 (3 ounce) boxes orange gelatin
2 cups boiling water
2 cups cold water
Several heaping tablespoons orange sherbet
1 can crushed pineapple, drained
Whipped topping

Combine all ingredients except whipped topping and pour into small glass dish to jell. When completely jelled pour into large dish to beat whipped topping in. Pour back into small dish and keep in refrigerator to stay cool.

Yum Yum

1 cup flour
1 cup pecans
½ cup margarine, melted

Mix together and press into 2-quart casserole dish to make crust. Bake until light brown.

1 (8 ounce) package cream cheese
1 cup powdered sugar
1 cup whipped topping

Combine above ingredients. Beat until smooth and spread on cooled crust.

1 (3 ounce) box chocolate instant pudding mix
1 (3 ounce) box vanilla instant pudding mix
3 cups milk

Mix together above ingredients; beat until thick enough for pudding. Place on top of cream cheese mixture in casserole dish. Top with remaining whipped topping. Sprinkle with pecans.

Cherry Crunch

1 large can crushed pineapple
1 (20 ounce) can cherry pie filling
1 box Duncan Hines butter cake mix
2 sticks butter
1 cup chopped pecans

OVEN 325°

Spread pineapple in bottom of 9x13-inch pan. Spread cherry pie filling on top of pineapple. Sprinkle dry cake mix over top. Melt 2 sticks butter and pour over mixture. When mixture starts to rise, sprinkle pecans on top. Bake 20 to 30 minutes, or until done.

Walnut Walkaways

1 (¼ ounce) package dry yeast
¼ cup warm water
2 (8 ounce) packages cream cheese
1½ cups sugar
2 teaspoons lemon juice
¾ cup margarine
2 cups sifted flour
¼ teaspoon salt
1 egg
1 cup chopped nuts

OVEN 375°

Soften yeast in water. Beat cream cheese, sugar, and lemon juice until smooth. Set aside. Cut margarine into flour and salt. Add yeast and egg. Mix well. Roll dough half at a time on floured surface. Spread cheese mixture on both pieces of dough. Sprinkle with nuts. Roll up like jelly roll and seal ends. Place seam down on greased cookie sheet. Cut both cakes halfway lengthwise. Bake for 25 minutes. Cool and slice.

Cream Torte

4 egg whites
½ cup sugar
4 tablespoons cold water
4 egg yolks
½ cup sugar
1 cup flour
2 teaspoons baking powder

OVEN 350°

Beat egg whites until stiff. Gradually add ½ cup sugar, beat, and set aside. Add cold water to egg yolks; beat. Add ½ cup sugar, flour, and baking powder. Fold egg whites into this mixture. Bake in two greased and floured 9-inch layer-cake pans for 25 minutes. Remove from pans and cool on rack. Split layers with thin knife.

Filling:
1 package vanilla instant pudding mix
1½ cups milk
4 ounces whipped topping
Powdered sugar

Mix pudding mix and milk. Fold in whipped topping. Spread between layers (using one-third of filling for each layer) and push powdered sugar through strainer (or sprinkle over a doily) to decorate top. Refrigerate several hours.

Serves at least 12.

Four-Layered Dessert

1 stick butter
1 cup flour
1 cup chopped pecans

OVEN 350°

Melt butter and mix with flour and pecans. Press in bottom of 9x13-inch pan and bake for 25 minutes. Let cool.

1 (8 ounce) package cream cheese
1 cup powdered sugar
8 ounces whipped topping

Mix all and pour over first layer.

2 (3 ounce) packages chocolate instant pudding mix
3 cups milk

Mix and pour over second layer.

8 ounces whipped topping

Spread over third layer. Refrigerate at least 6 hours.

Variation: You may put a layer of butterscotch pudding on top of chocolate pudding and then add whipped topping. It's very good with both flavors and nuts on top!

Heavenly Hash

1 bag miniature marshmallows
½ cup chopped pecans
1 large can chunk pineapple, drained
1 Washington State and 1 Granny Smith apple, diced
Small bottle red or green cherries, chopped and drained
1 (16 ounce) carton sour cream

Mix all ingredients; let stand at least overnight in refrigerator. Serve as salad or dessert.

Oreo Delight

1 (16 ounce) bag Oreo cookies, crushed
1 stick margarine, melted
3 cups milk
2 (3 ounce) packages vanilla instant pudding mix
1 tablespoon vanilla
8 ounces cream cheese, softened
8 ounces whipped topping

Crush Oreo cookies with rolling pin; then mix together with margarine. Pat into 9x13-inch pan, reserving some cookies for topping. Mix together milk, pudding mix, and vanilla; set aside. Mix together cream cheese and whipped topping; then add to pudding mixture. Pour over top of Oreo crust and sprinkle with remaining Oreo cookies; chill for 2 hours or more.

Cinnamon-Crusted Baked Apples

Butter-flavored cooking spray
⅓ cup water
5 medium cooking apples
⅓ cup firmly packed brown sugar
¼ cup flour
½ teaspoon ground cinnamon
¼ teaspoon ground nutmeg
2 tablespoons reduced-calorie margarine, softened

OVEN 350°

Coat 9x9-inch baking dish with spray. Pour water into dish. Peel, core, and slice apples. Arrange apples in prepared dish; coat apple slices lightly with cooking spray. Combine brown sugar, flour, cinnamon, and nutmeg; cut in margarine with pastry blender until mixture resembles coarse meal. Sprinkle mixture evenly over apples. Bake uncovered for 30 minutes or until apples are tender.

Raisin Puffs

1 cup raisins
1 cup water
1 cup shortening
1½ cups sugar
2 eggs
1 teaspoon vanilla
3½ cups flour
1 teaspoon soda
½ teaspoon salt

OVEN 350°

Cook raisins in water until dry. Mix shortening, sugar, eggs, and vanilla. Add raisins, then dry ingredients. Roll into balls. Dip in sugar. Put on cookie sheet. Bake for 12 to 15 minutes.

Butter Pecan Dessert

1 stick margarine
1 cup flour
1 cup chopped pecans
1 (8 ounce) package cream cheese
½ cup powdered sugar
1 (16 ounce) tub whipped topping
3 (3 ounce) boxes butter pecan instant pudding mix
4 cups milk

OVEN 350°

Melt margarine, mix in flour, put in 9x13-inch pan, and pat it down. Add pecans; bake for 10 minutes. Cool. Mix together cream cheese and powdered sugar; when creamy add half container of whipped topping and spread over crust. Mix 3 boxes of butter pecan instant pudding with milk and spread over whipped topping. Top with remaining whipped topping. Refrigerate.

Cherry Cream Cheese Turnovers

1 (8 ounce) package cream cheese
1 cup butter
1 teaspoon vanilla
2 cups sifted flour
Pinch salt
1 (20 ounce) can cherry pie filling
Powdered sugar

OVEN 350°

Blend cream cheese and butter in bowl; then stir in vanilla. Add flour and salt; mix well. Place in refrigerator for 1 hour. Roll out thin on floured surface and cut into 2-inch squares. Place 2 cherries from cherry pie filling in center of each square. Fold over and seal edges. Place on baking sheet. Bake for about 25 minutes. Cool and dust with powdered sugar.

Makes 50 turnovers.

Sweet Potato Delight

1 large can sweet potatoes, or 1 medium can mashed
½ stick margarine
2 eggs
½ cup evaporated milk
¾ cup sugar (more or less to taste)

Topping:
¾ stick margarine
¾ cup light brown sugar
½ cup flour
1 cup chopped nuts

OVEN 325°

Mix sweet potato ingredients together and put in glass casserole dish. Mix topping ingredients and spread on top of potato mixture. Bake about 45 minutes.

Sheen Island

1 (6 ounce) package lime gelatin
1 large can pineapple rings
1 large package cream cheese
1 small bag miniature marshmallows
Chopped nuts (optional)

Dissolve gelatin in hot water. Let gelatin partly set in refrigerator. In separate bowl, chop pineapple rings, saving juice. Blend juice with cream cheese. Add pineapple and cream cheese, then marshmallows, to gelatin.

Variations: Strawberry-banana gelatin can be used. Finely chopped nuts can be added to cream cheese mixture.

Angel Food Dessert

1 large angel food cake
1 (16 ounce) package strawberries
1 (3 ounce) package each strawberry, lime, and orange gelatin
½ gallon vanilla ice cream
1 (10 ounce) can crushed pineapple
1 (10 ounce) can mandarin oranges

Divide cake into thirds and crumble. In large tube pan, place one-third of crumbled cake over bottom, add strawberries mixed with dry strawberry gelatin, and cover with one-third of ice cream. Then add one-third cake and slightly drained pineapple mixed with dry lime gelatin; cover with one-third of ice cream. Add last one-third of cake and mandarin oranges mixed with dry orange gelatin. Top with last of ice cream. Freeze cake until ready to serve. Unmold and serve.

Strawberry Shortcake

Sugar
1 package Duncan Hines deluxe French vanilla cake mix
3 eggs
1¼ cups water
½ cup butter

OVEN 350°

Grease two 9-inch round cake pans with butter or margarine. Sprinkle bottom and sides with sugar. Combine cake mix, eggs, water, and butter in large bowl. Beat at medium speed with electric mixer for 2 minutes. Pour into pans. Bake for 30 to 35 minutes. Cool in pans for 10 minutes. Invert onto cooling rack. Cool completely.

Filling and Topping:
2 cups whipping cream, chilled
⅓ cup sugar
½ teaspoon vanilla
1 quart fresh strawberries, sliced
Mint leaves (optional)

In large bowl, beat whipping cream, sugar, and vanilla until stiff. Reserve ⅓ cup for garnish. Place one cake layer on serving plate. Spread with half of remaining whipped cream and half of sliced strawberries. Repeat with remaining layer and whipped cream and berries. Garnish with reserved whipped cream and mint leaves. Refrigerate until ready to serve.

Cherry Angel Dessert

1 angel food cake
1 (3 ounce) box vanilla instant pudding mix
2 cups milk
1 (20 ounce) can cherry pie filling

Pull apart angel cake into bite-size pieces. Prepare pudding according to box directions. Pour pudding over angel food cake pieces and stir until cake is moistened well. Pour into 2- or 3-quart glass dish. Spread mixture to cover bottom of dish. Pour cherry pie filling over cake and pudding mixture. Spread to cover. Refrigerate until ready to serve. Makes 6 to 8 servings.

Punch Bowl Dessert

2 (3 ounce) boxes vanilla instant pudding mix
3⅔ cups milk
1 (12 ounce) container whipped topping
1 box vanilla wafers
1 large can crushed pineapple, drained
3 to 4 bananas, sliced

Mix pudding with milk and half of whipped topping. Put layer of wafers in bowl; spread with half of pineapple, bananas, and pudding; repeat. Put remaining whipped topping on top. Garnish with nuts, cherries, and coconut if desired.

Hemmels Flutter

1 teaspoon vanilla
1 cup sugar
2 eggs
6 tablespoons flour
2 teaspoons baking powder
1 cup finely chopped dates
1 cup chopped nutmeats (not too finely chopped)

OVEN 325°

Mix a little flour with dates to keep them separated. Mix remaining ingredients in order given. Pour and spread out in ungreased 9x13-inch cake pan. Bake in slow oven 30 to 40 minutes. After baking, cut into squares and break up into bite-size pieces in dessert dishes. Spoon a couple of tablespoons of pineapple and some slices of banana over; top with whipped cream.

Fruit Pizza

1 box Duncan Hines golden sugar cookies, or 1 box (1 pound 1 ounce) Pillsbury sugar cookies
1 (8 ounce) package cream cheese
½ cup sugar
1 teaspoon vanilla
Fresh fruit

OVEN 350°

Follow directions on box for rolled sugar cookies. Spread on large ungreased pizza pan or jelly roll pan. Bake for 8 to 10 minutes. Cool. Mix cream cheese, sugar, and vanilla together. Spread over cooled cookie crust. Place fruit on top of cream cheese mixture. Pour fruit glaze on top of fruit (recipe follows).

Fruit Glaze:
1 cup water
¾ cup sugar
2 tablespoons cornstarch
2 tablespoons strawberry gelatin

Cook water, sugar, and cornstarch until thickened. Add gelatin. Let cool. The gelatin is for color and a little flavoring.

Note: A great fruit combination is strawberries, blueberries, raspberries, and blackberries. If you want to use bananas, dip them first in pineapple juice to prevent them from turning brown.

Apple Pie Pizza

Pastry for two-crust pie
7 to 8 medium apples, pared, cored, sliced
1½ tablespoons lemon juice
1 cup sugar, divided
1 teaspoon cinnamon
½ teaspoon nutmeg
¾ cup flour
½ cup butter, softened

OVEN 350°

Line 12x14-inch pizza pan with pastry dough. Place dough carefully to avoid tears in bottom. Arrange apples in attractive pattern in pastry shell. Sprinkle apple slices with lemon juice. Combine ½ cup sugar with spices; sprinkle over apple slices. Combine flour with remaining ½ cup sugar; cut in butter until crumbly. Sprinkle over apple slices. Bake 20 to 25 minutes, until crust is golden brown and apples are tender. Serve warm or cold.

Prune Whip

2 packages lemon gelatin (or more to taste)
5 jars baby food prunes
4 ounces whipped topping

Prepare gelatin according to package directions; set until semi-solid. Using mixer, mix gelatin, prunes, and whipped topping (don't overmix). Chill in refrigerator until set to pudding consistency.

Sugar-Free Fruit Crisp

2½ cups fruit, cut into bite-size pieces
5 tablespoons flour, divided
⅛ teaspoon cinnamon
1 cup organic muesli (or mix your own oats, raisins, and sunflower seeds to equal 1 cup)
¼ to ½ teaspoon fresh lemon zest
⅛ teaspoon cinnamon
3 tablespoons canola/corn oil blend
½ cup 100% pear juice

OVEN 375°

In 9-inch glass pie plate, combine fruit, 2 tablespoons flour, and ⅛ teaspoon cinnamon. In separate bowl, mix together muesli, 3 tablespoons flour, lemon zest, ⅛ teaspoon cinnamon, and oil. Spread over fruit mixture. Pour fruit juice over all. Bake for 45 minutes. Serve warm or cold. Flavor mellows and becomes sweeter if you refrigerate for 2 to 3 days.

Zucchini-Apple Crisp

½ cup packed brown sugar
2 teaspoons lemon juice
¼ cup water
1 teaspoon salt (optional)
1 teaspoon cinnamon
3 cups zucchini, peeled, quartered, seeded, and sliced to look like apples
3 cups apples, peeled and sliced
1 cup raisins (optional)

Topping:
½ cup flour
½ cup oats
½ cup brown sugar
1 teaspoon cinnamon
2 to 4 tablespoons oil

OVEN 375°

Mix first eight ingredients in large saucepan. Boil 10 minutes, stirring so zucchini is thoroughly mixed with apples. Pour into ungreased 9x13-inch baking dish. Mix topping with fork and sprinkle on top. Bake for 45 minutes. If desired, this can be served with whipped topping or ice cream. It is delicious hot or cold!

Variation: Substitute apple juice for lemon juice and water.

Rhubarb Crisp

3 cups diced rhubarb
1 egg
¾ cup sugar
2 tablespoons flour
¼ teaspoon mace

Topping:
¼ cup margarine
⅓ cup white or brown sugar
⅔ cup flour

OVEN 375°

Mix rhubarb, egg, sugar, 2 tablespoons flour, and mace; put in deep glass dish. Combine topping ingredients and cover rhubarb with topping. Bake 30 minutes.

Cinnamon Apple Crisp

6 medium apples, pared, cored, sliced
1 cup water
1 package white cake mix
1 cup firmly packed brown sugar
½ cup margarine, melted
1 teaspoon cinnamon
Whipped topping or ice cream

OVEN 350°

Arrange apple slices in ungreased 9x13-inch pan. Pour water over top. Combine cake mix, brown sugar, melted margarine, and cinnamon. Stir until thoroughly blended. (Mixture will be crumbly.) Sprinkle crumb mixture over apple slices. Bake for 50 to 55 minutes or until lightly browned and bubbly.

Variations: To reduce sweetness, use ½ cup brown sugar. You can substitute 2 (21 ounce) cans apple pie filling for fresh apples. Omit water.

Chocolate-Cherry Delicious

2 (20 ounce) cans cherry pie filling
1 box chocolate cake mix
¾ cup butter, melted

OVEN 350°

Spread pie filling in 9x13-inch pan. Sprinkle dry cake mix evenly over pie filling. Drizzle butter evenly over cake mix. The butter will leave some dry spots, but don't worry about them. Bake for 45 minutes until done. Serve warm or cold.

Ice Cream Dessert

Crust:
½ package (approximately 26) low-fat Oreo cookies
¼ cup margarine, melted

Filling:
½ gallon low-fat or fat-free ice cream

Topping:
1 (16 ounce) jar fat-free hot fudge sauce
1 (8 ounce) container low-fat whipped topping

Crush cookies and combine with margarine. Press in bottom of 9x13-inch pan and chill in freezer. Cut ice cream into thick slabs and cover crust. Heat topping for 1 minute in microwave. Spoon over ice cream and spread as much as possible. Cover with whipped topping and freeze. Cut into squares and top with cherries, chocolate curls, or chopped pecans.

Easy Chocolate Mint Chip Dessert

16 frozen waffles
½ gallon chocolate mint chip ice cream
Chocolate syrup
1 (12 ounce) container whipped topping

Separate waffles and put 8 in 9x13-inch pan (or put in plastic bag wrapped in aluminum foil when done). Cut ice cream into ½-inch slices and cut each slice in two, to fit waffles. Put slices on waffles and top each with another waffle. Put in your freezer until ready to use. When ready to serve, remove from freezer and top with a couple of tablespoons of chocolate syrup (or however much you prefer). Top this with large tablespoon of whipped topping.

Cranberry Nut Loaf

1 (8 ounce) package cream cheese
⅓ cup margarine
1¼ cups sugar
1 teaspoon vanilla
3 eggs
2 tablespoons lemon juice
1 teaspoon grated lemon peel
2¼ cups flour
2 teaspoons baking powder
½ teaspoon baking soda
1½ cups chopped cranberries
1 cup chopped walnuts or pecans

OVEN 325°

Beat cream cheese, margarine, sugar, and vanilla until well blended; add eggs one at a time. Mix in lemon juice and lemon peel, then flour, baking powder, and baking soda. Add cranberries and nuts. Bake for 1 hour 15 minutes.

Fruit Loaf

2 cups sugar
1 cup water
Lump of butter
1 teaspoon vinegar
Honey
1 pound (2 cups) mixed nuts
1 pound coconut
1 pound dates
½ pound figs
1 pound (2⅔ cups) powdered sugar

Syrup: Boil sugar, water, butter, and vinegar, adding honey for flavor, until it threads. Chop or grind nuts and fruit until fine. Mix well with syrup in large mixing bowl. Turn out onto board and mix with powdered sugar. Mix well with hands; form into loaf. Roll into several long rolls and refrigerate to cool. When cooled, cut into thin slices for serving. Keeps long while in refrigerator or may be frozen.

Chocolate Éclair Dessert

1 (6 ounce) package French vanilla instant pudding mix
3 cups milk
1 (8 ounce) carton whipped topping
1 (1 pound) box graham crackers

Frosting:
3 ounces margarine, melted
2 ounces unsweetened baking chocolate, melted
2 tablespoons light corn syrup
3 tablespoons milk
1 teaspoon vanilla
1½ cups powdered sugar

Mix pudding mix and milk as package directs; fold in whipped topping. In 9x13-inch pan place one layer of graham crackers. Cover with half of pudding mixture. Repeat once again. Beat together frosting ingredients; spread over top layer of graham crackers.

Pineapple Surprise

1 (16 ounce) can chunk pineapple, undrained
1 box yellow cake mix
3 tablespoons butter, melted
½ cup chopped walnuts

OVEN 350°

Butter glass or metal pan; add pineapple with juice. Spread half of cake mix evenly over pineapple; do not mix. Drizzle butter on top. Sprinkle walnuts on top. Bake 30 minutes for glass pan, 50 minutes for metal pan.

Note: Use other half of cake mix to repeat recipe. Freeze this dessert for later.

Pineapple Au Gratin

3 cans crushed pineapple, drained
6 tablespoons self-rising flour
2 cups shredded cheddar cheese
1 sleeve butter crackers (Ritz or Townhouse), crushed
1 stick margarine or butter, melted

OVEN 350°

Mix pineapple and flour in 9x13-inch baking dish. Stir in cheese. Spread crushed crackers on top and drizzle with melted butter. Bake until cheese melted on top is light brown (about 20 minutes).

Baked Pineapple

½ cup flour
⅓ cup sugar
1 egg
2 tablespoons butter
1 (20 ounce) can pineapple chunks, drained, juice reserved
½ pound processed cheese, chopped (Velveeta works well)
Miniature marshmallows

OVEN 350°

Combine flour, sugar, egg, butter, and pineapple juice in pan. Cook until thick. Add cheese. Stir in pineapple chunks. Pour in buttered baking dish. Top with marshmallows. Bake for 15 to 20 minutes.

Anytime Treats

1 to 2 packages graham crackers
Miniature marshmallows
Chocolate chips

OVEN 350°

Line cookie sheet with one package of graham crackers. Sprinkle graham crackers generously with marshmallows and chocolate chips. Put in oven for 5 minutes or until chocolate chips start to melt. Remove from oven and cool.

Note: To put in lunch boxes or wrap for gift giving, place another package of graham crackers on top of chocolate chips when you remove from oven.

Oreo Cookie Dessert

1 (1 pound) package Oreo cookies
1 stick butter, melted
1 (6 ounce) box vanilla instant pudding mix
2½ cups milk
1 (8 ounce) package cream cheese, softened
1 cup powdered sugar
1 (12 ounce) container whipped topping

Crush cookies (set aside ½ cup crushed cookies), add melted butter, and press into bottom of 9x13-inch pan. Beat pudding mix and milk together until thickened. Pour over crumb mixture and refrigerate. Beat softened cream cheese and sugar together. Fold in half of whipped topping. Remove mixture from refrigerator and spread cream cheese mixture on top of pudding. Spread remaining whipped topping on top and sprinkle with remaining ½ cup crushed Oreos.

Variations: Use vanilla or peanut butter cookies with chocolate pudding.

Apple Roll

1½ cups sugar
2 cups water
2 cups flour
½ teaspoon salt
2 tablespoons sugar
4 teaspoons baking powder
3 tablespoons shortening
¾ cup milk
4 medium apples, finely chopped

OVEN 350°

Combine sugar and water, cook to dissolve sugar, and pour into 9x11-inch cake pan. Combine next six ingredients. Roll flour mixture ½-inch thick. Spread apples over flour mixture. Roll up like jelly roll and cut slices 1 inch thick. Place in sugar water. Put small pieces of butter on top and sprinkle with cinnamon. Bake for 30 minutes.

Variation: Use peaches instead of apples.

Blackberry Grunt

4 cups blackberries
1 cup sugar
½ cup water
1½ tablespoons butter
1 cup flour
1½ teaspoons baking powder
Dash salt
2 tablespoons sugar
½ cup milk
2 tablespoons butter, melted

Combine berries, 1 cup sugar, water, and 1½ tablespoons butter in heat-proof casserole dish to be used on top of range. Bring to boil. In separate bowl, mix flour, baking powder, salt, remaining sugar, milk, and melted butter. Spoon dough over berry mixture and cover tightly. Simmer 12 minutes. When cooked, a knife inserted in center will come out clean.

Blueberry Delight

CRUST:
1 cup finely chopped walnuts
2 cups graham cracker crumbs or vanilla wafer crumbs
½ cup butter or margarine

FILLING:
2 (8 ounce) packages cream cheese
2 cups powdered sugar
1 package Dream Whip, prepared as directed
1 (20 ounce) can blueberry pie filling

OVEN 350°

Mix crust ingredients well and press into casserole dish. Bake until slightly brown. Cool.

To make filling, soften cream cheese and add sugar, then Dream Whip. Mix well using mixer. Pour filling into crust. Top with pie filling. Chill 2 to 3 hours.

Four-Layer Blueberry Delight

1½ cups flour
1½ sticks margarine, melted
1 cup chopped nuts

OVEN 350°

Mix crust ingredients and press into 9x13-inch pan. Bake 15 minutes.

2 (8 ounce) packages cream cheese
2 (14 ounce) cans condensed milk
⅔ cup lemon juice
2 teaspoons vanilla

Beat cream cheese until creamy; add other ingredients in order listed. Pour over cooled crust.

1 to 2 (20 ounce) cans blueberry pie filling
1 (8 ounce) whipped topping

Top cream cheese layer with filling, to taste. Top pie filling with whipped topping. Refrigerate.

Blueberry Buckle

2 cups sifted flour
3 teaspoons baking powder
½ teaspoon salt
½ cup butter or margarine, softened
½ cup sugar
2 eggs
¾ cup milk
2 cups blueberries, washed and drained

TOPPING:
⅓ cup flour
¼ cup butter
¾ cup brown sugar
2 teaspoons cinnamon

OVEN 375°

Grease and flour 9-inch square pan (or equivalent). Sift flour and baking powder with salt in large bowl. In another bowl, combine butter, sugar, and eggs; beat at high speed until fluffy. At low speed, add dry ingredients alternately with milk. Fold in berries last.

Turn into prepared pan. Mix topping ingredients to consistency of peas and sprinkle on top of batter. Bake 35 minutes or until done. Can be frozen for later use.

Spring Temptation

1 (3 ounce) package orange gelatin
1 cup hot water
1½ cups orange sherbet
1 small can crushed pineapple
1 small can mandarin oranges
1 cup miniature marshmallows

Mix together gelatin, hot water, and sherbet. Mix until sherbet is melted. Refrigerate until almost set. Stir in pineapple, mandarin oranges, and marshmallows. Refrigerate.

Cool Fruit

1 cup whipped topping
1 cup condensed milk
1 cup tidbit pineapple, drained
2 small cans mandarin oranges
1 cup miniature marshmallows
½ cup chopped walnuts
1 cup cherry pie filling

Mix all together and chill.

Strawberry-Nut Jell-O

2 (3 ounce) packages strawberry gelatin
1 cup boiling water
2 (10 ounce) packages sliced strawberries, thawed
1 large can crushed pineapple, drained
3 bananas, mashed
1 cup coarsely chopped walnuts
1 pint sour cream

Dissolve gelatin in water. Fold in strawberries with juice, pineapple, bananas, and walnuts. Put half in pan for first layer. Set 1½ hours; spoon sour cream on top evenly. Add remaining gelatin mixture and let set.

Sugar-Free Jell-O Dessert

2 (3 ounce) or 1 (6 ounce) sugar-free orange gelatin
1 (20 ounce) can crushed pineapple, undrained
2 cups buttermilk
1 (8 ounce) lite whipped topping

Heat gelatin and pineapple. Mix well until gelatin is dissolved. Add buttermilk and whipped topping. Mix well. Put in refrigerator until gelatin sets up.

Makes 4 to 6 servings.

Peaches and Cream

1 (16 ounce) can peaches
1 (12 ounce) can evaporated milk
1 cup sugar

Open can of peaches and set aside. Put milk in metal or glass bowl (not plastic). Put bowl and beaters in freezer for 20 minutes. Remove and beat milk on high speed. Then add sugar. Beat until smooth and frothy. Put peaches in individual bowls. Spoon on cream. Eat immediately. Will not keep.

Creamy Mocha Frozen Dessert

2 teaspoons instant coffee granules
1 tablespoon hot water
1 cup cream-filled chocolate cookie crumbs (about 7 cookies)
¾ cup chopped pecans, divided
¼ cup butter or margarine, melted
2 (8 ounce) packages cream cheese, softened
1 (14 ounce) can condensed milk
½ cup chocolate syrup
1 (8 ounce) container whipped topping

In small bowl dissolve coffee granules in hot water; set aside. In another bowl, combine cookie crumbs, ½ cup pecans, and butter. Pat into bottom of 9x13-inch baking pan. In mixing bowl, beat cream cheese until light and fluffy. Blend in coffee mixture, milk, and chocolate syrup. Fold in whipped topping; spread over crust. Sprinkle remaining pecans on top. Freeze.

Million-Dollar Pudding

1 (3 ounce) box sugar-free instant pudding (vanilla or butterscotch)
1 cup whipping cream
4 ounces whipped topping
3 ounces cream cheese
1 cup unsweetened pineapple
1 package artificial sweetener
½ cup chopped walnuts

Blend pudding and whipping cream; add rest of ingredients and chill.

"Lil's" Creamy Rice Pudding

1⅓ cups uncooked rice
2⅔ cups sugar
2 teaspoons salt
14 cups milk
4 eggs
4 teaspoons vanilla
Nutmeg or cinnamon to taste

Heat rice, sugar, salt, and milk in top of double boiler over direct heat until milk is scalded. Occasionally stir rice from bottom of pan with fork. Place over boiling water in bottom of double boiler. Cover and cook for 2½ to 3 hours, stirring occasionally. Beat eggs; add small amount of hot pudding to eggs first, so not to scramble eggs. Then add egg mixture a small amount at a time. Add flavorings. Serve hot or cold.

Caramel Pudding

3 cups hot water
2 cups brown sugar
1 tablespoon butter
1½ teaspoons vanilla
½ cup milk
½ cup sugar
1 tablespoon margarine
1½ cups flour
1½ teaspoons baking powder
Pinch salt
Vanilla

Combine first four ingredients and boil for 10 minutes. Mix rest of ingredients. Drop by spoonfuls into first mixture and boil for 30 minutes, covered.

Lemon Delight

Crust:
2 cups flour
2 sticks margarine, softened or melted
1 cup chopped pecans

Filling:
2 cups powdered sugar
1 (8 ounce) package cream cheese
2 (3 ounce) packages lemon instant pudding mix
3 cups milk
1 carton whipped topping

OVEN 375°

Mix crust ingredients; may be crumbly. Press into 9x13-inch pan. Bake for 15 to 20 minutes. Cool.

Combine powdered sugar and cream cheese. Chill 15 minutes and spread over cooled crust. Whisk together pudding and milk. Let set a few minutes after mixture thickens. Spread over cream cheese mixture. Cover with whipped topping. Place twist of lemon in center for garnish.

Cherry Icebox Dessert

24 large marshmallows
½ cup hot milk
20 graham crackers
3 tablespoons powdered sugar
1 stick butter or margarine, melted
½ pint whipping cream or 1 pint whipped topping
1 (20 ounce) can cherry pie filling

Melt marshmallows in hot milk on top of double boiler. Cool. Crush graham crackers very fine. Add sugar and melted butter to cracker crumbs; press into bottom of 8x12-inch dish. Whip cream, sweetened to taste, and fold into cooled marshmallow mixture. Spread half of whipped cream mixture on top of crust. Spoon on entire can of cherry pie filling. Top with remaining whipped cream mixture. Chill at least 6 hours; overnight is best.

My Pistachio Delight

1 (16 or 20 ounce) can crushed pineapple
1 (3 ounce) package pistachio instant pudding mix
½ (10 ounce) package miniature marshmallows
1 (8 ounce) tub whipped topping

Put crushed pineapple in bottom of large mixing bowl. Add pudding and mix well. Add marshmallows and mix well. Place in small bowl; refrigerate until firm. Top with whipped cream.

Hot Fudge Pudding

1 cup flour
¼ teaspoon salt
2 tablespoons cocoa
2 teaspoons baking powder
¾ cup sugar
½ cup milk
2 tablespoons shortening
1 cup chopped nuts
4 tablespoons brown sugar
2 tablespoons cocoa

OVEN 350°

Mix first five ingredients in bowl. Stir in milk, shortening, and nuts. Spread in 9x9-inch pan. Mix brown sugar and additional cocoa and sprinkle over mixture. Pour 2 cups hot water on top and bake for 40 minutes. Serve with ice cream, whipped cream, or whipped topping.

Apple Pudding

Apples, peeled and sliced
¼ to ½ cup sugar
Cinnamon
Butter
½ cup sugar
2 eggs
⅓ cup flour
¼ teaspoon baking powder

OVEN 350°

Butter 1- or 1½-quart casserole dish. Fill baking dish half full of apples. Put ¼ to ½ cup sugar over apples. Sprinkle with cinnamon and dot with butter. Make batter of ½ cup sugar, eggs, flour, and baking powder; pour over apples; do not stir. Bake for 30 minutes or until apples are tender.

My Original Banana Pudding

¾ cup sugar, divided
½ cup flour
Dash salt
4 eggs, separated
2 cups milk
½ teaspoon vanilla
Vanilla wafers
5 to 6 medium bananas, sliced

OVEN 425°

Combine ½ cup sugar, flour, and salt in double boiler. Stir in 4 egg yolks and milk. Cook, uncovered, over boiling water. Stir constantly until mixture thickens. Reduce heat and cook 5 more minutes. Remove from heat and add vanilla. Spread on bottom of dish and layer with wafers and bananas. Repeat this process several times.

Beat egg whites until stiff peaks form.

Add remaining sugar and beat until dissolved. Cover entire top of banana pudding and seal sides. Bake for 5 minutes or until brown on top. Add cookie crumbs on top for garnish.

Big-as-Texas Banana Pudding

2 packages vanilla instant pudding mix
4 cups milk
1 (8 ounce) package cream cheese
1 can Eagle brand fat-free milk
1 container fat-free whipped topping
8 bananas, sliced
1 box vanilla wafers

Beat together pudding and milk; set aside. Mix cream cheese and fat-free milk. Mix together cream cheese and pudding mixtures. Fold in whipped topping and bananas. Layer in dish with wafers.

Peach Pudding

¼ cup sugar
1 tablespoon cornstarch
2 eggs
¼ cup water
1 large can peaches, drained, juice reserved
1 tablespoon vanilla
½ pint whipped cream or 1 (8 ounce) container whipped topping

Mix sugar, cornstarch, and eggs with water. Heat juice from peaches and sugar mixture. Cook until thick; cool. Cut peaches in dish and add cooled mixture; add vanilla and whipped cream.

Walnut Pudding

1 cup sugar
1 cup milk
½ cup raisins
1 teaspoon cloves
1 teaspoon nutmeg
2 tablespoons butter
1 teaspoon baking powder
1 cup chopped walnuts
1 teaspoon cinnamon
2 cups flour

Sauce:
2 tablespoons butter
3 cups brown sugar
5 cups boiling water

OVEN 350°

Combine pudding ingredients except flour. Add flour until stiff. Combine sauce ingredients in deep pan; drop batter into sauce by spoonfuls. Bake for 1 hour.

Graham Cracker Pudding

½ cup margarine
1 cup brown sugar
1½ cups water
2 rounded tablespoons flour
2 rounded tablespoons cornstarch
½ cup sugar
2 egg yolks
1 cup milk
1 (8 or 12 ounce) container whipped topping

Crumbs:
12 graham crackers, crushed
2 tablespoons butter, melted
¼ cup white sugar

Melt margarine, add brown sugar, and let come to boil. Add water and let almost come to boil again. Combine flour, cornstarch, sugar, egg yolks, and milk. Stir into hot mixture. On low heat, stir and cook until it thickens. Cool. Mix cracker crumbs, butter, and sugar. Layer crumbs, chilled pudding, and whipped topping in clear bowl. Refrigerate.

S'more Pudding Dessert

9 full-size graham crackers, crushed
1 (5 ounce) box vanilla pudding mix
3¼ cups milk
3 (1¼ ounce) chocolate candy bars
2 cups miniature marshmallows

Line bottom of 1½-quart baking dish with one-third of graham cracker crumbs. Using 3¼ cups milk, cook pudding as directed on package; cool 5 minutes. Spread half of pudding over crackers. Top with second layer of one-third of crackers. Place candy bars on crackers. Spread remaining pudding over candy. Top with remaining crackers. Sprinkle with marshmallows. Broil until golden brown. Serve warm or chilled in refrigerator.

Fruit and Nut Bread Pudding

16 slices day-old bread, torn into 1-inch pieces
2 cups sugar
4 eggs
3 cups milk
2 teaspoons ground cinnamon
½ teaspoon salt
2 tablespoons vanilla
1 (21 ounce) can apple pie filling, slices cut in half
2 cups coarsely chopped pecans
1 cup golden raisins
¾ cup butter or margarine, melted
Whipped cream (optional)

OVEN 350°

In large bowl, combine bread and sugar. Set aside. In another bowl, beat eggs, milk, cinnamon, salt, and vanilla until foamy. Pour over bread and sugar; mix well. Cover and refrigerate for 2 hours.

Stir in remaining ingredients except cream. Pour into greased 9x13-inch baking pan. Bake for 45 to 50 minutes or until firm. Cut into squares. Serve warm or cold, with whipped cream, if desired.

Makes 12 to 15 servings.

Mousse in Minutes

1½ cups cold skim milk
1 package (4 servings) fat-free, sugar-free chocolate instant pudding mix
2 cups lite whipped topping

Combine skim milk and pudding in large bowl; whisk 1 minute. Stir in whipped topping. Garnish as desired.

Makes 6 servings.

Custard Raisin Bread Pudding

4 or 5 slices raisin bread
2 cups milk, scalded
1 tablespoon butter
¼ teaspoon salt
½ cup sugar
2 eggs, lightly beaten
1 teaspoon vanilla
Ground cinnamon

OVEN 350°

Soak bread in scalded milk for 5 minutes. Add butter, salt, sugar, eggs, and vanilla. Mix well. Pour into greased 1-quart casserole dish. Sprinkle lightly with cinnamon. Place casserole in pan of hot water in middle of oven. Bake for 45 to 50 minutes or until center is firm.

Orange Bread Pudding

3 eggs, beaten
1⅓ cups sugar
¼ teaspoon salt
1½ cups orange juice
4 cups bread cubes, cut from day-old bread with crusts removed
¼ cup coconut
2 tablespoons raisins

OVEN 350°

Grease 1-quart casserole. In medium bowl combine beaten eggs, sugar, salt, and orange juice. Add bread cubes, coconut, and raisins; mix. Place in buttered casserole and bake 40 to 45 minutes or until set. Increase heat to 450° for 2 to 3 minutes to brown peaks. Spoon into dessert dishes and serve with orange sauce (recipe follows).

Orange Sauce:
1 tablespoon cornstarch
½ cup sugar
1 teaspoon grated orange peel
1 cup orange juice
1 teaspoon lemon juice
2 tablespoons butter or margarine

In pan combine cornstarch, sugar, orange peel, and orange juice. Bring to boil and cook over medium heat for 5 minutes, stirring constantly. Remove from heat; stir in lemon juice and butter until butter is melted and sauce is smooth.

Raisin-Nut Pudding

2 tablespoons butter
2 teaspoons sugar
1 cup flour
2 teaspoons baking powder
⅛ teaspoon salt
½ teaspoon cinnamon
1 cup raisins
½ cup chopped nuts
½ cup milk
1 cup brown sugar
1 tablespoon butter
1¾ cups boiling water

OVEN 375°

Cream butter and sugar. Sift flour, baking powder, salt, and cinnamon; add to creamed mixture. Blend until mealy. Add raisins and nuts. Stir in milk. Stir only until blended. Put in greased casserole. Mix together brown sugar, butter, and boiling water and pour over batter. Bake for 35 to 40 minutes.

Tapioca Dessert

5 cups boiling water
1 cup small-ball tapioca
1 (3 ounce) box gelatin, any flavor
1 scant cup sugar
1 (20 ounce) can crushed pineapple, undrained
Whipped topping
Miniature marshmallows

Combine boiling water and tapioca; boil 10 minutes. Remove from heat. Keep covered 10 minutes. Add gelatin, sugar, and pineapple. Add whipped topping and miniature marshmallows to taste.

Note: You can use any kind of canned or frozen fruit. Nuts can be added also.

Easy Custard

6 eggs
1 (14 ounce) can condensed milk
2½ cans warm water
¼ teaspoon salt
1 teaspoon vanilla
Nutmeg
Whipped topping

OVEN 325°

Beat eggs until frothy. Add condensed milk, water, salt, and vanilla; beat well. Pour into coated 9-inch baking dish. Sprinkle with nutmeg. Bake approximately 1 hour or until knife comes out clean. (The warmer the water, the faster it bakes.) Custard will finish cooking after you take it out. Cool. Top with whipped topping.

Easy Jelly Roll

1 cup margarine
1½ cups sugar
4 eggs
2 cups flour
1 teaspoon vanilla
1 (8 ounce) can prepared pie filling
Powdered sugar

OVEN 350°

Cream margarine and gradually add sugar; add one egg at a time and beat after each addition; add flour and vanilla. Spread in 11x14-inch jelly roll pan. Drop pie filling into batter. Bake for 35 minutes. Cool on rack. After 15 minutes sprinkle powdered sugar on top. When using blueberry filling, substitute lemon juice for vanilla.

Hawaiian Delight

2 cups crushed cinnamon graham crackers
½ cup margarine, melted

Mix and press into 9x13-inch pan; set aside.

2 (3 ounce) packages banana instant pudding mix
3 cups milk
¾ cup coconut

Mix pudding and milk; then add coconut and spread onto first layer.

2 large bananas, sliced and quartered

Spread onto second layer.

1 (20 ounce) can of crushed pineapple, drained
1 (8 ounce) whipped topping

Mix together pineapple and whipped topping and spread on top of other layers. Chill.

Hawaiian Delight

1 (18¼ ounce) box yellow cake mix
3 (3 ounce) packages vanilla instant pudding mix
4 cups cold milk
1½ teaspoons coconut extract
1 (8 ounce) package cream cheese, softened
1 (20 ounce) can crushed pineapple, well drained
2 cups heavy cream, whipped and sweetened
2 cups flaked coconut, toasted

OVEN 350°

Mix cake batter according to box directions. Pour into two greased 9x13-inch baking pans. Bake for 15 minutes or until done. Cool completely. In large mixing bowl, combine pudding mixes, milk, and coconut extract; beat for 2 minutes. Add cream cheese and beat well. Stir in pineapple. Spread over cooled cakes. Top with whipped cream. Sprinkle with coconut. Chill at least 2 hours.

Makes 24 servings.

My Mother's Snow Ice Cream

2 cups milk
2 eggs
½ teaspoon salt
1½ cups sugar
½ teaspoon salt

Mix all ingredients and gently fold in clean, fresh snow until mix is at saturation. Should yield about one gallon. You can halve the recipe.

Pavlova

6 egg whites
1½ cups sugar
1 tablespoon vinegar
1 tablespoon vanilla
2 tablespoons cornmeal
Whipped cream
Fruit (bananas, kiwi, strawberries, with passion fruit juice squeezed over all, or just fresh fruit salad)

OVEN 300°

Beat egg whites until stiff meringue consistency, then slowly add sugar until you cannot see sugar grains. One at a time fold in vinegar, vanilla, and then cornmeal. Spread onto piece of aluminum foil that has been lightly greased and place on baking tray. Cook for 1½ hours. Allow to cool in oven—preferably overnight. When ready to serve, top with whipped cream and your choice of fruit.

Lamingtons

Cook your favorite 2-egg sponge cake in 10x12-inch pan and when cool, freeze. (Or if in a hurry, buy your sponge slab cake from the nearest bakery and pop it straight into the freezer!)

Chocolate Icing:

1 large tablespoon butter
½ cup water (approximately)
3 cups powdered sugar
⅓ cup cocoa
½ teaspoon vanilla
2 cups coconut (approximate—have more on hand)

Place all ingredients except coconut into small saucepan. Bring almost to boil on low heat. Make sure butter is melted but do not boil, as icing will become too hard when cool. The icing must be thin enough so that squares of cake can be readily and rapidly coated, but not so thin that it soaks into cake too much—add more sugar or less water as required. While mixture is heating, cut frozen cake into approximately 30 small squares. Using long, two-pronged carving fork to hold each square, plunge one at a time into hot icing; drop onto pile of coconut, quickly roll until coated, and leave to dry on plate. Before serving, cut in half and put whipped cream in center or leave uncut and pipe whipped cream on top, placing a strawberry or cherry to garnish.

Note: Using frozen cake prevents it from crumbling into icing. Cut a few squares at a time to prevent pieces from thawing out too much before being iced. It is much easier for two (or three) people to roll squares. When cooking alone, make up half of icing at a time so it is not cooled too quickly by frozen cake.

English Trifle

4 sponge dessert shells (often featured in produce department in markets)
⅓ cup raspberry jam
1 (3 ounce) package raspberry gelatin
2 cups fresh fruit
1 envelope Bird's custard-style dessert mix (found in markets featuring imported products)
3 tablespoons sugar
1½ cups milk
½ cup heavy cream, whipped

Slice dessert shells horizontally and spread four halves with jam. Replace tops and arrange shells in bottom of glass serving dish. Prepare gelatin according to package directions and pour half over dessert shells. Reserve remaining gelatin for other use. When gelatin is set, arrange fruit over gelatin.

Combine dessert mix and sugar in saucepan. Add 2 tablespoons milk and mix until smooth. Add remaining milk. Bring mixture to full boil over medium heat, stirring constantly. Remove from heat and cool a few minutes, stirring occasionally. Pour over layers in glass bowl. Chill. Top with whipped cream and decorate top with fruit and nuts.

Serves 6.

Cheesecake Dessert

Crust:

2 cups graham cracker crumbs
6 tablespoons sugar
½ cup butter or margarine, melted

Filling:

2 cups powdered sugar
2 (8 ounce) packages cream cheese
1 teaspoon vanilla
1 (8 ounce) tub whipped topping
1 (20 ounce) can cherry pie filling

Mix crust ingredients well and press into bottom of 9x13-inch pan. Combine sugar, cream cheese, and vanilla; mix well. Add whipped topping. Pour over crust. When set, pour cherry pie filling on top.

Creamy Fruit and Cake Delight

1 cup Entenmann's fat-free golden loaf cake cubes (½ inch)
½ cup diced banana
½ cup sliced strawberries (fresh or frozen, unsweetened)
¾ cup boiling water
1 package (4 serving size) sugar-free gelatin, any red flavor
½ cup cold water
Ice cubes
1 cup whipped topping

Divide cake cubes and fruit evenly among 6 dessert glasses, reserving several strawberry slices for garnish, if desired. Stir boiling water into gelatin in large bowl 2 minutes or until completely dissolved. Mix cold water and ice cubes to make 1¼ cups. Add to gelatin, stirring until slightly thickened. Remove any remaining ice. Stir whipped topping into gelatin with wire whisk until well blended. Let stand 5 minutes or until thickened. Spoon into dessert glasses. Refrigerate 1 hour or until firm. Garnish with reserved strawberry slices.

Cherry Cheesecake

1 package Dream Whip mix
1 (8 ounce) package cream cheese
2 cups powdered sugar
1 premade graham cracker crust
Cherries

Follow instructions on package of Dream Whip. Mix in one bowl until mixture forms peaks when beaters are removed. In separate bowl mix cream cheese and sugar. This must peak also. Add Dream Whip to cream cheese mixture. Make sure it peaks when you remove beaters. Place into graham cracker crust. Top with cherries. Chill in refrigerator for 2 hours before serving.

Frozen Peppermint Cheesecake

1 (8 ounce) package cream cheese, softened
1 (14 ounce) can condensed milk
1 cup crushed hard peppermint candy
2 cups whipping cream, whipped
1 (9 inch) premade chocolate piecrust

In large mixing bowl, beat cheese until fluffy. Gradually beat in condensed milk. Stir in crushed candy. Fold in whipping cream. Pour into crust. Garnish as desired. Freeze 6 hours or until firm. Return leftovers to freezer.

Ideas for garnishes: Crushed peppermint candies, milk chocolate shavings (use a peeler).

Chocolate Chip Cheesecake

3 (8 ounce) packages cream cheese, softened
3 eggs
¾ cup sugar
1 teaspoon vanilla
3 tubes refrigerated chocolate chip cookie dough

OVEN 350°

Beat together cream cheese, eggs, sugar, and vanilla until well mixed. Set aside. Slice cookie dough into ⅓-inch slices. Arrange slices from 1½ rolls on bottom of greased 9x13-inch glass baking dish. Press together so there are no holes. Spoon cream cheese mixture evenly over top. Top with remaining dough. Bake for 45 to 50 minutes or until golden and center is slightly firm. Remove from oven. Let cool, then refrigerate. Cut when well chilled.

Cheesecake

1 (3 ounce) package any flavor gelatin
1 cup boiling water
1 (12 ounce) can evaporated skim milk (refrigerated for 24 hours)
1 (8 ounce) package cream cheese, softened to room temperature
1 cup sugar

CRUST:
3 cups crushed graham crackers
½ cup sugar
1 teaspoon cinnamon (optional)
1 cup margarine, melted

Mix gelatin and water. Set aside to cool. Prepare graham cracker crust by mixing crust ingredients together; press into greased 9x13-inch pan. Whip milk until peaks form. Mix cream cheese and sugar; add to whipped milk. Mix gelatin with cream cheese and milk. Pour mixture over crust. Refrigerate until set.

Peach Cheesecake

1 envelope unflavored gelatin
¼ cup cold water
1 (16 ounce) can lite peaches, drained, juice reserved
1 (8 ounce) lite cream cheese, softened
6 packets artificial sweetener
1 (8 inch) prepared graham cracker crust

In blender sprinkle gelatin over cold water; let stand 2 minutes. In small saucepan, bring reserved juice to boil. Add hot juice to blender and process at low speed until gelatin is completely dissolved, about 2 minutes. Add peaches, cream cheese, and artificial sweetener. Process at high speed until blended; pour into prepared crust. Chill until firm, about 3 hours. Garnish if desired.

Pineapple Cheesecake

FILLING:
2 (8 ounce) packages cream cheese, softened
⅓ cup lemon juice
1 (16 ounce) tub of whipped topping
2 large cans chilled, crushed pineapple, drained

CRUST:
3 tablespoons melted butter
4 tablespoons brown sugar
3 cups graham cracker crumbs
1 cup finely chopped pecans, divided

OVEN 325°

Beat cream cheese until smooth and creamy; beat in lemon juice. Fold half of whipped topping into cheese mixture. Stir in 1 can pineapple until mixed well. To make crust, mix butter, sugar, graham cracker crumbs, and ¾ cup pecans; press in bottom of 9x13-inch dish. Bake 15 minutes, let cool. When crust is cool, spread half of filling over crust, then spread remaining pineapple over filling. Then spread remaining cheese mixture over pineapple. Top with remaining whipped topping. Sprinkle remaining pecans on top. Chill and eat.

Impossible Cheesecake

¾ cup milk
2 teaspoons vanilla
2 eggs
1 cup sugar
½ cup baking mix
2 (8 ounce) packages cream cheese, softened

OVEN 350°

Place milk, vanilla, eggs, sugar, and baking mix in blender. Cover and blend on high for 15 seconds. Add cream cheese. Cover; blend on high for 2 minutes. Pour into greased 9x13- or 10x14-inch pan. Bake until center is firm, about 40 to 45 minutes.

Peaches and Cream Cheesecake

¾ cup flour
1 teaspoon baking powder
3 tablespoons butter, softened
1 egg
½ cup milk
1 package vanilla pudding mix (not instant)
1 large can sliced peaches, drained, juice reserved
¾ cup sugar
1½ (8 ounce) packages cream cheese
1 tablespoon sugar
½ teaspoon cinnamon

OVEN 350°

Combine flour, baking powder, butter, egg, milk, and vanilla pudding mix; pour into greased deep-dish pie plate. Arrange drained peach slices over batter. Combine sugar, cream cheese, and 5 tablespoons juice; spoon within 1 inch of edge. Mix cinnamon and sugar and sprinkle on top. Bake for 30 to 35 minutes.

Low-Fat Cheesecake

⅓ cup graham cracker crumbs
2 (8 ounce) cartons non-fat cream cheese
⅔ cup sugar
3 eggs (or ¾ cup egg substitute)
2 tablespoons almond extract

OVEN 350°

Spray 9-inch pan with cooking spray. Sprinkle crumbs in pan. Mix together cream cheese, sugar, eggs, and almond extract. Spread over crumbs. Bake for 30 to 35 minutes.

Topping:
8 ounces non-fat sour cream
3 tablespoons sugar
1 teaspoon vanilla

Combine topping ingredients and spread over baked cake. Return to oven for additional 10 minutes. Let cool.

Makes about 9 servings.

Very Low-Fat Cheesecake

1¼ cups crushed low-fat graham crackers
2 tablespoons sugar
3 tablespoons fat-free spread
2½ (8 ounce) packages fat-free cream cheese
1 cup sugar
1 teaspoon lemon juice
¼ teaspoon vanilla
¾ cup egg substitute
1 can favorite fruit topping

OVEN 350°

Mix crumbs, 2 tablespoons sugar, and fat-free spread. Spray 9-inch springform pan with cooking spray and press crumb mixture into bottom. Bake 10 minutes. Cool. Reheat oven to 300°. Beat cream cheese in large bowl. Gradually add sugar, beating until fluffy. Add lemon juice and vanilla. Beat in egg substitute, ¼ cup at a time. Pour over crumb mixture. Bake until center is firm, about 1 hour. Cool to room temperature. Loosen edges of cake from pan with knife before removing side of pan. Refrigerate at least 3 hours but no longer than 10 days. Top with favorite fruit topping!

Low-Fat, Sugar-Free Cheesecake

1 (8 ounce) package fat-free cream cheese
3 packages artificial sweetener
⅓ cup lemon juice
½ teaspoon vanilla
1 (8 ounce) container fat-free whipped topping
1 (9 inch) fat-free graham cracker crust

Mix softened cream cheese with artificial sweetener. Add lemon juice; mix, then add vanilla; mix well. Mix with whipped topping and pour into graham cracker crust. Let set 45 minutes to 1 hour.

Miniature Cheesecakes

2 eggs
2 (8 ounce) packages cream cheese
½ cup sugar
1 teaspoon vanilla
1 (20 ounce) can cherry pie filling

OVEN 350°

Beat first four ingredients until smooth. Line small muffin pans with paper liners. Fill each cup three-quarters full with mixture. Bake for 15 minutes. When cool, top each with one cherry from can of cherry pie filling.

Makes approximately 48 servings.

Cakes

Crumb Cake

2 cups brown sugar
¾ cup shortening
2½ cups flour
1 egg, beaten
1 cup sour milk or buttermilk
1 teaspoon baking soda
1 cup chopped nuts
1 cup raisins
½ teaspoon ginger
½ teaspoon cinnamon

OVEN 350°

Blend sugar, shortening, and flour until crumb consistency; set aside ½ cup for topping. Add remaining ingredients. Pour into greased and floured 9x13-inch pan. Put reserved ½ cup dry mix on top. Bake 30 to 40 minutes.

Donna's Crumb Cake

3 cups flour
1 cup shortening
1 cup sugar

Mix into crumbs. Take out 1 cup crumbs and set aside for topping.

1 teaspoon baking soda
1 pint buttermilk
1 cup white sugar
2 eggs
1 teaspoon cloves
1 teaspoon cinnamon
1 teaspoon allspice
1 teaspoon nutmeg
½ teaspoon salt

OVEN 350°

In another bowl dissolve baking soda in buttermilk; add remaining ingredients. Stir well by hand. Pour into 9x13-inch pan. Sprinkle reserved cup of crumbs on top. Bake 45 minutes. Freezes well.

Lemon Crumb Cake

1 package lemon cake mix
1 (6 ounce) can frozen lemonade, undiluted
1 (14 ounce) can sweetened condensed milk
1 (8 ounce) container whipped topping
1 (7 ounce) bag coconut

Mix and bake cake, according to package directions, in 9x13-inch pan; let cool. Crumble half of cake into 9x13-inch pan. Blend together lemonade and condensed milk. Pour over crumbs in pan. Crumble remaining cake. Sprinkle and press down rest of crumbs over milk mixture. Spread whipped topping over all; sprinkle coconut on top. Keep refrigerated.

Apple Cake

1 box white cake mix
1 (20 ounce) can prepared apple pie filling

OVEN 350°

Prepare cake batter according to box instructions. Spread half of batter in bottom of 9x11-inch pan. Spoon pie filling over batter in pan. Cover filling with remainder of cake batter. Bake at 350° until knife comes out clean.

Easy and Delicious Apple Cake

2 cups diced apples
1 cup sugar
1 egg
1 cup flour
1 teaspoon baking soda
Dash salt
1½ teaspoons cinnamon
½ cup chopped nuts

OVEN 350°

Mix together apples and sugar; let stand. Add egg to apple mixture. Mix together dry ingredients and add to apple mixture. Add nuts. Bake 40 minutes at 350° in greased and floured 9-inch square pan.

Apple Cake

2 eggs
¼ cup shortening
1 teaspoon vanilla
1 cup sugar
1 cup flour
1 teaspoon baking soda
1 teaspoon cinnamon
4 apples, diced

OVEN 350°

Cream together eggs, shortening, vanilla, and sugar. Sift three times, flour, soda, and cinnamon. Mix all ingredients together; add apples. Bake at 350° until brown. May top with light powdered sugar icing. Nuts or raisins may be added to batter if desired.

Fresh Apple Cake

3 eggs, beaten
½ teaspoon salt
2 cups sugar
2 teaspoons vanilla
3 cups flour
1 teaspoon cinnamon
1½ cups oil
3 to 4 raw apples, finely diced
1 cup chopped pecans
1 cup raisins (optional)

Topping:
1 cup evaporated milk
¾ cup butter
1 cup sugar
½ cup coconut
½ cup chopped pecans

OVEN 350°

Mix all ingredients except topping in large bowl. Bake for 30 to 45 minutes. To make topping, boil milk and butter 8 to 10 minutes; add sugar and boil 8 to 10 minutes. Add coconut and pecans. Spread over warm cake.

Fresh Apple Cake

3 cups diced apples
1 cup coconut
1 cup raisins
1 cup chopped nuts
3 cups self-rising flour, divided
1½ cups oil
2 cups sugar
3 eggs

Topping:
½ cup buttermilk
½ stick margarine
½ cup sugar

OVEN 325°

Dust apples, coconut, raisins, and nuts with 1 cup flour; set aside. Blend oil, sugar, and eggs. Sift remaining flour and add to egg mixture; fold in apple mixture. Turn into 10-inch tube pan. Bake at 325° for 1 hour and 15 minutes. To make topping, boil ingredients rapidly for 2 minutes, stirring constantly. Pour over cake.

Raw Apple Cake

1½ cups flour
½ teaspoon salt
1 teaspoon baking soda
1 teaspoon baking powder
1 teaspoon cinnamon
1 cup sugar
½ cup oil
½ cup milk
2 eggs
1 teaspoon vanilla
3 cups chopped raw apples
½ cup chopped walnuts

OVEN 350°

Sift dry ingredients. Mix with remaining ingredients until crumbly. Pat into 9x13-inch pan. Bake at 350° for 40 to 45 minutes. Great for freezing. No icing necessary.

Topping (optional):

4 teaspoons margarine
½ cup brown sugar
1 teaspoon shortening
2 teaspoons flour
½ cup finely chopped nuts

Mix together well. Spread over cake before baking.

Note: This recipe is for ripe apples. For tart apples use 2 teaspoons baking soda and no baking powder.

Banana Cupcakes

1⅓ cups sugar
3 very ripe bananas, mashed
½ cup shortening
2 eggs
2 cups plus 2 tablespoons flour
1 teaspoon baking powder
1 teaspoon baking soda
1 cup milk
1 teaspoon vanilla

OVEN 350°

Cream sugar, bananas, shortening, and eggs until smooth. Add flour, baking powder, and baking soda, then milk and vanilla. Beat 5 minutes. Fill paper muffin cups half full. Bake at 350° for 30 minutes or until done.

Blushing Apple Cake

1¼ cups flour
2 tablespoons sugar, divided
1 teaspoon baking powder
½ teaspoon salt
½ cup shortening or butter
1 egg, beaten
1 tablespoon milk
4 cups sliced apples
1 (3 ounce) package strawberry gelatin

Topping:
1 cup flour
1 cup sugar
½ cup margarine

OVEN 350°

Mix flour and 1 tablespoon sugar with baking powder and salt. Cream shortening or butter. Mix in dry ingredients. Combine beaten egg and milk and add to shortening mixture. Press into greased 9x13-inch pan. Add sliced apples. Mix remaining tablespoon of sugar in gelatin; sprinkle over apples in pan. Mix topping ingredients until crumbs form. Sprinkle over cake. Bake at 350° until done.

Strawberry Pop Cake

1 box yellow cake mix
1 (3 ounce) package strawberry gelatin
1 can strawberry soda pop
1 large container strawberries
1 (3 ounce) package vanilla instant pudding mix
1½ cups milk
1 (16 ounce) tub whipped topping

Prepare cake mix according to package directions. Punch holes in top of cake with meat fork; dissolve gelatin in soda pop and pour over cake. Pour strawberries and juice over cake. Mix pudding with milk. When pudding is firm, mix with whipped topping and spread over cake.

Pineapple Cake

2 eggs
2 cups sugar
2 tablespoons oil (optional)
2 cups flour
½ teaspoon salt
2 teaspoons baking soda
1 (20 ounce) can crushed pineapple, with juice
1 teaspoon vanilla
½ cup chopped nuts (pecans or walnuts)

OVEN 350°

Beat eggs. Add sugar and oil. Sift flour, salt, and baking soda. Add alternately with pineapple. Stir in vanilla and nuts. Bake 30 to 45 minutes at 350° in 9x13-inch pan. Cool and frost.

Frosting:
1 (8 ounce) package cream cheese
½ cup shortening or butter
1 teaspoon vanilla
2 cups powdered sugar
½ cup chopped nuts (optional)

Beat all ingredients well, adding additional sugar if necessary to get proper spreading consistency.

Topping variation:
½ cup butter
½ cup milk
1 cup sugar
1 teaspoon vanilla

Boil 5 minutes and pour over cake while still hot.

Strawberry Cake

1 box white cake mix
½ cup oil
3 eggs
1 (3 ounce) box strawberry gelatin
½ cup water, minus 2 tablespoons
½ cup mashed berries

OVEN 350°

Mix together all ingredients; pour into greased 9x13-inch pan and bake at 350° for 25 to 30 minutes.

Icing:
1 box powdered sugar
1 stick butter, softened
½ cup mashed berries

Beat together all ingredients and frost cooled cake.

Frosted Apple Sheet Cake

2 cups sugar
2 teaspoons vanilla
2 eggs
1 cup vegetable oil
3 cups unsifted flour
1 teaspoon salt
2 teaspoons cinnamon
2 teaspoons baking soda
4 cups finely chopped apples
½ cup chopped nuts (optional)
½ cup raisins (optional)

OVEN 350°

Combine sugar, vanilla, and eggs with mixer; add vegetable oil; mix well. Add dry ingredients, apples, nuts, and raisins (optional). Bake in large greased and floured pan at 350° for 35 to 45 minutes. Cool; spread with Cream Cheese Frosting.

Cream Cheese Frosting:

1 (8 ounce) package cream cheese, room temperature
½ cup shortening, softened
1 teaspoon vanilla
1 pound powdered sugar

Mix cream cheese, shortening, and vanilla together; then add powdered sugar. Spread on cooled cake.

Lemon Cake Pie

1 cup sugar
3 tablespoons flour
3 tablespoons butter
2 eggs, separated
Juice and rind of 1 lemon
1 cup milk
1 unbaked pie shell

OVEN 350°

Cream sugar, flour, and butter; stir in beaten egg yolks. Add lemon juice, rind, and milk slowly. Beat egg whites and fold into mixture. Pour into unbaked pie shell and bake in 350° oven for 30 minutes or until firm.

Lemon Nut Cake

1 pound butter
2 cups sugar
6 eggs, separated
1 teaspoon baking powder dissolved in 1 tablespoon water
3 cups flour
1 quart chopped pecans
1 pound golden raisins
2 ounces lemon extract

OVEN 250°

Cream butter and sugar; add egg yolks and dissolved baking powder. Combine flour, nuts, and raisins. Add this mixture to creamed mixture; then add lemon extract. Beat egg whites until stiff. Fold into mixture. Pour into tube pan lined with waxed paper. Set in pan of water in oven and bake at 250° for 2 hours and 45 minutes.

Banana Split Cake

2 egg whites
2 cups powdered sugar
1 stick butter, softened
2 cups graham cracker crumbs
1 stick butter, melted
¼ cup sugar
3 bananas, sliced
1 (20 ounce) can crushed pineapple, drained, juice reserved
12 ounces whipped topping
Chopped nuts (optional)
1 small jar sliced cherries, drained and halved

Use stand mixer to beat egg whites, powdered sugar, and softened butter for 18 minutes. In the meantime, mix crumbs, melted butter, and sugar. Place this crumb mixture in deep casserole dish. Spread creamed mixture on top of crumb mixture. Arrange bananas for next layer. Place pineapple on top of bananas and whipped topping on top of pineapple. Sprinkle with nuts and top with halved cherries.

Note: Soak bananas in pineapple juice to keep them from turning brown.

Cherry Nut Cake

⅔ cup shortening
2 cups sugar
3 cups cake flour
3 teaspoons baking powder
½ teaspoon salt
½ cup chopped maraschino cherries, with juice
½ cup milk
1 teaspoon vanilla
½ teaspoon almond extract
5 egg whites, beaten
½ cup chopped nut meats

OVEN 350°

Cream together shortening and sugar. Sift together flour, baking powder, and salt; add alternately with ½ cup maraschino cherry juice and milk. Add vanilla and almond extract. Fold in beaten egg whites. Add chopped cherries and nuts. Pour into three 9-inch layer pans. Bake at 350° for 35 minutes. Very good with fluffy white frosting.

Cherry Spice Cake

2 cups sugar
1 cup butter or oil
2 eggs
1 teaspoon vanilla
1 cup dried apples, cooked and sweetened
3 cups flour
1 teaspoon baking soda
1 teaspoon baking powder
1 teaspoon cinnamon
1 teaspoon allspice
1 teaspoon cloves
1 cup buttermilk
1 cup cherries
1 cup chopped nuts

OVEN 325°

Cream sugar and butter. Add eggs and vanilla and beat together. Add apples. Sift dry ingredients together and add alternately with buttermilk. Flour cherries and nuts and fold in. Bake about 1 hour.

Blueberry Buckle Cake

½ cup butter
1 cup sugar
2 eggs
4 cups sifted flour
4 teaspoons baking powder
1 teaspoon salt
1 cup milk
4 cups washed fresh blueberries

Topping:
½ cup soft butter
¾ cup sugar
⅔ cup flour
1 teaspoon cinnamon

OVEN 375°

Mix cake ingredients. Mix topping and sprinkle over top of cake. Bake at 375° for 50 minutes.

Weary Willie Blueberry Cake

1½ cups flour
1 cup sugar
2 teaspoons baking powder
½ teaspoon salt
1 cup blueberries
⅓ cup shortening, melted
1 egg
Milk
1 teaspoon vanilla
2 tablespoons sugar
Cinnamon

OVEN 350°

Sift together flour, sugar, baking powder, and salt. Put blueberries in flour mixture and stir. Put shortening in one-cup measure and add egg; fill cup to top with milk. Add to flour and blueberries. Mix well, gently. Add vanilla. Pour into greased and floured 8-inch square pan; sprinkle top with sugar and cinnamon mixture. Bake at 350° for 35 minutes.

Peach Cake

1 stick margarine
2 cups sugar
2 eggs
2 cups flour
1 teaspoon baking soda
1 teaspoon baking powder
1 teaspoon cinnamon
1 large can peaches, drained and cut small

OVEN 350°

Cream margarine, sugar, and eggs. In another bowl mix flour, baking soda, baking powder, and cinnamon. Mix with creamed ingredients; add peaches. Bake at 350° for 35 minutes.

ICING:
½ cup sugar
½ cup evaporated milk
1 stick shortening
1 teaspoon vanilla

Cook until thick; cool down a little and spread on cooled cake.

Easy Peach Cake

1 (29 ounce) can peaches, cut up, with juice
1 box yellow cake mix
1 cup chopped walnuts
1 stick butter or margarine, melted

OVEN 350°

Place peaches in ungreased 8x12-inch baking pan or long oven-safe glass dish, juice and all. Sprinkle cake mix on top of peaches and juice in the pan. Sprinkle nuts on top of mixture. Melt butter or margarine and dribble on top. Bake at 350° for 1 hour.

Mandarin Orange Cake

1 box butter cake mix
1 (11 ounce) can mandarin oranges, with juice
4 eggs
½ cup corn oil

OVEN 325°

Mix together cake mix, mandarin oranges with juice, eggs, and oil. Pour into two 9-inch round cake pans, floured and greased. Bake in 325° oven for 30 minutes or longer if necessary.

Topping:
12 ounces whipped topping
1 (3 ounce) package vanilla instant pudding mix
1 (20 ounce) can crushed pineapple, with juice

Whip together; spread small amount on bottom layer then place other round cake on top and finish putting topping on top and sides.

Orange Slice Cake

3½ cups flour, divided
1 pound orange slice candy, cut up
2 cups chopped pecans
1 cup flaked coconut
1 (8 ounce) package chopped dates (optional)
1 cup butter
2 cups sugar
4 eggs
1 teaspoon baking soda
½ cup buttermilk
½ teaspoon salt

Topping:
1 cup orange juice
2 cups powdered sugar, sifted

OVEN 300°

Mix together orange juice and powdered sugar. Set aside. Use ½ cup flour to toss and coat evenly orange slices, nuts, and coconut. Set aside. Cream butter and sugar together. Add eggs one at a time, beating well after each addition. Combine baking soda and buttermilk. Add alternately with remaining flour and salt. Add floured candy mixture. Mix well. Spoon into greased and floured 10-inch tube pan. Bake until inserted toothpick comes out clean. When done, remove from oven and immediately pour topping over hot cake. Let stand overnight before removing from pan.

Sunny Orange Cake

1 package yellow cake mix
1 package lemon instant pudding mix
¾ cup water
¾ cup oil
4 eggs

Icing:
2 cups powdered sugar
⅓ cup orange juice
2 tablespoons warm water
2 tablespoons butter, melted

OVEN 325°

Blend dry cake mix and pudding mix. Add water slowly. Then add oil. Add eggs one at a time. Mix on high speed. Pour into 8x12-inch pan. Bake at 325° for 35 to 40 minutes. Prick hot cake with fork in many places. Mix together icing ingredients. Drizzle icing over warm cake.

Apricot Preserve Cake

2 cups sugar
2 sticks margarine, softened
4 eggs
1 cup apricot preserves
1 teaspoon baking soda
1 cup buttermilk
3 cups flour
1 teaspoon cinnamon
1 cup chopped pecans
1 (8 ounce) package chopped dried apricots

OVEN 325°

Cream sugar and margarine; add eggs one at a time, beating thoroughly after each addition. Add preserves and blend. Dissolve baking soda in buttermilk. Sift flour and cinnamon and add to creamed mixture alternately with buttermilk. Stir in pecans and apricots. Pour into greased and floured Bundt pan. Bake at 325° for 1 to 1¼ hours. Cool only a few minutes before removing from pan.

Blackberry Spice Cake

1 (20 ounce) can blackberry pie filling
1 box spice cake mix
4 eggs

OVEN 350°

Grease and flour 9x13-inch cake pan. Mix ingredients until well mixed. Pour into cake pan. Bake for 40 to 45 minutes. Top with vanilla or sour cream icing if desired.

Dark Fruitcake

3 eggs
1 cup brown sugar
½ cup butter or shortening
½ cup molasses
½ cup prepared coffee
2 cups flour
¼ teaspoon allspice
¼ teaspoon cinnamon
¼ teaspoon cloves
1 teaspoon baking soda
½ teaspoon nutmeg
½ cup raisins
1 cup fruit-flavored nuts

OVEN 350°

Beat eggs, brown sugar, butter or shortening, molasses, and cooled coffee. Sift dry ingredients. Add to creamed mixture. Fold in fruit last. Beat 3 minutes. Flour and grease pan (size your preference). Bake at 350° for 1 hour or until done.

Cranberry Sauce Cake

1½ cups whole cranberry sauce
1 cup mayonnaise
Grated rind of 1 orange
⅓ cup orange juice
1 cup chopped nuts
3 cups sifted flour
1½ cups sugar
1 teaspoon baking soda
1 teaspoon salt

OVEN 350°

Mix together and bake at 350° until cake is done, about 1 hour and 15 minutes. Cool; frost.

Frosting:
2 tablespoons margarine
2 cups powdered sugar
¼ cup whole cranberry sauce

Cream together margarine and sugar; add cranberry sauce. Beat until very creamy.

Gumdrop Fruitcake

1 cup shortening
1½ cups sugar
2 eggs, beaten
1½ teaspoons baking soda
1 cup applesauce
½ teaspoon salt
1 pound gumdrops, no black
1 pound golden raisins
1 cup broken walnuts
1 teaspoon vanilla
2½ to 3 cups flour

OVEN 350°

Cream shortening; add sugar and beaten eggs. Add baking soda to applesauce and salt; add to creamed mixture. Add gumdrops, raisins, broken walnuts, vanilla, and flour. Mix well. Put in 2 medium bread tins or 3 small greased pans; line bottom with waxed paper. Bake at 350° for 1 hour.

Fruit Cocktail Cake

1 egg, beaten
1 (20 ounce) can fruit cocktail, with juice
1¼ cups flour
1 cup sugar
1 teaspoon baking soda

Topping:
½ teaspoon salt
½ cup brown sugar
½ cup nut meats

OVEN 350°

Combine cake ingredients. Combine brown sugar and nut meats; sprinkle on top of cake ingredients before baking. Bake in 9x9-inch pan at 350° for 40 minutes. Serve warm or cold with whipped cream or ice cream.

Easy Fruitcake

1 egg
1 cup warm water
1 package Pillsbury bread mix (date, nut, cranberry, or your choice)
1 cup chopped walnuts
1 cup raisins
1 package fruitcake mix

OVEN 350°

Stir all together. Stir until mixture is well blended. Put into greased 5x9-inch loaf pans. Bake at 350° for 65 to 70 minutes.

Makes 2 loaves.

Festive Fruitcake

2 eggs
2 cups water
¼ cup oil
2 packages Pillsbury date bread mix
2 cups finely chopped pecans
2 cups raisins
2 cups (1 red, 1 green) candied cherries
1 (16 ounce) can fruit cocktail, drained
1 cup bananas

OVEN 350°

Combine eggs, water, and oil. Combine date bread mix, pecans, raisins, cherries, fruit cocktail, and bananas; add to egg mixture. Bake at 350° in greased and floured Bundt pan for 75 to 85 minutes, until tests done. Cool in pan 30 minutes, loosen edges, and remove from pan. Cool completely; wrap in plastic wrap or foil. Refrigerate 2 weeks or freeze for up to 3 months. Glaze with warm corn syrup before serving. Decorate with frosting, candied cherries, and nuts.

Holiday Cake

2 cups sifted flour
2 teaspoons baking soda
½ teaspoon salt
½ teaspoon cinnamon
¼ teaspoon cloves
1 cup mixed candied fruit
1 cup seedless raisins
1 cup chopped nuts
½ cup butter or margarine
1 cup sugar
1 egg
1 teaspoon vanilla
1½ cups applesauce

OVEN 325°

Sift together flour, baking soda, salt, and spices. Combine ½ cup flour mixture with fruits and nuts. Cream butter and sugar. Stir in egg, vanilla, and applesauce. Add dry ingredients gradually; mix well. Stir in fruit. Pour into greased cake pan or loaf pan. Bake at 325° for 1½ hours. Cool and decorate.

Easy-to-Please Fruitcake

1 pound pitted dates, cut in small pieces and softened
8 ounces candied pineapple, chopped
8 ounces candied cherries, chopped
3 cups chopped pecans
1 cup sifted flour
1 cup sugar
1 teaspoon baking powder
¼ teaspoon salt
4 eggs, beaten
1 teaspoon vanilla

OVEN 325°

Mix all ingredients well. Place in paper-lined angel food cake pan. Bake at 325° approximately 1½ hours, or until done.

Rhubarb Cake

3 tablespoons butter, melted
½ cup sugar
Few drops red food coloring
1 pound rhubarb, finely diced
1 package (1 layer size) white cake mix

OVEN 375°

Combine butter, sugar, and food coloring. Add rhubarb and toss lightly; spread in 8x12-inch pan. Prepare cake mix using package directions; pour over fruit. Bake at 375° for about 35 minutes or until done. Immediately run spatula around edge of pan and invert onto serving plate. Before lifting off pan, let syrup drain onto cake for 3 to 5 minutes. Cut while warm. Top with whipped cream.

Rhubarb Upside-Down Cake

5 cups diced rhubarb
1 to 1½ cups sugar
1 (3 ounce) package raspberry or strawberry gelatin
3 cups miniature marshmallows
1 package yellow, strawberry, or cherry cake mix

OVEN 350°

Put rhubarb in greased 9x13-inch cake pan. Sprinkle sugar and dry gelatin on rhubarb. Top with marshmallows. Prepare cake mix as directed on package; spread evenly over rhubarb mix. Bake at 350° for 50 minutes or until done. Cool 10 to 15 minutes then turn out upside down onto tray. Serve warm with whipped cream.

Carrot Cake

1¾ cups flour
¼ teaspoon salt
½ teaspoon baking soda
1½ cups sugar
1 teaspoon cinnamon
½ teaspoon nutmeg
3 eggs
1 cup corn oil
1 cup grated carrots
1 cup ground pecans

OVEN 350°

Sift all dry ingredients. Add eggs and oil; mix well and add carrots and pecans. Mix well and bake in tube pan at 350° for 55 minutes.

Pineapple-Coconut Carrot Cake

1 cup oil
1½ to 2 cups sugar
3 eggs (4 if small)
2 cups flour
2 teaspoons baking soda
½ teaspoon salt
2 teaspoons cinnamon
1 cup crushed pineapple
2 cups shredded carrots
1 cup flaked coconut
1 cup chopped nuts
1 teaspoon vanilla
1 cup raisins (optional)

OVEN 350°

Mix oil, sugar, and eggs. Add remaining ingredients. Pour into 9x13-inch pan and bake for 50 minutes at 350°.

FROSTING:

½ cup soft butter or margarine
1 (8 ounce) package cream cheese
2 cups powdered sugar
2 teaspoons vanilla
1 cup chopped nuts

Cream first four ingredients with electric mixer. Fold in nuts. Spread on cooled cake.

Pumpkin Cake

1 package yellow cake mix
½ cup salad oil
¼ to ½ cup water
4 eggs, beaten
1 can pumpkin
Dash nutmeg
1 teaspoon cinnamon
½ to ¾ cup sugar

OVEN 350°

Mix ingredients in order given; beat with mixer for about 3 minutes. Pour into greased tube pan. Bake at 350° for 1 hour and 10 minutes.

Pumpkin Bundt Cake

1 cup salad oil
3 cups sugar
3 large eggs
1 (16 ounce) can pumpkin
3 cups flour
½ teaspoon salt
2 teaspoons baking powder
¼ teaspoon baking soda
2 teaspoons allspice
1 teaspoon cinnamon

OVEN 350°

In mixer bowl blend salad oil and sugar thoroughly. Add eggs one at a time, beating well after each addition. Add pumpkin and mix thoroughly. Turn mixer to lowest speed and blend in dry ingredients. Pour into greased and floured 10-inch tube pan. Bake for 1 hour. Make a glaze or frosting of powdered sugar and water; drizzle over cake.

Pumpkin Pie Cake

1 (16 ounce) can pumpkin
4 eggs, beaten
1½ cups sugar
1 teaspoon salt
2 teaspoons pumpkin pie spice
1 (12 ounce) can Milnot nondairy canned milk
1 box yellow cake mix
2 sticks shortening, melted
1 cup chopped pecans

OVEN 350°

Mix pumpkin, eggs, sugar, salt, spice, and Milnot. Pour into ungreased 9x13-inch pan. Sprinkle cake mix over filling. Pour melted shortening over top of cake mix. Sprinkle with pecans. Bake at 350° for 1 to 1½ hours or until knife comes out clean when inserted in center. Cut into squares. Serve warm or cold with or without topping (whipped topping or whipped cream).

Pumpkin Cake

2 cups sugar
1 (16 ounce) can pumpkin
1 cup vegetable oil
4 eggs, beaten
2 cups flour
1 teaspoon salt
2 teaspoons baking soda
2 teaspoons baking powder
2 teaspoons cinnamon
½ cup coconut
½ cup chopped pecans

OVEN 350°

Combine sugar, pumpkin, oil, and eggs; beat 1 minute. In separate bowl combine next five ingredients. Add to pumpkin mixture. Beat until smooth and creamy. Stir in coconut and pecans. Pour into three 8-inch greased pans. Bake at 350° for 25 to 30 minutes.

FROSTING:
½ cup butter, softened
1 (8 ounce) package cream cheese
1 pound powdered sugar
2 teaspoons vanilla
½ cup coconut
½ cup chopped pecans

Combine butter and cream cheese. Beat until light and fluffy. Add sugar and vanilla; mix well. Stir in coconut and pecans. Stack and frost cooled layers.

Pumpkin Pie Cake

1 box yellow cake mix (reserve 1 cup for topping)
1 stick melted shortening or ½ cup oil
2 eggs, beaten

OVEN 350°

To cake mix add melted shortening or oil and beaten eggs. Mix well and press into pan as piecrust.

Filling:
1 large can pumpkin
3 eggs
½ cup light brown sugar plus ¼ cup white sugar (or 1 cup white sugar)
⅔ cup milk
1½ teaspoons cinnamon
½ teaspoon nutmeg

Mix filling ingredients and spread over crust.

Topping:
1 cup reserved cake mix
½ cup sugar
½ cup chopped nuts
½ stick shortening

Mix topping ingredients together and sprinkle on top. Bake at 350° for 55 minutes or longer.

Sweet Potato Crisp

2 cups sweet potatoes
1 (12 ounce) can evaporated milk
1 cup sugar
3 eggs
½ teaspoon cinnamon
1 box yellow cake mix
1 cup chopped nuts
2 sticks butter, melted

OVEN 325°

Line 9x13-inch pan with waxed paper. Mix potatoes, milk, sugar, eggs, and cinnamon. Pour on waxed paper. Spread dry cake mix evenly over mixture. Sprinkle nuts over mix. Pour melted butter on top. Bake 50 to 60 minutes. Turn cake onto plate or board. Peel off waxed paper; completely cool. Frost.

Frosting:
1 (8 ounce) package cream cheese
¾ cup whipped topping
2 cups powdered sugar

Nanny's Pound Cake

2 cups sugar
2 cups flour
2 sticks butter, softened
6 eggs
1 teaspoon vanilla
Chopped nuts (optional)
½ teaspoon lemon juice (optional)

OVEN 325°

Mix sugar and flour with butter. Beat with electric mixer; add one egg at a time, beating about 2 minutes each. Add vanilla. Batter is thick. Add nuts if desired. Spray tube pan with nonstick spray; sprinkle with sugar. Put batter in tube pan. Bake at 325° for 1 hour. Can be served with lemon sauce or ice cream.

Blackberry Wine Pound Cake

1 box white cake mix
1 (3 ounce) box blackberry gelatin
4 eggs
1 cup corn oil
1 cup blackberry wine

OVEN 325°

Mix cake and dry gelatin; add eggs, oil, and wine; beat mixture until smooth. Bake in Bundt pan at 325° for 40 to 50 minutes. Let set 5 to 8 minutes then turn out onto plate and glaze.

Glaze:
1½ cups powdered sugar
4 to 5 tablespoons blackberry wine

Stir together until smooth. Spoon over hot cake.

Black Walnut Pound Cake

½ pound butter
½ cup shortening
3 cups sugar
5 eggs
3 cups cake flour
1 cup chopped black walnuts
2½ teaspoons vanilla
1 teaspoon baking powder
1 cup milk

OVEN 325°

Cream together butter, shortening, sugar, and eggs. Flour nuts and add them and rest of ingredients to creamed mixture; mix well. Bake at 325° for 1 hour and 20 minutes.

Millie's Pound Cake

3 sticks margarine, softened
3 cups sugar
12 ounces cream cheese
6 eggs
1 teaspoon vanilla
½ teaspoon almond flavoring
½ teaspoon anise flavoring
3 cups flour

OVEN 300°

Cream margarine, sugar, and cream cheese until fluffy. Add eggs one at a time; then flavorings and flour. Beat well after adding each ingredient. Place in cold oven and bake 1½ hours at 300°.

Banana Pound Cake

4 eggs
⅓ cup oil
½ cup water
1 box yellow cake mix
1 package vanilla instant pudding
1 teaspoon cinnamon
½ teaspoon nutmeg
1⅓ cups very ripe, mashed bananas

OVEN 350°

Beat well eggs, oil, and water; then add dry ingredients. Last add mashed bananas. Bake in large Bundt pan or five mini pans at 350° until tests done. Freezes very well and is moist.

7-UP Pound Cake

2 sticks margarine
½ cup butter-flavored shortening
3 cups sugar
5 eggs
1 teaspoon vanilla
3 cups flour
1 teaspoon salt
1 cup 7-UP

OVEN 325°

Cream margarine and shortening; add sugar and cream together. Add eggs one at a time, then vanilla. Add flour slowly and salt. Add 7-UP. Bake in greased and floured angel food cake pan at 325° for 1 hour or until tests done. Will stay fresh for at least one week or longer if covered.

Blueberry Pound Cake

1 (8 ounce) package) cream cheese
1 box butter-flavor cake mix
3 eggs
½ cup oil
2 cups fresh or frozen blueberries

OVEN 350°

Cream cheese. Add other ingredients except blueberries and mix well. Fold in berries. Bake in sprayed Bundt or tube pan at 350° until done. Cool in pan 5 minutes. Turn out onto plate. You may glaze with powdered sugar glaze if desired.

Brownie Cake

1 cup water
4 tablespoons cocoa
2 sticks margarine
2 cups sugar
2 cups flour
1 teaspoon baking soda
Dash salt
2 eggs, beaten
½ cup buttermilk

OVEN 350°

Bring water, cocoa, and margarine to boil. Mix remaining ingredients into margarine mixture. Beat 2 minutes. Pour into greased and floured 9x13-inch pan. Bake for 40 to 45 minutes.

Frosting:
½ cup margarine
3 tablespoons cocoa
3 tablespoons milk
1 pound powdered sugar

Bring first three ingredients to boil. Add sugar.

Mudslide Cake

1 box chocolate cake mix
1 (14 ounce) can sweetened condensed milk
6 ounces SKOR baking pieces
1 jar hot fudge ice-cream topping
1 (8 ounce) container whipped topping

Prepare and bake chocolate cake per instructions in 9x13-inch pan. While cake is still hot, poke holes all over it with wooden spoon handle. Drizzle entire can of milk into holes. Sprinkle with SKOR pieces. Spread hot fudge topping over entire cake. Cool cake in refrigerator. One to four hours before serving, spread whipped topping on top.

Heath Bar Cake

1 box German chocolate cake mix
1 (14 ounce) can sweetened condensed milk
1 jar caramel ice cream topping
1 (8 ounce) tub of whipped topping
3 to 6 Heath bars, crushed

Bake cake according to package directions. While cake is still hot, poke holes in cake about 1 inch apart using handle of wooden spoon. Pour sweetened condensed milk and ice cream topping mixture over cake, making sure cake is completely covered. Refrigerate overnight. When serving, garnish with whipped topping and sprinkle with Heath bar crumbs.

Note: You can easily crush candy bars by freezing them first, then breaking them with hammer.

Mississippi Mud Cake

2 cups sugar
1 cup shortening
4 eggs
1½ cups flour
¼ teaspoon salt
⅓ cup cocoa
1 cup chopped pecans
3 teaspoons vanilla
7 ounces marshmallow cream

OVEN 350°

Cream sugar and shortening; add eggs one at a time. Sift flour, salt, and cocoa and add to creamed mixture. Mix and add nuts and vanilla. Bake at 350° for 30 minutes in 9x13-inch pan. Spread marshmallow cream on top as soon as cake comes out of oven. Cool. Frost.

Frosting:
2 sticks margarine (not melted)
1 box powdered sugar
1 teaspoon vanilla
½ cup chopped nuts
¼ cup canned milk

Mix and put on cake. Keep refrigerated.

Chocolate Fudge Upside Down Cake

2 tablespoons shortening
1 cup milk
1 teaspoon salt
2 teaspoons baking powder
1½ cups sugar
2 cups flour
1 teaspoon vanilla
3 tablespoons cocoa

Topping:
2 cups sugar
½ cup cocoa
2½ cups boiling water

OVEN 375°

Mix together all ingredients and place in cake pan; sprinkle with nuts if desired. Set aside. To make topping, mix sugar with cocoa and spread over batter in pan. Then pour boiling water over top. Bake 30 minutes at 375°.

Oatmeal Chocolate Chip Cake

1¾ cups boiling water
1 cup oats
1 cup brown sugar
1 cup sugar
½ cup margarine
2 large eggs or 3 small eggs
1¾ cups flour
1 teaspoon baking soda
½ teaspoon salt
1 tablespoon cocoa
1 cup chocolate chips
¾ cup chopped walnuts

OVEN 350°

Pour boiling water over oats; let stand at room temperature for 10 minutes. Add both sugars and margarine to oatmeal. Stir with spoon until margarine melts. Add eggs and mix well. Add flour, baking soda, salt, and cocoa, stirring until well blended. Add half of chocolate chips. Pour batter into greased 9x13-inch pan. Sprinkle chopped nuts and rest of chocolate chips on top. Bake at 350° for 40 minutes. Needs no other frosting.

No-Fat Chocolate Cake

3 cups flour
2 cups sugar
6 tablespoons cocoa
2 teaspoons baking soda
2 teaspoons vanilla
2 tablespoons vinegar
2 cups water
1 teaspoon salt
¾ cup applesauce or fat-free mayonnaise

OVEN 350°

Preheat oven to 350°. Mix all ingredients together. Beat for 10 minutes. Pour into 9x13-inch greased and floured pan. Bake for 30 minutes or until done. Frost as desired.

Oatmeal Cake

1 cup oats
1¼ cups boiling water
½ cup butter
1 cup brown sugar
1 cup white sugar
2 eggs (can use 1 egg and 2 whites)
1⅓ cups flour
1 teaspoon baking soda
½ teaspoon salt
½ teaspoon nutmeg
½ teaspoon cinnamon

OVEN 350°

Combine oats and boiling water; let cool. Beat butter into oatmeal and water mixture. Combine both sugars and add to oatmeal mixture, beating well. Add eggs and beat well. Sift flour, baking soda, salt, nutmeg, and cinnamon; add to oatmeal mixture, beating well. Bake at 350° for 35 to 40 minutes. When done, add topping.

Topping:
6 tablespoons margarine or butter
¾ cup brown sugar
¼ cup milk (can use ⅓ cup cream or evaporated milk)
1 teaspoon vanilla
1 cup chopped nuts
1 cup coconut (optional)

Mix all topping ingredients except nuts in saucepan, allowing margarine or butter to melt. Remove from stove and add nuts and coconut. Spread over cake after cake is done. Put under broiler to brown topping.

Chocolate Chip Cake

1 box yellow cake mix
1 (3 ounce) package chocolate instant pudding mix
1 cup sour cream
4 eggs
½ cup water
½ cup oil
1 (6 ounce) package chocolate chips

OVEN 350°

Mix all ingredients; pour into floured Bundt pan. Bake at 350° for 45 to 55 minutes. Glaze while warm.

Glaze:
½ stick butter or margarine
3 tablespoons milk
2 tablespoons cocoa
½ (1 pound) box powdered sugar
½ teaspoon vanilla

Bring butter or margarine, milk, and cocoa to boil. Add sugar and vanilla. Drizzle on cake.

Dan's Chocolate Cake

2 sticks margarine
1 cup water
4 tablespoons cocoa
2 cups flour
2 cups sugar
2 eggs
½ teaspoon baking soda
⅛ teaspoon baking powder
½ cup buttermilk*
1 teaspoon vanilla

OVEN 350°

Melt margarine; add water and cocoa. Bring mixture to boil then cool. Add flour and sugar, sifted together. Beat in eggs one at a time. Add baking soda and baking powder dissolved in buttermilk. Add vanilla. Bake at 350° for at least 30 minutes.

*You may use dry buttermilk, adding the required water and the buttermilk powder to dry ingredients.

Chocolate Chiffon Cake

2 cups hot water
⅓ cup cocoa
2 cups flour
4 teaspoons baking powder
½ teaspoon baking soda
1 teaspoon salt
2 cups sugar
½ cup corn oil
1 teaspoon vanilla
6 eggs, separated
½ teaspoon cream of tartar

OVEN 350°

Combine hot water and cocoa. Boil 1 minute. Cool. Sift flour, baking power, baking soda, salt, and sugar in bowl. Add cooled cocoa syrup, corn oil, vanilla, and egg yolks. Blend until smooth. Beat egg whites and cream of tartar until very stiff. Fold egg whites into first mixture carefully. Bake in ungreased tube pan at 350° for about 50 minutes. (Frosting recipe follows.)

Cocoa Frosting:

1½ cups cold milk
1 envelope whipped topping mix
1 package (4 serving size) chocolate fudge instant pudding mix

Pour cold milk into mixing bowl; add whipped topping and pudding mix. Beat on low for 1 minute. Slowly increase speed and beat for 4 to 6 minutes.

Hershey Cake

12 ounces cream cheese
2 sticks butter
2 (1 pound) boxes powdered sugar
1 (8 ounce) bar German sweet chocolate
¼ cup water
¼ cup shortening
3 whole eggs
2¾ cups flour
1 teaspoon baking soda
1 teaspoon vanilla
1 teaspoon salt
1 cup buttermilk

OVEN 350°

Cream together cream cheese and butter. Add powdered sugar. Melt German chocolate in water and add to creamed mixture. Reserve half of this mixture for icing. To other half of this mixture add shortening, eggs, flour, baking soda, vanilla, salt, and buttermilk. Bake at 350° for about 45 minutes.

Reese's Cup Cake

1 box chocolate or yellow cake mix
1 (3 ounce) box chocolate instant pudding mix
1 to 3 cups crumbled Reese's cups (according to how many you want)
¼ cup water

OVEN 325°

Preheat oven to 325°. Mix cake according to directions on box. Add pudding mix. Add crumbled Reese's cups. Add water. Bake for about 45 minutes. Ice.

Icing:

1 (8 ounce) package cream cheese, softened
3 to 4 tablespoons peanut butter
1 (8 ounce) tub whipped topping
1 (1 pound) box powdered sugar

Mix together, spread on cake, and top with crumbled Reese's cups.

Hershey Syrup Cake

1 cup sugar
1 stick butter
4 eggs
1 cup flour
1 teaspoon baking powder
½ teaspoon salt
1 (16 ounce) can Hershey syrup
1 cup chopped nuts (optional)

OVEN 350°

Cream sugar and butter; add eggs. Combine flour, baking powder, and salt; add to creamed mixture; add syrup. Mix 2 minutes. Use greased 9x13-inch pan. Bake until done.

Frosting:
⅓ cup evaporated milk
½ stick butter
1 cup sugar
1 cup milk chocolate chips

Combine milk, butter, and sugar in saucepan. Bring to boil over medium heat. Cook for 2 minutes, stirring constantly. Remove from heat; add chocolate chips and stir until melted. Spread over cake.

Oreo Cookie Cake

1 (16 ounce) package Oreo cookies
1 cup margarine, melted
1 (8 ounce) package cream cheese, softened to room temperature
1 cup powdered sugar
2 (8 ounce) containers whipped topping
1 (6 ounce) package chocolate instant pudding mix

Crush cookies; set aside ½ cup. Combine remaining cookie crumbs and melted margarine. Mix and press into 9x13-inch pan. Refrigerate for 1 hour. Mix softened cream cheese, powdered sugar, and 8 ounces whipped topping together and spread on cookie layer. Refrigerate 1 hour. Make pudding as package directs; spread on cream cheese layer and refrigerate 1 hour. Spread other 8 ounces whipped topping on top of pudding layer; sprinkle with extra cookie crumbs.

German Chocolate Cake

2 cups flour
2 cups sugar
½ teaspoon salt
2 sticks margarine
3 tablespoons cocoa
1 cup water
2 eggs
1 teaspoon baking soda
½ cup buttermilk
1 teaspoon vanilla

OVEN 350°

Sift together twice, flour, sugar, and salt. In saucepan combine margarine, cocoa, and water. Bring to boil; stir until butter is melted. Beat this mixture slowly into flour mixture. Beat together eggs, baking soda, buttermilk, and vanilla. Add to other mixture and mix well. Bake in 10x13-inch pan at 350° for 30 to 45 minutes.

Frosting:
1 cup canned cream
1 cup sugar
3 egg yolks
¼ pound margarine
1 teaspoon vanilla
1 cup coconut
1 cup chopped pecans

Combine all ingredients except coconut and pecans in saucepan. Cook, stirring, over medium heat for 12 minutes or until mixture thickens. Remove from heat. Add coconut and pecans. Beat until cool. Spread on cake in pan.

Grandmother Yutz's One Egg, One Bowl Chocolate Cake

OVEN 350°

Prepare two 8-inch cake pans (cut out waxed paper liners if you are going to ice cake, or spray with cooking spray). This will also make a sheet cake or about 19 cupcakes.

In large bowl, sift together:
1½ cups flour
1 cup sugar
1 teaspoon baking soda
2 heaping tablespoons cocoa
1 generous pinch salt

Make hole in center and drop in:
1 egg
1 cup sour milk (add 1 teaspoon vinegar to milk and let it set short time)
½ cup cooking oil
1 heaping teaspoon vanilla

Mix well and beat for 3 minutes. Bake cupcakes at 350° about 20 minutes and cake layers about 30 minutes.

Dirt Cake

1 (16 ounce) package Oreo cookies
1 (8 ounce) package cream cheese
1 stick butter
1 cup powdered sugar
1 (8 ounce) tub whipped topping
2 (3 ounce) packages vanilla instant pudding mix
3 cups milk
1 teaspoon vanilla

Crush cookies and put half of crumbs in 9x13-inch pan. Mix cream cheese and butter until smooth. Mix in powdered sugar. Fold in whipped topping. In separate bowl mix pudding mix, milk, and vanilla. Fold in cream cheese mixture. Stir both batters together well. Pour batter on top of crumbs. Sprinkle remaining crumbs on top. Refrigerate.

Apple Dump Cake

1 large can crushed pineapple with juice
1 cup apple pie filling
¼ teaspoon cinnamon
¼ pound margarine
1 package yellow cake mix
½ cup chopped walnuts
1 cup coconut

OVEN 350°

Pour pineapple with juice and apple filling in 9x13-inch pan. Sprinkle with cinnamon. In bowl mix margarine, cake mix, and nuts. Spread over fruit in pan. Sprinkle top with coconut. Cover and bake 30 minutes at 350°. Uncover and bake another 15 minutes.

Chocolate Sheet Cake

2 cups flour
1½ teaspoons baking soda
2 cups sugar
½ teaspoon salt
2 sticks butter
4 tablespoons cocoa
1 cup water
½ cup buttermilk
2 eggs
1 teaspoon vanilla

OVEN 350°

Sift together flour, soda, sugar, and salt. Melt butter; add cocoa and water. Bring to boil and pour over dry ingredients. Add buttermilk, eggs, and vanilla. Mix and pour into greased 10x16-inch sheet cake pan. Bake at 350° for 15 to 20 minutes. Ice. (Icing recipe follows.)

Icing:

1 stick butter
4 tablespoons cocoa
6 tablespoons buttermilk
1 (1 pound) box powdered sugar
1 cup chopped nuts
1 teaspoon vanilla

Melt butter, cocoa, and buttermilk; bring to boil and add powdered sugar, nuts, and vanilla. Pour over cake while hot.

Zucchini Chocolate Cake

4 ounces unsweetened chocolate
½ cup vegetable oil
½ cup butter, room temperature
2 cups sugar
3 eggs, beaten
1 tablespoon vanilla
2 cups sifted unbleached flour
⅓ cup cocoa
2 teaspoons baking soda
2 teaspoons baking powder
1 teaspoon salt
⅓ cup buttermilk or sour cream
3 cups coarsely grated zucchini or summer squash
½ cup chopped nuts

OVEN 350°

Melt chocolate and oil in small saucepan over very low heat. Cream butter until light; add sugar, eggs, and vanilla. Beat well. Add melted chocolate and mix well. Sift together dry ingredients and stir them into batter with buttermilk. Mix zucchini and nuts into batter. Divide batter between two greased and floured 9-inch cake pans. Bake on middle rack of oven for 40 minutes until tests done. Cool cake completely before frosting with whipped cream or your favorite frosting.

Dump Cake

1 can chunk pineapple
1 (20 ounce) can cherry pie filling
1 box yellow cake mix
Coconut (optional)

OVEN 350°

Combine pineapple and cherry pie filling; dump dry cake mix on top (do not mix). Add coconut if desired. Bake in greased and floured pan for 45 minutes. It's best if you use glass baking dish. You can eat it right out of oven. Serve with ice cream.

Stir Crazy Cake

2½ cups flour
1½ cups sugar
½ cup cocoa
2 teaspoons baking soda
½ teaspoon salt
⅔ cup oil
2 tablespoons vinegar
1 tablespoon vanilla
2 cups cold coffee
¼ cup sugar
½ teaspoon cinnamon or nutmeg

OVEN 350°

Put first five ingredients in 9x13-inch pan. Stir with fork to mix. Form three wells. Pour oil in one well, vinegar in another well, and vanilla in another. Pour cold coffee over all. Stir with fork until well mixed. Do not beat. Combine sugar, cinnamon, or nutmeg. Sprinkle over batter in pan. Bake at 350° for 35 to 40 minutes.

Note: Batter will be thin. May look like it is ready to boil. Not to worry—comes out fine.

Crazy Cake

3 cups flour
2 cups sugar
⅓ cup cocoa
2 teaspoons baking soda
1 teaspoon salt
2 tablespoons vinegar
1 teaspoon vanilla
¾ cup salad oil
2 cups cold water

OVEN 350°

Stir together ingredients. In ungreased 9x13-inch pan bake at 350° for 45 to 50 minutes or until cake springs back when you touch middle. No need to grease your pan. Or makes 30 to 36 cupcakes. Delicious with cream cheese frosting!

Wacky Cake

1½ cups flour
½ teaspoon salt
3 tablespoons cocoa
1 teaspoon baking soda
1 cup sugar
1 teaspoon vanilla
1 teaspoon vinegar
5 tablespoons salad oil
1 cup water

OVEN 350°

Stir together in ungreased 8x8-inch pan: flour, salt, cocoa, baking soda, and sugar. Make three holes in ingredients. In first hole put vanilla; in second, put vinegar; in third, salad oil. Pour water over all and mix well. Bake at 350° for 25 to 30 minutes.

Jewish Coffee Cake

1 package yellow cake mix
1 (3 ounce) package vanilla instant pudding mix
½ cup vegetable oil
4 eggs
1 cup sour cream
½ teaspoon vanilla
½ cup sugar
1 teaspoon cocoa
1 teaspoon cinnamon
½ cup chopped pecans

OVEN 350°

Mix cake mix, pudding mix, oil, eggs, sour cream, and vanilla; set aside. Mix together sugar, cocoa, cinnamon, and pecans. Pour half of cake mixture into greased tube pan or two loaf pans. Sprinkle with half of sugar mixture; add remaining cake batter. Sprinkle remaining sugar mixture on top. Take knife and make zigzag lines through batter. Bake at 350° for 50 to 55 minutes.

Granny's Crazy Cake

1 egg
1 cup sugar
½ cup milk
½ cup cocoa
½ cup shortening
½ teaspoon salt
1 teaspoon baking powder
1½ cups flour
½ cup boiling water

OVEN 325°

Put all ingredients in bowl; after adding boiling water, stir and mix. Pour into greased and floured pan and bake at 325° for 30 minutes. Makes 9-inch square or round layer pan. Double recipe for 9x13-inch pan.

Red Velvet Cake

2 ounces red food coloring
3 tablespoons milk chocolate cocoa
½ cup shortening
1½ cups sugar
2 eggs
1 cup buttermilk
2½ cups flour
½ teaspoon salt
1 teaspoon vanilla
1 tablespoon vinegar
1 teaspoon baking soda

OVEN 350°

Mix food coloring with cocoa. Cream shortening with sugar; add eggs and colored cocoa. Mix and beat well. Add buttermilk, flour, salt, and vanilla. Beat again. Remove from mixer and add vinegar and baking soda. Mix by hand. Pour into two greased and floured 8-inch pans. Bake at 350° for 25 to 35 minutes. Cut each layer in half while still warm. Ice.

American Beauty Icing:
4 tablespoons flour
1 cup milk
Pinch salt
1 cup sugar
½ cup margarine
½ cup shortening
2 teaspoons vanilla

Cook flour, milk, and salt until thick and put in refrigerator to cool. When cooled, add sugar, margarine, shortening, and vanilla; mix at high speed with electric mixer.

Jelly Roll Coffee Cake

2½ cups flour
½ teaspoon salt
½ teaspoon cinnamon
¾ cup sugar
1 cup brown sugar
¾ cup salad oil
1 cup buttermilk, divided
1 egg
1 teaspoon baking soda
1 teaspoon baking powder

OVEN 350°

Mix first six ingredients to fine crumb mixture, then divide equally into two bowls. Add to one mixture ½ cup buttermilk, egg, baking soda, and baking powder. Beat for 2 minutes then add remaining ½ cup buttermilk and beat for 2 more minutes. Pour into greased 12x18-inch jelly roll pan. Put leftover crumb mixture on top. Bake at 350° for approximately 20 minutes.

Cowboy Coffee Cake

2½ cups flour
1½ cups brown sugar
½ teaspoon salt
⅔ cup shortening
2 teaspoons baking powder
½ teaspoon baking soda
½ teaspoon cinnamon
½ teaspoon nutmeg
½ teaspoon allspice
2 eggs
1 cup sour milk

OVEN 375°

Combine flour, brown sugar, and salt. Cut in shortening until very fine. Take out 1½ cups of crumbs to be put on top of cake. To remaining crumbs add baking powder, baking soda, and spices. Mix well. Add eggs and milk to dry mixture; mix well (batter will be thin). Pour into well-greased and floured 9x11-inch pan. Sprinkle with reserved crumbs. Bake at 375° for 45 minutes.

Bubble Coffee Cake

1 (3 ounce) package butterscotch instant pudding mix
1 teaspoon cinnamon
1 loaf frozen bread dough, thawed
1 cup pecans
½ cup brown sugar
½ cup shortening

OVEN 350°

Mix pudding mix and cinnamon together in bowl. Pinch off small balls of bread dough and roll in pudding and cinnamon mixture. Place in greased Bundt pan with nuts in bottom. Pour any remaining mixture over top. Bring brown sugar and shortening just to boil and pour over. Cover and allow to rise until doubled. Bake uncovered at 350° for 40 minutes or until done when tested.

Éclair Cake

Cake:
1 (16 ounce) box graham crackers
2 (4 serving size) packages vanilla instant pudding mix
3 cups milk
1 (16 ounce) tub of nondairy whipped topping

Sauce:
1 cup sugar
¼ cup cocoa
¼ cup milk
½ stick butter

Butter bottom of 9x13-inch pan. Line pan with crackers; do not crush. Prepare pudding with milk, beating at medium speed until well blended (approximately 2 minutes). Carefully fold in whipped topping. Pour half of mixture over crackers. Cover with another layer of crackers; pour remaining pudding mixture over crackers. Cover with more crackers. Refrigerate at least 2 hours.

To make sauce, mix sugar, cocoa, and milk in saucepan; boil for 1 minute, stirring occasionally. Take off heat; add butter; beat with spoon until thickened. Pour on top of crackers.

Variation: Carefully spread can of chocolate or lemon frosting on top.

Note: Recipe can easily be halved.

Sour Cream Coconut Cake

1 box yellow cake mix
1 pound powdered sugar
1 (8 ounce) package sour cream
1 small package flaked coconut
Whipped topping

Prepare cake mix according to package directions. Bake in two round cake pans. Split layers. To make filling, mix together sugar, sour cream, and coconut. Ice between layers. Save some filling. Mix whipped topping with remains. Ice cake. This cake is more moist the longer it sits.

Twinkie Cake

1 box yellow cake mix
3 tablespoons cornstarch
1 cup water
1 cup margarine
1 cup sugar
1 teaspoon vanilla

Prepare cake mix according to package directions. Bake in oblong cake pan or two square pans. Let cool and cut into two layers; lay top aside. Cook cornstarch, water, margarine, sugar, and vanilla until clear; cool. Spread on bottom of cake and lay top back on. It keeps well for a week. These freeze well for later use.

Note: Any kind of cake mix can be used.

Reese's Peanut Butter Cake

- 2 sticks margarine
- 1 cup water
- 2 eggs, beaten
- ¼ cup cocoa (unsweetened)
- ½ cup buttermilk
- 2 cups sugar
- 2 cups flour
- 1 teaspoon baking soda
- 1 teaspoon vanilla
- 1 cup peanut butter
- 1 tablespoon oil

OVEN 350°

Heat margarine, water, beaten eggs, cocoa, and buttermilk until bubbly. Add sugar, flour, baking soda, and vanilla. Bake at 350° for 25 to 30 minutes in greased and floured 9x13-inch pan. Mix 1 cup peanut butter with 1 tablespoon oil; spread over cooled cake. Ice.

Icing:

- ½ cup margarine
- ¼ cup cocoa
- 6 tablespoons buttermilk
- 1 box (4 cups) powdered sugar
- 1 teaspoon vanilla

Heat margarine, cocoa, and buttermilk until bubbly. Add sugar and vanilla; beat until smooth and spreading consistency. Spread on top of peanut butter layer.

Lemon Twist Coffee Cake

- ¾ cup milk
- 1 (¼ ounce) package dry yeast
- ¼ cup lukewarm water
- 1 tablespoon plus ½ cup sugar
- 1 stick margarine
- 3 eggs
- 4½ cups flour, divided
- ¾ teaspoon lemon extract
- 1 tablespoon grated lemon peel
- White frosting mix
- Red (or red and green) candied cherries
- Chopped nuts (optional)

OVEN 375°

Scald milk; let cool. Dissolve dry yeast in lukewarm water. Put 1 tablespoon sugar in water/yeast mixture and let stand for 5 minutes. Cream margarine and ½ cup sugar. Add eggs; mix in scalded milk and yeast mixture. Add 2 cups flour and lemon extract. Beat with beaters and add remaining 2½ cups flour and grated lemon peel. Knead 1 minute. Let stand in greased bowl overnight, preferably in warm area. In morning, divide dough into two sections. Take one section and divide it again into two sections. Roll out like tubes and braid. Place on cookie sheet in two circles or horseshoe shapes. Place in warm spot to raise for about 1½ hours until double in size. Bake at 375° for 12 to 15 minutes. Frost when cool. Add cherries and nuts.

Unbake Cake

2 cups finely chopped pecans
1 cup finely chopped walnuts
1 cup finely chopped Brazil nuts
2 packages vanilla wafers (or 1 pound), crushed
1 (14 ounce) can condensed milk (NOT evaporated milk)

Mix thoroughly. Shape in loaf; wrap in foil. Keeps in refrigerator for four days.

Crunch Cake

2 cups flour
2 cups sugar
1 cup cooking oil
7 large eggs
1 tablespoon vanilla

OVEN 275°

Sift 1 cup flour and 1 cup sugar into mixing bowl. Sift remaining flour and sugar into bowl. Add other ingredients and beat 12 minutes on high speed. Pour batter in tube pan lined with waxed paper. Bake 1 hour and 30 minutes at 275°. Do not open oven door until done, because it will fall. Take out of oven, turn over, and let it sit for about 30 minutes. Flip over and cut loose from side of pan; turn out onto cloth until it cools.

Coffee Cake Swirl

Cake:
1 cup flour
¼ cup sugar
¼ cup brown sugar
½ teaspoon baking soda
½ teaspoon baking powder
¼ teaspoon salt
½ teaspoon cinnamon
½ cup buttermilk
⅓ cup shortening
1 egg

Topping:
¼ cup brown sugar
½ teaspoon cinnamon
¼ teaspoon nutmeg

Glaze:
½ cup powdered sugar
3 to 4 teaspoons milk
¼ teaspoon vanilla

OVEN 350°

Grease and flour bottom of 9-inch round pan. Combine all cake ingredients. Blend at low speed until moistened. Beat 3 minutes at medium speed. Spread in pan. Blend topping ingredients. Sprinkle over batter, cover, and refrigerate overnight (or bake immediately). Heat oven to 350°; uncover and bake for 20 to 25 minutes or until toothpick comes out clean. Blend glaze ingredients until smooth. Drizzle over cake.

Or you can make muffins instead of cake; bake about 15 minutes.

*To make your own buttermilk, in measuring cup add 2 teaspoons lemon juice or vinegar then milk to make ½ cup total.

Peanut Butter Tandy Cake

1½ cups sugar
2 cups flour
2 teaspoons baking powder
¼ teaspoon salt
2 teaspoons shortening
4 eggs
1 cup milk
1 tablespoon vanilla
1 small jar peanut butter
1 (8 ounce) chocolate bar

OVEN 350°

Combine first five ingredients; mix thoroughly. Beat eggs; add milk and vanilla. Add liquid to dry ingredients. Pour into greased pan. Bake at 350° for 25 minutes. While hot, spread peanut butter on top. Cool. Spread melted chocolate bar over peanut butter. Put cake in refrigerator. Serve when chocolate is firm.

7-UP Cake

3 cups sugar
1½ cups butter (3 sticks)
5 eggs
3 cups flour
2 tablespoons lemon extract
¾ cup 7-UP

OVEN 325°

Cream sugar and butter together and beat until light and fluffy. Add eggs one at a time; beat well. Add flour and beat well. Beat in lemon extract and 7-UP. Pour batter into well-greased and floured jumbo fluted tube pan or large Bundt pan. Bake at 325° for 1¼ hours. Remove from oven and let cool for 15 minutes; turn upside down on cake rack. Ice with your favorite icing.

Sour Cream Coffee Cake

½ cup butter
1 cup sugar
2 eggs
1 teaspoon vanilla
1 cup sour cream
2 cups flour
1 teaspoon baking soda
1 teaspoon baking powder
1 teaspoon salt

Topping:
½ cup chopped walnuts
1 teaspoon cinnamon
½ cup sugar

OVEN 350°

Cream butter and sugar. Add eggs to creamed mixture. Add vanilla and sour cream. Sift dry ingredients and add to creamed mixture. Mix walnuts, cinnamon, and sugar together. Pour half of batter into greased and floured tube pan; sprinkle with half of nut mixture. Pour remaining batter in pan and top with remaining nut mixture. Bake 45 minutes at 350°.

Variation: Add ¼ cup brown sugar, being sure to double all batter ingredients except salt.

Special Coconut Cake

1 box yellow cake mix
1 (14 ounce) package coconut
1 (15 ounce) can Coco Lopez cream of coconut
1 (8 ounce) container whipped topping

Mix cake according to directions. Then stir in half package of coconut. Bake in 9x13-inch pan according to directions. While cake is baking, put can of Coco Lopez in pan and cover with hot water. Immediately after removing from oven, poke holes 1 inch apart all over cake using an instrument about the size of pencil. (The handle of a spatula works well.) Pour Coco Lopez over top of hot cake, making sure some liquid goes into each hole. When cake is cool, top with whipped topping. Then add remaining coconut.

Variations: Use white cake mix. Add 1 can sweetened condensed milk and use 1 cup piña colada instead of Coco Lopez.

Hornet's Nest Cake

1 (4¾ ounce) package vanilla pudding mix
2⅔ cups milk
1 teaspoon vanilla
1 (18 ounce) box yellow or French vanilla cake mix
1 (6 ounce) package butterscotch chips
1 cup chopped nuts

OVEN 350°

Cook pudding, milk, and vanilla until thick. Pour over cake mix. Beat with mixer. Will be like whipped cream. Pour into greased 9x13-inch pan. Sprinkle with butterscotch chips and nuts. Bake at 350° for 25 to 30 minutes or until done. Serve plain or with whipped topping.

Elegant Angel Food Cake

8 ounces cream cheese, softened
8 ounces powdered sugar
8 ounces whipped topping
1 angel food cake cut in thirds lengthwise
1 can blueberry or cherry pie filling

Blend cream cheese and sugar together. Add whipped topping. Stir until well blended. Frost between layers of cake, top, and sides. Top with cherry or blueberry pie filling. Refrigerate until ready to serve.

Eggless Cake

2 cups sugar
2 cups water
½ cup butter
2 teaspoons cloves
2 cups raisins
2 teaspoons baking soda
4 scant cups flour
1 teaspoon baking powder

OVEN 350°

Cook all ingredients except flour and baking powder until boiling. Remove from stove and let cool. Add flour and baking powder. Bake at 350° until cake springs back when pressed. Do not overbake.

Coca-Cola Cake

2 cups flour
2 cups sugar
2 sticks butter
3 tablespoons cocoa
1 cup Coca-Cola
½ cup buttermilk
2 eggs
1 teaspoon baking soda
1 teaspoon vanilla
1½ cups miniature marshmallows

OVEN 350°

Combine flour and sugar in mixing bowl. Heat butter, cocoa, and Coca-Cola to boiling and pour over flour and sugar. Mix well. Add buttermilk, eggs, baking soda, vanilla, and marshmallows. Mix well. The batter will be thin. Bake in greased and floured 9x13-inch pan for 30 to 35 minutes at 350°. When you turn cake out, top should be up. Very moist! Ice while hot.

Icing:
½ cup butter
3 tablespoons cocoa
6 tablespoons Coca-Cola
1 pound powdered sugar
1 cup roasted pecans, chopped

Combine and heat to boiling butter, cocoa, and Coca-Cola. Pour over powdered sugar. Beat well. Add pecans. Spread over hot cake.

Jell-O Cake

¾ cup oil
¾ cup water
4 eggs
1 package lemon gelatin (dry)
1 package white or lemon cake mix
1½ cups powdered sugar
⅓ cup concentrated lemon juice

OVEN 350°

Mix first five ingredients together. Beat 4 minutes. Bake in lightly greased 9x13-inch pan at 350° for 30 minutes. Remove from oven; wait a few minutes; prick top of cake with fork. Mix sugar and lemon juice. Pour over cake while warm.

Cream Puff Cake

1 cup water
1 stick butter
¾ cup flour
4 eggs
3 (3 ounce) boxes vanilla instant pudding mix
3¼ cups milk
1 (8 ounce) package cream cheese, softened
1 (8 ounce) container whipped topping

OVEN 350°

Heat water and butter together until butter melts. Add flour and eggs, one at a time; beat. Grease pan, pour in batter, and smooth out. Bake at 350° for 45 minutes. Cake will be lumpy and bumpy. Make sure cake is cooled, then beat pudding and milk; add cream cheese. Put pudding mix on cake. Spread whipped topping on top. Keep refrigerated.

Old-Fashioned Teacakes

2 cups sugar
3 eggs
1 cup butter (no substitute)
3 teaspoons baking powder
⅛ teaspoon salt
Enough flour to make stiff dough

OVEN 375°

Combine ingredients; mix well. Roll to ½-inch thickness and cut with 2½-inch round cutter; place on baking sheet. Bake at 375° for 7 to 12 minutes or until set.

Upside-Down Raisin Cake

1⅓ cups sugar
4 teaspoons baking powder
¼ teaspoon salt
1 teaspoon vanilla
½ cup shortening, melted
1 cup raisins
⅔ cup milk
2 eggs
2 cups flour
2 cups boiling water
1 cup brown sugar

OVEN 350°

Mix all ingredients except for water and brown sugar together in 9x13-inch pan. Mix together boiling water and brown sugar; pour over cake. Do not stir in! Bake at 350° for 30 minutes.

Plum Cake

2 cups sugar
3 eggs
1 cup oil
2 small baby food jars plums
1 teaspoon vanilla
1 teaspoon red food coloring
2 cups flour
½ teaspoon baking soda
Pinch salt
1 teaspoon cloves
1 teaspoon cinnamon
1 cup chopped nuts

OVEN 350°

Mix together sugar, eggs, oil, plums, vanilla, and coloring. Sift together dry ingredients. Combine flour mixture with plum mixture and stir in nuts. Bake 1 hour at 350° in greased Bundt pan. Drizzle with glaze when cooled.

Glaze:
2½ cups powdered sugar
3 tablespoons lemon juice
1 teaspoon melted margarine

Wafer Cake

2 sticks margarine
2 cups sugar
6 eggs
1 (12 ounce) box vanilla wafers, crushed
½ cup sweet milk
1 (7 ounce) can flaked coconut
1 cup chopped pecans

OVEN 325°

Cream margarine; add sugar and eggs, one at a time, mixing well after each addition. Add milk and crushed wafers alternately to creamed mixture while beating. Add coconut and pecans; mix well. Bake in greased tube pan 1 hour and 15 minutes at 325°.

Almond Poppy Seed Cake

3 cups flour
2 cups sugar
1½ teaspoons baking powder
1½ teaspoons salt
2 tablespoons poppy seed
¼ teaspoon baking soda
1½ cups milk
1 cup cooking oil
3 eggs
1½ teaspoons vanilla
1½ teaspoons almond extract

OVEN 350°

Combine flour, sugar, baking powder, salt, poppy seed, and baking soda in large mixer bowl. Add milk, oil, eggs, vanilla, and almond extract. Beat on low speed just until moistened. Beat on high speed for 2 more minutes. Pour into greased and floured 10-inch tube pan. Bake at 350° for 1 to 1¼ hours. Cool in pan on rack for 15 minutes. Turn out into pan.

Cheesecake

Cake:

1 stick butter, melted
1 egg, beaten
1 box white cake mix

Topping:

1 (8 ounce) package cream cheese, softened
2 eggs, beaten
1 (1 pound) box powdered sugar

OVEN 350°

Melt butter in 9x13-inch pan. Beat egg and add to butter. Add dry cake mix; press in pan (batter will be stiff). To make topping, beat together cream cheese and eggs; add sugar and pour on top of batter. Bake in 350° oven for 40 to 45 minutes.

Icebox Cake

1 large package chocolate pudding mix (not instant)
1 large package vanilla pudding mix (not instant)
1 box graham crackers
½ cup chopped walnuts

Following package directions, prepare both puddings separately. Let cool 15 minutes, stirring often. In 9x13-inch glass dish, layer following: graham crackers (setting side by side), vanilla pudding, nuts, graham crackers, chocolate pudding, nuts; repeat all layers. Place in refrigerator until chilled.

Checkerboard Cake

2½ cups flour
2 teaspoons baking powder
½ teaspoon baking soda
½ teaspoon salt
¾ cup shortening
2 cups sugar, divided
1 tablespoon vanilla
1⅓ cups buttermilk or sour milk
5 egg whites, room temperature
⅓ cup unsweetened cocoa powder
1 tablespoon milk
Chocolate frosting

OVEN 350°

No special pan is needed. Grease and flour three 8½-inch round baking pans. In bowl combine flour, baking powder, baking soda, and ½ teaspoon salt. In very large bowl beat shortening with electric mixer on medium speed for 30 seconds; add 1⅔ cups sugar and vanilla; beat until combined. Alternately add flour mixture and buttermilk, beating after each addition just until combined.

Thoroughly wash beaters. Beat egg whites on medium speed until soft peaks form (tips curl). Gradually add remaining sugar, beating on medium to high until stiff peaks form (tips stand straight). Gently fold half of egg white mixture into beaten mixture. Fold in remaining egg white mixture. Spoon half of batter (about 3¼ cups) into bowl. Sift cocoa powder over remaining batter. Stir in 1 tablespoon milk.

Set ¾ cup white batter aside. Spoon 1¼ cups remaining white batter around outer edge of each of two prepared pans. Spoon ¾ cup chocolate batter in ring right next to inner edge of white batter in each of pans. Spoon half of remaining white batter into center of each pan. In third pan, using 1¼ cups chocolate batter, make outer ring; using reserved ¾ cup white batter, make inner ring. Fill center with remaining chocolate batter.

Bake in 350° oven about 25 minutes or until cakes test done. Cool in pan for 10 minutes. Remove and cool. Place cake layer with white outer ring on serving plate. Frost top with ½ cup frosting. Place cake layer with chocolate outer ring on top. Frost sides and top with remaining frosting.

Serves 16.

Frosting:
¼ cup margarine
2 cups sifted powdered sugar
3 squares (3 ounces) unsweetened chocolate
½ cup milk
1 teaspoon vanilla
2½ to 3 cups sifted powdered sugar

Beat together margarine and 2 cups powdered sugar. Beat in chocolate, melted and cooled; add milk and vanilla. Beat in rest of powdered sugar to reach desired consistency.

Makes 4 cups.

Funnel Cake

1 cup self-rising flour
½ teaspoon ground cinnamon
1 egg
½ cup milk

Mix ingredients with fork until smooth, pancake batter consistency. Holding finger under funnel opening, pour about ¼ cup batter into funnel. Allow batter to pour from funnel into 1 inch of hot oil, moving funnel in circle to form spiral shape. Fry 1 minute, turn cake, and fry until golden brown. Remove to paper towel and drain. Sprinkle with powdered sugar.

Plain Cake

2 cups flour
1 cup sugar
2 teaspoons baking powder
2 eggs
½ cup cooking oil or 1 stick shortening, melted
1 teaspoon vanilla
1 cup milk (enough to thin dough)
1 cup coconut (optional)

OVEN 350°

Combine ingredients and hand beat until well mixed. Pour into greased and floured sheet pan or loaf pan. Bake at 350° for 35 minutes or until cake is light brown and tests done.

Date Cake Dessert

1⅛ cups flour
1 teaspoon soda
½ teaspoon salt
1 tablespoon butter
1 cup sugar
1 egg, beaten
½ pound dates, chopped
1 cup boiling water

OVEN 375°

Sift dry ingredients together. Blend butter and sugar and add egg. Cover chopped dates with boiling water. Add to creamed mixture alternately with flour mixture. Pour into greased 7x7-inch pan. Bake for 25 minutes or until it springs back to touch.

Lane Cake

1 cup butter
3 cups sugar
1 cup milk
3 cups flour
3 teaspoons baking powder
Vanilla
8 egg whites

OVEN 350°

Cream butter and sugar. Add milk, flour, and baking powder. Then add vanilla. Beat egg whites until stiff; fold into creamed mixture. Pour into three layer pans. Bake at 350° for 30 minutes.

Filling:
½ cup butter
1½ cups sugar
11 egg yolks
1 cup chopped pecans
1 teaspoon vanilla

Melt butter in double boiler. Add sugar, egg yolks, and pecans. Cook until thick, stirring continuously, about 10 minutes. Add vanilla. Spread on each layer of cake before icing.

Icing:
3 egg whites
½ cup sugar
1 cup white corn syrup

Beat egg whites. Cook sugar and corn syrup until it starts thickening, approximately 5 minutes. Add to beaten egg whites, beating as you pour sugar and corn syrup into mixing bowl. Mix until it becomes thick enough to ice cake. Top each layer with cake filling and then cake icing. After third layer ice sides also.

Mom's Guess Cake

4 cups flour
¼ cup cocoa
2 teaspoons cinnamon
3⅔ teaspoons baking soda
1 teaspoon salt
Buttermilk or sour milk for thinning
2 cups sugar
1 cup shortening
1 box raisins
1 box dates, cut up
1 cup chopped walnuts

OVEN 350°

Sift dry ingredients into bowl; add enough sour milk or buttermilk to make batter thin enough for baking. Cream sugar and shortening; add to batter mixture. Add raisins, dates, and nuts. Bake at 350° for 45 minutes, then at 375° until done. Frost with chocolate fudge frosting.

Pea Pickin' Cake

1 box butter cake mix
4 eggs
1 cup corn oil
1 can mandarin oranges, with juice

OVEN 350°

Mix together cake mix, eggs, oil, and mandarin oranges with juice. Bake in three layer pans for 15 to 20 minutes.

Topping:
1 large can crushed pineapple, with juice
1 (16 ounce) carton whipped topping
1 (3 ounce) package vanilla instant pudding mix

Mix carefully; do not beat. Put between layers and on top. Keep refrigerated.

Pig Picking Cake

1 box yellow cake mix
3 eggs
¾ cup applesauce
1 (12 ounce) can mandarin oranges, with juice

OVEN 350°

Mix all together. Bake at 350° for 35 to 45 minutes.

Icing:
1 (16 ounce) container whipped topping
1 (12 ounce) can crushed pineapple, drained
1 (3 ounce) box vanilla instant pudding mix

Mix icing ingredients. Refrigerate for 45 minutes.

Scripture Cake

4½ cups 1 Kings 4:22
1 cup Judges 5:25b
2 cups Jeremiah 6:20
2 cups 1 Samuel 30:12
2 cups Nahum 3:12
2 cups Numbers 17:8
1 tablespoon 1 Samuel 14:25
1 teaspoon Leviticus 2:13
6 Jeremiah 17:11
½ cup Judges 4:19b
2 teaspoons Amos 4:5
2 teaspoons 2 Chronicles 9:9

OVEN 325°

Follow mixing directions for any basic fruitcake. Bake slowly in moderate oven.

Punch Bowl Cake

1 box cake mix
1 (20 ounce) can cherry pie filling
1 (3 ounce) box vanilla instant pudding mix
1 can crushed pineapple, drained
Whipped topping
Chopped pecans (for garnish)
Maraschino cherries (for garnish)

Prepare cake mix as directed on package. Pour into two layer pans. Bake and cool. In punch bowl put one layer of cake on bottom. Cover with layers of cherry pie filling, prepared pudding, pineapple, and whipped topping. Put second layer of cake on top and layer with cherry pie filling, pudding, pineapple, and whipped topping. Garnish with pecans and maraschino cherries. Cool before serving.

Makes 30 servings.

Italian Love Cake

1 box chocolate cake mix
2 (16 ounce) containers ricotta cheese
4 eggs
1 teaspoon vanilla
¾ cup sugar
1 (6 ounce) box chocolate instant pudding mix
1 cup milk
1 (8 ounce) container whipped topping

OVEN 350°

Mix cake as directed on box. Pour into greased and floured 9x13-inch pan. In separate bowl combine ricotta cheese, eggs, vanilla, and sugar. Mix well and spoon over top of unbaked cake. Bake at 350° for 1 hour. Cake will rise to top. Cool. Mix pudding with milk; fold in whipped topping. Spread over cooled cake and refrigerate.

Sally Lunn (Quick Version)

1 cup flour
½ cup sugar
3 tablespoons baking powder
1 teaspoon salt
1 egg
1 cup milk
¼ cup oil

OVEN 400°

Blend dry ingredients. Add egg, milk, and oil. Mix slightly; do not over mix. Pour into greased 9-inch pan. Bake for 20 to 25 minutes. Frost with butter. Cut into wedges.

Amish Cake

3 cups brown sugar
1 stick shortening, room temperature
2 teaspoons baking soda
2 cups buttermilk
3 cups self-rising flour, sifted
2 teaspoons vanilla

Topping:
⅔ cup brown sugar
1 cup chopped walnuts
1 cup shredded coconut
2 tablespoons shortening, melted
½ cup canned milk
1 tablespoon vanilla

OVEN 370°

Cream together sugar and shortening. Add baking soda to buttermilk; add milk, flour, and vanilla. Mix well. Bake at 370° for 40 to 45 minutes or until done. Remove from oven.

Topping: Mix together topping ingredients. Spread on cake. Place back in oven for 10 minutes or until topping is bubbly.

Sauerkraut Cake

½ cup butter or shortening
1¼ cups sugar
3 eggs
2 teaspoons vanilla
¼ teaspoon salt
2 cups flour
1 teaspoon baking soda
½ cup quick cocoa mix
½ cup sour cream
½ cup water
1 cup sauerkraut, rinsed, drained, and chopped

OVEN 350°

Grease and flour 9x13-inch cake pan. In large bowl, cream butter, and sugar until light. Beat in eggs and vanilla. Sift dry ingredients together. Mix sour cream and water together; add to creamed mixture alternately with dry ingredients. Fold in sauerkraut and pour into pan. Bake at 350° for 40 minutes. Frost with chocolate frosting.

Frosting:
2 cups powdered sugar
3 to 4 tablespoons vanilla
3 to 4 tablespoons cocoa, not too dark
¼ stick shortening, softened
3 ounces cream cheese

Mix and frost cooled cake.

Magic Cake

2 teaspoons baking soda
2 cups sugar
2 cups flour
2 eggs
1 teaspoon vanilla
1 (20 ounce) can crushed pineapple, with juice

OVEN 350°

Stir and pour into greased and floured 9x13-inch pan. Bake at 350° for 45 minutes. Top with cream cheese icing.

Popcorn Cake

4 quarts popped corn
1 pound gumdrops
½ package M&M's candy
½ pound salted peanuts
½ cup butter or margarine
1 pound marshmallows
½ cup oil

Mix popcorn, gumdrops, M&M's, and nuts in large bowl. Melt butter, marshmallows, and oil. Pour over popcorn mixture and stir. Press firmly into greased cake pan and cool.

Tomato Soup Cake

1 cup sugar
½ stick shortening
1 cup chopped walnuts
1 (10¾ ounce) can tomato soup
½ cup boiling water
2 cups flour
1 teaspoon nutmeg
1 teaspoon baking soda
1 teaspoon cinnamon
2 teaspoons baking powder
½ cup sour milk

OVEN 350°

Cream together sugar and shortening. Add walnuts, soup, and boiling water. Add flour, nutmeg, baking soda, cinnamon, and baking powder. Then add sour milk. Bake in 9x13-inch pan at 350° for 40 minutes.

Easy Caramel Frosting:

1½ cups brown sugar
¼ cup plus 2 tablespoons milk
1 teaspoon vanilla

Bring ingredients to boil and boil 3 minutes, stirring constantly. Remove from heat; add vanilla. Cool until lukewarm. Beat until creamy and thick enough to spread. Add more milk if necessary for spreading.

Poor Man's Cake

⅔ cup shortening
1½ cups sugar
1½ cups milk
2 eggs
2½ cups flour
5 teaspoons baking powder
¼ teaspoon salt
2 teaspoons vanilla

OVEN 350°

Cream shortening and sugar; then add milk and eggs. Add dry ingredients; add vanilla. Pour into greased 9x13-inch pan. Bake at 350° for 25 to 30 minutes.

Mom's Gingerbread

1 stick butter or margarine
1 cup sugar
1 cup molasses
⅔ cup milk
2 eggs
½ teaspoon salt
3 cups flour
2 teaspoons baking soda
2 teaspoons cinnamon
2 teaspoons ginger

OVEN 325°

Mix together. Put in loaf pan. Bake at 325° until springs back when lightly touched. Serve plain or topped with lemon sauce or whipped topping.

Easy Lemon Sauce:
1 package lemon pudding mix
½ cup sugar
3 cups water, divided
1 egg

Combine pudding mix, sugar, and ¼ cup of water in saucepan. Add egg; blend well. Add remaining 2¾ cups water. Cook and stir over medium heat until it comes to full boil. Serve warm over gingerbread.

Pies

Best Pastry

5 cups flour
2 teaspoons baking powder
2 teaspoons salt
1 pound lard or shortening
1 egg, beaten well
1 tablespoon vinegar with enough water to equal 1 cup

Makes 5 single shells or 4 double shells.

Nanny's Piecrust

5 pounds flour plus 2 cups
3 teaspoons light salt or 2 teaspoons salt
3 pounds shortening
2½ cups water

Mix flour, salt, and shortening until mixture is coarse as cornmeal. Add water and mix. Follow directions below.

Mix all in large bowl and take out enough for one piecrust. Then place this ball in plastic bag and flatten. Do this until all dough is used. Freeze bags and take out what you need for baking. Let crust thaw for a few hours or defrost it in microwave until pliable enough to work with.

Yields 15 to 20 crusts.

Never Fail Piecrust

1 egg
2 tablespoons vinegar
Water to blend
4 cups flour
2 cups shortening

Break egg into measuring cup. Beat egg. Add vinegar and fill up with water; add flour and shortening. Blend with piecrust blender; shape into ball. Refrigerate for 30 minutes. Cut off and roll into crusts.

Summer Cool and Easy Pie

1 package gelatin
⅔ cup boiling water
10 ice cubes
1 (8 ounce) container whipped topping
1 (8 inch) crumb crust

Stir gelatin into boiling water until dissolved. Stir in ice cubes until it begins to thicken; dip out remaining cubes. Whisk whipped topping in until smooth. Pour into crust. Chill 6 hours. Top with thin layer of whipped topping or fruit, or both.

Jell-O Pie

1 (8 ounce) container whipped topping
1 (12 ounce) carton cottage cheese
1 cup coconut
1 (14 ounce) can fruit cocktail, drained
1 (3 ounce) package orange gelatin
1 graham cracker crust

Combine whipped topping, cottage cheese, coconut, and fruit cocktail. Sprinkle gelatin over all; stir to mix well and pour into crust.

Chess Pie

½ cup butter or margarine, softened
1 cup sugar
2 to 3 eggs (depending on size), beaten
1 cup walnut meats
1 cup raisins, currants, or dates
Pinch salt
½ teaspoon flavoring

OVEN 350°

Cream butter or margarine and sugar; add beaten eggs, then other ingredients. Fill pastry-lined cupcake tins. Bake at 350° for 20 to 30 minutes until browned.

Frozen Coconut Pie

½ stick margarine
1 cup chopped pecans
7 ounces coconut
16 ounces whipped topping
8 ounces cream cheese
1 (14 ounce) can condensed milk
2 deep-dish pie shells, baked
Caramel topping

Brown margarine, pecans, and coconut in skillet; let cool. Mix together whipped topping, cream cheese, and milk until smooth and creamy. Layer pie shell with half of whipped topping mixture and of half pecan mixture. Drizzle caramel topping over. Repeat. Put in freezer. Keep frozen. Will keep up to 3 months in freezer.

Tropical Pie

6 egg whites
1 teaspoon baking powder
2 cups sugar
34 Ritz crackers
2 cups chopped pecans
1 teaspoon vanilla

OVEN 350°

Beat egg whites until foamy. Beat in baking powder until stiff. Add sugar and beat until well mixed. Roll Ritz crackers until fine; fold in with chopped pecans and vanilla. Put into well-greased 9x13-inch pan. Smooth out and bake at 350° for 25 minutes.

Optional: After pie is cooled, cover top with 2 envelopes prepared whipped topping mix. Store in refrigerator overnight.

Brown Sugar Pie

3 cups brown sugar
½ cup butter or margarine
3 eggs
4 tablespoons flour
1 cup milk
2 unbaked pie shells
Black walnuts, hickory nuts (optional)

OVEN 350°

Combine brown sugar, butter or margarine, eggs, and flour. Mix well with milk and pour into pie shells. Bake at 350° until brown on top. Let cool. Garnish with nuts.

Creeping Crust Pie

½ cup margarine or butter
1 cup flour
1 teaspoon baking powder
1 cup sugar
½ cup milk
2 cups berries
1 cup, or less, sugar for berries

OVEN 350°

Melt butter or margarine in 10-inch baking dish. Mix together flour, baking powder, and sugar; add milk and mix; pour or spoon over melted butter. Heat berries with sugar; let cool and pour over batter. Bake in 350° oven until golden brown, approximately 30 minutes.

Hospitality Pie

1 stick margarine, melted
1½ cups chopped pecans
2 cups coconut (7 to 8 ounces)
1 (14 ounce) can condensed milk
8 ounces cream cheese
16 ounces whipped topping
3 graham cracker crusts
1 small jar caramel or butterscotch ice cream topping

OVEN 350°

Melt margarine in 9x13-inch pan at 350°. Stir in nuts and coconut. Stir every 5 minutes until brown. Cool. Mix milk and cream cheese with electric mixer on low speed until smooth. Fold in whipped topping. Layer in crusts one-sixth of cream cheese mixture, coconut, and nuts. Drizzle with caramel topping. Repeat layers once and freeze.

Vinegar Pie

4 tablespoons flour
1 cup sugar
1 cup boiling water
1 to 2 eggs, beaten
3 tablespoons vinegar
1 teaspoon lemon extract
1 baked piecrust

Mix flour and sugar together. Add boiling water and cook for 5 minutes, stirring constantly. Add beaten eggs and cook 2 minutes longer. Add vinegar and lemon extract; cook 2 minutes more. Pour into baked crust and let cool.

Low-cholesterol variation: Use ½ cup egg substitute. Also, for more lemony flavor, use 1 tablespoon real lemon juice and 2 tablespoons vinegar.

My Favorite Cream Pie

1 cup plus 2 to 3 tablespoons water
½ stick margarine
1 (12 ounce) can evaporated milk
½ cup sugar
3 tablespoons cornstarch
Salt to taste
3 egg yolks
1 cup coconut
1 baked piecrust

Heat 1 cup water and margarine together; bring to boil. Add milk. Separately, mix sugar, cornstarch, salt, egg yolks, and 2 to 3 tablespoons water. Add to milk mixture. Cook until thick, stirring constantly. Boil 2 minutes. Add coconut. Pour into baked piecrust.

Butternut Brownie Pie

3 egg whites
⅛ teaspoon baking powder
1 cup sugar
1 packet graham crackers, crushed
1 cup chopped pecans
½ pint whipping cream
¼ cup sugar
1 teaspoon vanilla

OVEN 350°

Beat egg whites to stiff peaks with baking powder. Gradually add 1 cup sugar. Fold in crushed graham crackers and pecans. Bake in buttered pie plate for 20 to 25 minutes at 350°. Beat whipping cream and fold in sugar and vanilla. Spread over cooled crust.

Three-Minute Pie

½ stick margarine, melted
1 cup sugar
1 cup coconut
3 eggs
1 teaspoon vanilla
¼ cup buttermilk
1 unbaked pie shell

OVEN 325°

Combine melted margarine, sugar, coconut, eggs, vanilla, and buttermilk. Mix well. Pour into unbaked pie shell. Bake at 325° for 35 to 45 minutes. Insert knife in center to test for doneness.

Million-Dollar Pie

¼ cup concentrated lemon juice
1 (14 ounce) can sweetened condensed milk
1 large can crushed pineapple
12 ounces whipped topping
1 (7 ounce) bag coconut
Chopped pecans (optional)
2 graham cracker crusts

Mix lemon juice and condensed milk. Drain pineapple and add to milk and all other ingredients. Mix well and pour into crusts. Refrigerate for several hours or overnight.

Crumb Pie

1 cup warm water
1 cup brown sugar (½ molasses and ½ dark corn syrup)
1 teaspoon baking soda
3 cups flour
1 cup sugar
1 cup shortening
2 pie shells

OVEN 350°

Mix water, brown sugar, and baking soda in saucepan. Separately, mix flour, sugar, and shortening until fine like flour. Put liquid in shells and add crumbs on top. Bake at 350° for 20 to 30 minutes until crumb mixture starts to brown. This will burn quite easily so do not get too hot. Heat until boiling. Put liquid on to cook first and then prepare crumbs.

Foolproof Meringue

3 egg whites
Dash salt
1 cup (½ of 7 ounce jar) marshmallow creme

OVEN 350°

Beat egg whites and salt until soft peaks form. Gradually add marshmallow creme, beating until stiff peaks form. Spread over pie filling, sealing to edge of crust. Bake at 350° for 12 to 15 minutes or until lightly browned. Cool.

Rhubarb Custard Pie

2 cups diced uncooked rhubarb
1 cup brown sugar
2 tablespoons flour or cornstarch
1 tablespoon water
2 egg yolks, beaten
Lump of butter
1 unbaked pie shell

OVEN 375°

Combine rhubarb, brown sugar, and flour or cornstarch. Add water to beaten egg yolks; pour over rhubarb mixture; add lump of butter. Pour into pie shell and bake at 375° for 35 minutes. Whip meringue (recipe follows); add to top of pie and brown.

Meringue

3 egg whites
1 teaspoon vanilla
1 teaspoon cream of tartar
6 tablespoons sugar

OVEN 350°

Beat egg whites with vanilla and cream of tartar until soft peaks form. Gradually add sugar, beating until stiff and glossy peaks form and all sugar is dissolved. Spread meringue over hot filling in 9-inch pie shell, sealing to edge of pastry. Bake at 350° for 12 to 15 minutes, or until meringue is golden. Cool.

Variation: For 8-inch pie use only 2 egg whites and 4 tablespoons sugar with same amount of vanilla and cream of tartar.

Note: Wet knife before cutting a meringue-topped pie.

Kentucky Derby Pie

4 eggs
1 stick butter
¾ cup brown sugar
1 cup white corn syrup
1 cup chocolate chips
1 cup chopped pecans
1 teaspoon vanilla
1 teaspoon flour
1 unbaked pie shell

OVEN 350°

Beat eggs. Melt butter. Mix all ingredients and pour into pie shell. Bake at 350° for 40 to 45 minutes.

Variation: Use 2 eggs and substitute 1 cup sugar for brown sugar.

Black Forest Pie (Low-Fat)

1 (3 ounce) package sugar-free black cherry gelatin
1 (3 ounce) package sugar-free vanilla pudding mix (cook style)
1½ cups water
1 pound dark, sweet, pitted fresh or frozen cherries
½ teaspoon almond extract
1 baked chocolate piecrust

Cook gelatin and pudding in water until thick and clear, about 1½ minutes in microwave. Add cherries; cook until just about to boil. Add almond extract; pour into chocolate piecrust and refrigerate.

Topping:
8 ounces fat-free cream cheese, softened
1 cup fat-free whipped topping
1 teaspoon vanilla
2 teaspoons sugar or sweetener
Chopped nuts (optional)

Blend together and pour over firm pie filling; sprinkle with chopped nuts if desired.

Egg Custard Pie

5 eggs, well beaten
¾ cup sugar
1 cup sweet milk
1 teaspoon vanilla
1 tablespoon butter or cooking oil
1 unbaked pie shell

OVEN 350°

Mix first five ingredients well and pour into unbaked pie shell. Bake for 45 minutes or until filling is firm.

Note: Mix all ingredients in blender for faster mixing, then pour into pie shell and bake.

Shoo-Fly Pie

1 cup flour
⅔ cup brown sugar
1 tablespoon butter
1 cup dark molasses
¾ cup boiling water
1 teaspoon baking soda
1 egg, beaten
1 unbaked pie shell

OVEN 375°

Mix flour, brown sugar, and butter until crumbly. In separate bowl mix molasses, boiling water, baking soda, and beaten egg. Mix molasses mixture with half of crumb mixture, but do not beat. Put combined mixture into pie shell and cover with remaining crumbs. Bake for 11 minutes at 375° and then 30 minutes longer at 350°.

Buttermilk Pie

½ cup butter, softened
1½ to 2 cups sugar
2 to 3 rounded tablespoons flour
3 eggs, unbeaten
½ to 1 cup buttermilk
1 teaspoon vanilla
Dash nutmeg (optional)
1 (9 inch) unbaked pie shell

OVEN 350°

Cream together butter and sugar, mixing well. Add flour and eggs; beat well. Stir in buttermilk, vanilla, and nutmeg. Pour into unbaked pie shell. Bake for 45 to 50 minutes at 350° or until firm. Place on wire rack to cool completely before serving.

Impossible Buttermilk Pie "On the Run"

1½ cups sugar
1 cup buttermilk
½ cup baking mix
⅓ cup butter
1 teaspoon vanilla
3 eggs

OVEN 350°

Heat oven to 350°. Grease pie plate. Beat all ingredients until smooth. Pour into pie plate. Bake 30 minutes or until knife inserted in center comes out clean. Cool 5 minutes. Serve with mixed fruit if desired.

Chocolate Chip Rocky Road Pie

½ cup butter
1 cup dark brown sugar
1 egg, slightly beaten
2 tablespoons hot water
1 teaspoon vanilla
1 cup sifted flour
½ teaspoon baking powder
¼ teaspoon salt
⅛ teaspoon baking soda
½ cup chopped nuts
1 cup mini semisweet chocolate chips
1 cup miniature marshmallows

OVEN 350°

Melt butter over low heat; then stir in brown sugar until well blended. Add egg, hot water, and vanilla. Stir together flour, baking powder, salt, and baking soda. Add to sugar mixture; mix well. Mix in nuts, half of chocolate chips, and half of marshmallows. Spread mixture into two 9-inch pie plates; sprinkle with remaining chips and marshmallows. Bake for 20 minutes. Cool.

Makes 2 pies.

Four-Layer Chocolate Mud Pie

2 sticks margarine
1 cup chopped nuts
2 cups flour

OVEN 350°

Stir together and press onto bottom and sides of 10-inch pie pan. Bake for 10 to 15 minutes at 350°. Cool.

1 (8 ounce) package cream cheese
1 cup powdered sugar
1 cup whipped topping

Beat together until creamy; spread half of mixture into crust.

1 cup sugar
4 tablespoons flour
6 tablespoons cocoa
¼ teaspoon salt
2 cups milk
2 slightly beaten egg yolks
4 tablespoons butter or margarine
1 teaspoon vanilla

In saucepan, blend sugar, flour, cocoa, and salt; add milk. Cook and stir over medium heat. Stir small amount of mixture into egg yolks; return to hot mixture; cook. Add butter and vanilla. Let cool; then spread on top of second layer.

Spread whipped topping on top of third layer. Sprinkle with nuts. Refrigerate until ready to serve.

Variation: Substitute first layer (crust) with vanilla wafer crust (recipe follows).

Vanilla Wafer Crust:

Mix together 1½ cups crushed vanilla wafers (36 wafers) and 6 tablespoons melted butter or margarine. Press into 9-inch pie plate. Chill until set.

Chocolate Almond Pie

½ cup milk
16 large marshmallows
6 chocolate almond candy bars
½ pint whipping cream, whipped
1 (9 inch) baked pie shell

Heat milk in saucepan until hot; dissolve marshmallows in hot milk. Break and add candy bars. Stir until melted. Remove from heat and cool. Fold in whipped cream. Pour into baked 9-inch pie shell. Refrigerate until set. Serve with sweetened whipped cream and chocolate curls.

Turtle Pie

¼ cup butter, melted
24 Oreo cookies, crushed
1 cup chocolate fudge sauce
6 cups pecan praline ice cream
½ cup caramel sauce
½ cup chopped pecans

Mix butter and cookie crumbs. Press into 9-inch pie plate and freeze for 30 minutes. Spread chocolate sauce over bottom. Spread on softened ice cream. Freeze 3 to 4 hours; drizzle on caramel sauce and chopped nuts. Freeze covered until ready to serve.

Smearcase Pie

3 eggs
½ teaspoon nutmeg
½ cup sugar
Pinch salt (about ¼ teaspoon)
1 tablespoon flour
1 cup canned milk (undiluted)
16 ounces cottage cheese (large or small curd)
1 pie shell

OVEN 375°

Combine pie ingredients and beat until blended (use fork). Pour into unbaked pie shell. Sprinkle cinnamon on top. Bake at 375° for 50 to 60 minutes or until knife inserted in center comes out clean. Cool before serving.

Lemonade Pie

1 (6 ounce) can frozen lemonade, partially thawed (can be pink)
1 (14 ounce) can sweetened condensed milk
1 (8 ounce) carton whipped topping
1 graham cracker or shortbread piecrust, baked
1 teaspoon grated lemon rind (optional)

Mix lemonade and sweetened condensed milk together. Stir in whipped topping. Pour into pie shell. Refrigerate overnight.

Option: Add green or yellow food coloring for effect.

Glazed Strawberry Pie

1 quart strawberries
¼ cup cornstarch
1¼ cups cold water
1⅓ cups sugar
⅛ teaspoon salt
1 tablespoon lemon juice
Few drops red food coloring
2 baked pie shells
Whipped cream

Wash, drain, and hull berries. Dissolve cornstarch in water. Add sugar and salt. Place these ingredients in pot and cook over low heat. Stir constantly until thickened and clear. Remove from heat and add lemon juice and coloring to make bright red shade. Pour hot mixture over berries. Mix gently; pour into baked pie shells. Garnish with whipped cream.

Variations: Peaches, blueberries, etc.

Out of This World Pie

1 (20 ounce) can cherry pie filling
¾ cup sugar
1 (20 ounce) can crushed pineapple, with juice
1 tablespoon cornstarch
1 teaspoon red food coloring
1 (3 ounce) box cherry gelatin
4 bananas, sliced
1 cup chopped pecans
2 baked pie shells
Whipped topping

In saucepan combine cherry pie filling, sugar, pineapple with juice, cornstarch, and food coloring. Cook until thick. Remove from heat and add dry gelatin. Allow to cool. Add bananas and pecans. Pour into baked pie shells. Top with whipped topping. Chill.

Fresh Strawberry Pie

Fresh strawberries, washed and sliced (about 4 cups)
1 cup sugar
1 cup water
2 tablespoons cornstarch
⅛ teaspoon salt
3 tablespoons corn syrup
3 tablespoons strawberry gelatin
1 baked pie shell

Spread strawberries in pie shell. Cook next five ingredients slowly for 5 minutes. Add strawberry gelatin. Cool. Pour over fresh berries in pie shell.

Variations:

1. Use raspberries with raspberry gelatin.
2. Add 1 tablespoon cornstarch; slowly add 1 cup 7-UP.

Lemon Sponge Pie

1 cup sugar
1 tablespoon margarine or butter, softened
1 tablespoon flour
¼ teaspoon salt
3 eggs, separated
1 cup milk
1 lemon, for juice and zest
1 unbaked pie shell

OVEN 425°

Cream sugar, margarine, flour, salt, and egg yolks; slowly add milk and zest and juice of lemon. Fold in well-beaten egg whites; pour into pie shell. Bake at 425° for 10 minutes then at 350° for 20 minutes more until light brown on top and knife drawn through pie comes out clean. Cool.

Fresh Peach Pie

¾ cup sugar
3 heaping tablespoons flour
3 tablespoons butter
2 eggs
2 cups fresh peaches, sliced
1 (9 inch) unbaked piecrust

OVEN 400°

Mix first four ingredients together; fold in peaches. Pour into pie shell. Bake at 400° for 35 minutes.

Husband's Peach Pie

Crust:
2⅔ cups flour
1 teaspoon salt
1 cup shortening
7 to 8 tablespoons cold water

Filling:
1 (29 ounce) can peaches in heavy syrup
3 tablespoons reserved peach syrup
3 tablespoons cornstarch
1 cup sugar, divided
3 eggs
⅓ cup buttermilk
½ cup butter, melted
1 teaspoon vanilla

Glaze:
2 tablespoons butter, melted
Sugar

OVEN 400°

Crust: Spoon flour into measuring cup and level. Combine flour and salt in medium bowl. Cut in shortening using pastry blender (or 2 knives) until flour is blended to form pea-size chunks; sprinkle with water, 1 tablespoon at a time. Toss lightly with fork until dough forms ball. Roll out half on floured surface and press into bottom of 10-inch pie plate. Do not bake. Heat oven to 400°.

Filling: Drain peaches; reserve 3 tablespoons syrup; set aside. Cut peaches into small pieces and place in large bowl. Combine cornstarch and 2 to 3 tablespoons sugar. Add reserved peach syrup. Add remaining sugar, eggs, and buttermilk. Mix well. Stir in ½ cup melted butter and vanilla. Pour over peaches. Stir until peaches are coated. Pour filling into unbaked piecrust. Moisten pastry edge with water. Cover pie with top crust. Cut slits or designs in top crust to allow steam to escape.

Glaze: Brush with 2 tablespoons melted butter. Sprinkle with sugar. Bake for 45 minutes or until filling in center is bubbly and crust is golden brown. Cool. Refrigerate leftover pie.

Cherry Cheesecake Pie

1 (8 ounce) package cream cheese, softened
½ cup sugar
1 (8 ounce) tub whipped topping
1 (9 inch) unbaked graham cracker crust
1 (20 ounce) can cherry pie filling

Beat together cream cheese and sugar until creamy. Blend in whipped topping. Pour into crust. Top with cherry pie filling. Chill 3 hours before serving.

Variations: Fat-free/cholesterol-free ingredients may be used. Regular baked piecrust may be substituted for graham cracker crust.

Cherry Cream Cheese Pie

- 1 (8 ounce) package cream cheese (regular, low-fat, or fat-free)
- 1 (14 ounce) can sweetened condensed milk (also regular, low-fat, or fat-free)
- ⅓ cup lemon juice
- 1 teaspoon vanilla
- 1 (9 or 10 inch) graham cracker crust
- 1 can cherries, blueberries, or pineapple

Whip together cream cheese and milk until light; add juice and vanilla; blend. Pour into crust and top with canned fruit. Chill.

Key Lime Pie

- 1 (14 ounce) can sweetened condensed milk (can be fat-free)
- ½ cup key lime or regular lime juice
- 1 (8 ounce) container whipped topping
- 1 graham cracker crust

Beat milk and lime juice at medium speed until smooth and thick. Fold in whipped topping. Cover and refrigerate at least 1 hour.

Key Lime Pie

- 4 egg yolks
- 1 (14 ounce) can sweetened condensed milk
- ½ cup lime juice
- ½ teaspoon cream of tartar
- 6 egg whites
- ¾ cup sugar
- 1 (9 inch) baked pie shell

OVEN 330°

Beat egg yolks until lemon colored. Blend in condensed milk slowly. Add lime juice and mix well. Add cream of tartar to egg whites and beat until foamy. Continue beating, adding sugar 1 tablespoon at a time, until egg whites peak, to make meringue. Fold 6 tablespoons meringue into filling mixture. Pour into baked pie shell. Top with meringue and bake at 330° until golden brown.

Walnut Pie

½ cup brown sugar
½ cup butter
¾ cup sugar
3 eggs
¼ teaspoon salt
¼ cup light corn syrup
½ cup light cream
1½ cups chopped walnuts
½ teaspoon vanilla
1 (8 inch) unbaked pie shell
Whipped topping

OVEN 350°

In double boiler cream together brown sugar and butter. Stir in sugar, eggs, salt, corn syrup, and cream; cook over hot water for 5 minutes, stirring constantly. Remove from heat. Stir in nuts and vanilla. Pour into pie shell. Bake at 350° for 50 minutes. Cool. Top with whipped topping and serve.

Southern Pecan Pie

1 cup light corn syrup
⅔ cup sugar
3 eggs, slightly beaten
1 teaspoon vanilla
⅓ cup butter or margarine
Dash salt
¾ to 1 cup chopped pecans
1 unbaked pie shell
6 pecan halves

OVEN 350°

Mix all ingredients together, adding pecans last. Pour mixture into pie shell. Top with pecan halves. Bake at 350° for approximately 50 minutes.

Serves 6 to 8.

Chocolate Pecan Pie

2 squares unsweetened chocolate
2 tablespoons butter
3 eggs
½ cup sugar
¾ cup dark corn syrup (may use ½ amount of light syrup)
1 cup pecan halves
1 (9 inch) pie shell

OVEN 375°

Melt chocolate and butter together. Beat eggs, sugar, chocolate mixture, and syrup together. Mix in pecans. Pour into pie shell. Bake 40 to 50 minutes, just until set. Serve slightly warm, or cold, with ice cream or whipped cream.

Jell-O Pudding Pecan Pie

- 1 (6 ounce) package vanilla instant pudding mix
- 1½ cups corn syrup
- 1 cup plus 1 tablespoon evaporated milk
- 2 eggs, slightly beaten
- 1½ cups chopped pecans
- 1 (9 inch) unbaked pie shell

OVEN 375°

Blend pudding mix with corn syrup; add milk and eggs; mix well. Add pecans and pour into pie shell. Bake at 375° until top is firm and begins to crack, about 45 to 50 minutes. Cool about 3 hours. Garnish with whipped topping.

Pecan Pie

- ¼ cup butter
- ¾ cup sugar
- 1 tablespoon flour
- Dash salt
- 1 teaspoon vanilla
- 4 eggs
- 1 cup light corn syrup
- ¼ cup dark corn syrup
- 1 cup broken pecans
- 1 unbaked pie shell

OVEN 450°

Cream butter; add sugar and flour gradually. Cream until fluffy. Add salt, vanilla, and eggs. Beat thoroughly; add syrups, beating well. Spread pecans over bottom of unbaked pie shell. Bake 10 minutes at 450°. Add filling. Lower heat to 350° and bake 50 minutes until set.

Peanut Butter Pudding Pie

- 1 cup powdered sugar
- ½ cup creamy peanut butter
- 1 (3 ounce) box vanilla instant pudding mix
- 1 graham cracker crust
- 1 (8 ounce) tub whipped topping

Mix powdered sugar and peanut butter until crumbly. Mix instant pudding as directed on package for pie filling. Sprinkle ⅓ cup peanut butter crumbs on bottom of piecrust. Empty pudding on top. Sprinkle ⅓ cup peanut butter crumbs on top of pudding. Put whipped topping on top and put remaining crumbs on top of whipped topping. Chill in refrigerator.

Chocolate Peanut Butter Pie

2 cups crunchy peanut butter
1 (8 ounce) package fat-free cream cheese, softened
2 cups powdered sugar
1 cup skim milk
3 (8 ounce) containers whipped topping
3 chocolate piecrusts

Mix peanut butter and cream cheese until smooth. Add powdered sugar, milk, and 12 ounces whipped topping (1½ containers). Blend thoroughly and pour into piecrusts, spreading evenly. Top each pie with 4 ounces whipped topping. These pies freeze and keep well. For added freshness, store pies in 1-gallon freezer bags.

Low-Fat, Sugar-Free Peanut Butter Pie

1 (8 ounce) package fat-free cream cheese
½ to ¾ cup low-fat peanut butter
24 packages artificial sweetener
½ cup skim milk
12 ounces low-fat whipped topping
2 graham cracker crusts

Beat cream cheese and peanut butter at room temperature until smooth. Add artificial sweetener. Add milk slowly and continue beating; fold in whipped topping. Keep in freezer. Remove from freezer 30 to 40 minutes before serving.

Peanut Butter Pie

1 (8 ounce) package cream cheese
1 cup powdered sugar
1 cup peanut butter
12 ounces whipped topping
1 graham cracker crust

Mix ingredients, reserving small amount of whipped topping for garnish, if desired. Pour into graham cracker crust.

Peanut Butter Cream Pie

2 egg yolks
4 tablespoons cornstarch
¾ cup sugar
3 tablespoons warm water
2½ cups milk
⅔ cup peanut butter
2 tablespoons butter
1 teaspoon vanilla
1 (9 inch) baked pie shell

Combine egg yolks, cornstarch, sugar, and water. Mix into paste and add milk. Cook over medium heat, stirring constantly, until mixture begins to thicken. Remove from heat and beat in peanut butter, butter, and vanilla. Pour into pie shell; top with meringue.

Crunchy Peanut Butter Pie

3 eggs, separated
1 cup sugar
2 tablespoons cornstarch
2 cups milk
2 heaping tablespoons crunchy peanut butter
⅛ teaspoon salt (optional)
1 baked pie shell or graham cracker crust

OVEN 350°

Beat egg yolks until creamy. Mix sugar and cornstarch. Add to egg yolks. Add milk, peanut butter, and salt. Cook until thick. Pour batter into pie shell. Beat egg whites and place on top of pie. Bake in 350° oven until top is brown.

Raisin Cream Smoothie Pie

Crust:
1 cup flour
¼ teaspoon salt
⅓ cup shortening
2 to 3 tablespoons cold water

Cut together until crumbly. Sprinkle with cold water. Toss lightly with fork until dough is moist enough to hold together. Form into ball. Roll out on floured board to 11-inch circle. Fit loosely into 9-inch pie pan. Fold edge to form standing rim; flute.

Filling:
3 eggs, slightly beaten
1¼ cups sugar
⅓ teaspoon salt
1 teaspoon cinnamon
¼ teaspoon cloves

1¼ cups sour cream
1½ cups raisins

Mix eggs, sugar, salt, cinnamon, and cloves thoroughly. Blend in sour cream and raisins. Pour into pastry-lined pan. Bake at 400° for 10 minutes, then at 325° for 30 to 35 minutes, until tests done.

Raisin Cream Pie

1 box Jiffy piecrust mix (2 crusts)
1 zucchini, peeled and sliced like apple pie-size pieces
Cinnamon to taste
Nutmeg to taste
Salt to taste
2 tablespoons flour
Juice of 1 lemon (optional)
⅔ cup sugar
2 to 3 tablespoons margarine

OVEN 350°

Mix and roll out dough for bottom crust for 8- or 9-inch pie plate. Sprinkle zucchini with cinnamon, nutmeg, and salt. Add flour and lemon juice, if desired. Roll out top crust; spread margarine over crust. Press on top of zucchini. Run water over top. Sprinkle sugar over top crust. Make cuts throughout top crust. Bake at 350° for 1 hour; leave in warm oven 30 minutes.

Best-Ever Sweet Potato Pie

1 cup cooked mashed sweet potatoes
⅓ cup butter, melted
2 eggs, beaten
⅓ cup milk or half-and-half
½ teaspoon baking powder
Pinch salt
1 teaspoon ground nutmeg
1 teaspoon vanilla
1 cup sugar, or less if desired
1 unbaked pie shell

OVEN 400°

Blend all ingredients with electric mixer or by hand with wooden spoon. Pour into unbaked pie shell. Bake at 400° for about 30 minutes or until golden brown and puffy.

Sugar-Free Pumpkin Pie

3 ounces light cream cheese
1 cup plus 1 tablespoon skim or low-fat milk
1½ cups whipped topping
1 graham cracker crust
1 (6 ounce) package vanilla sugar-free instant pudding mix
1 teaspoon cinnamon
¼ teaspoon cloves
½ teaspoon nutmeg
1 (16 ounce) can pumpkin

Mix cream cheese and 1 tablespoon milk with wire whisk until smooth. Gently stir in whipped topping. Spread on bottom of crust. Add pudding to 1 cup milk and beat until smooth. Add remaining ingredients and mix well. Spread on cream cheese layer and refrigerate at least 2 hours. Garnish with whipped cream or nuts.

Impossible Pumpkin Pie

¾ cup sugar
½ cup baking mix
2 tablespoons margarine or butter
1 (12 ounce) can evaporated milk
2 eggs
1 (16 ounce) can pumpkin
2½ teaspoons pumpkin pie spice, or any spice you like
2 teaspoons vanilla

OVEN 350°

Lightly grease 10-inch pie plate. Beat all ingredients until smooth, 1 minute in blender on high speed or 2 minutes by hand beater. Pour into pie plate. Bake until golden brown and tests done, 50 to 55 minutes. Refrigerate leftovers.

Honey Pumpkin Pie

2 cups pumpkin
1 cup honey, plus ¼ cup brown sugar
3 eggs
1 (12 ounce) can evaporated milk
½ teaspoon salt
½ teaspoon ginger
1 teaspoon cinnamon
½ teaspoon nutmeg (optional)
⅛ teaspoon cloves (optional)
1 unbaked pie shell
1 cup chopped pecans

OVEN 450°

Mix together first nine ingredients and pour into unbaked pie shell; add pecans. Bake at 450° for 10 minutes, then at 325° for 45 minutes.

Mock Apple Pie

2 cups water
1½ cups sugar
2 teaspoons cream of tartar
24 Ritz crackers
1 (9 inch) unbaked piecrust
¼ stick butter or margarine
1 teaspoon cinnamon

OVEN 425°

Combine water, sugar, and cream of tartar in saucepan. Bring to boil. Add Ritz crackers and boil for 2 minutes. Do not stir! Let cool and pour into unbaked piecrust. Dot with butter or margarine over top. Sprinkle with cinnamon. Bake at 425° until crust is browned. Let cool completely. Serve with scoop of ice cream on each slice of pie, if desired.

Apple Cream Pie

¾ cup sugar
2 tablespoons flour
1 cup sour cream
1 egg, beaten well
½ teaspoon vanilla
⅛ teaspoon salt
2 cups finely chopped tart apples
1 unbaked pie shell

OVEN 450°

Combine sugar and flour. Add sour cream, egg, vanilla, and salt; beat until smooth. Add apples. Mix thoroughly. Pour into pie shell. Bake at 450° for 15 minutes. Reduce heat to 325° and bake for 30 more minutes. Remove from oven.

Topping:
⅓ cup sugar
1 teaspoon cinnamon
⅓ cup flour
¼ cup butter, softened

Combine all topping ingredients and mix thoroughly. Sprinkle over pie. Return to oven. Bake at 325° for additional 20 minutes.

Swedish Apple Pie

Enough apples peeled and sliced to fill pie pan two-thirds full
1 tablespoon sugar
1 teaspoon cinnamon
¾ cup butter, melted
1 cup sugar
1 cup flour
1 egg
½ cup chopped nuts
Pinch salt

OVEN 350°

Fill pie pan two-thirds full with apples. Combine 1 tablespoon sugar with cinnamon; sprinkle over apples. In small bowl combine butter, 1 cup sugar, flour, egg, nuts, and salt; mix thoroughly and spoon over apples. Bake in 350° oven for 35 minutes or until golden brown.

Caramel Crunch Apple Pie

1 (9 inch) piecrust
36 caramels
2 tablespoons water
4 cups apples, peeled and sliced

OVEN 375°

Roll piecrust out to 12 inches; place in pie pan and flute edge. Melt caramels in 2 tablespoons water until smooth. Place apple slices in piecrust, pour caramel over.

Topping:
¾ cup flour
⅓ cup sugar
½ teaspoon cinnamon
⅓ cup margarine
½ cup chopped walnuts

Mix together flour, sugar, and cinnamon; cut in margarine, then add nuts. Sprinkle over top of caramel and bake for 40 to 45 minutes.

Serves 8.

English Apple Pie

Heavy cream or half-and-half (optional)
½ cup margarine
½ cup packed brown sugar
1 cup flour
2 teaspoons cinnamon, divided
3 tablespoons water
½ cup chopped pecans
4 large cooking apples, peeled and sliced (about 6 cups)
½ cup sugar

OVEN 370°

Mix and beat cream (optional), margarine, and brown sugar until fluffy. Stir in flour, 1 teaspoon cinnamon, and water until smooth and thick. Stir in pecans. Mound apples in 9-inch pie plate. Mix sugar with remaining teaspoon cinnamon. Sprinkle over apples. Spoon pecan topping over apples in dollops. Bake on lowest rack for 45 to 50 minutes until apples are tender when pierced. Top with favorite topping and serve in bowls if desired.

Crustless Apple Pie

¼ cup butter
1 cup sugar
1 egg
1 cup flour
½ teaspoon baking powder
½ teaspoon baking soda
½ teaspoon nutmeg
¼ teaspoon salt
1 teaspoon cinnamon
2 cups apples, peeled and thinly sliced
½ cup chopped nuts

OVEN 350°

Cream together butter, sugar, and egg. Sift together in another bowl flour, baking powder, soda, nutmeg, salt, and cinnamon. Add to creamed mixture. Fold in apples and nuts. Put in greased pie plate. Bake 40 to 45 minutes at 350°. Serve warm with vanilla ice cream or whipped topping.

Diabetic Spiced Pumpkin Pie

Pastry for 9-inch shell
1 (16 ounce) can pumpkin
1 (12 ounce) can evaporated skim milk
3 eggs
5½ teaspoons liquid artificial sweetener, or 18 packets artificial sweetener
¼ teaspoon salt
1 teaspoon ground cinnamon
½ teaspoon ground ginger
¼ teaspoon ground nutmeg
⅛ teaspoon ground cloves

OVEN 425°

Roll pastry on floured surface to circle 1 inch larger than inverted pie dish. Ease pastry into dish; trim and flute edge. Beat pumpkin, evaporated milk, and eggs in medium bowl; beat in remaining ingredients. Pour mixture into pastry shell. Bake at 425° for 15 minutes. Reduce heat to 350°. Bake about 40 minutes.

Sugarless Apple Pie

1 tablespoon cornstarch
1 (12 ounce) can apple juice concentrate
4 cups sliced Golden Delicious apples
½ tablespoon butter
Dash salt
1 teaspoon apple pie spice
1 unbaked pie shell
3 packets artificial sweetener

OVEN 400°

Mix cornstarch and apple juice. Cook over medium heat, stirring until mixture begins to clear. Stir in apples, butter, salt, and pie spice. Pour into unbaked pie shell. Sprinkle sweetener on top. Bake at 400° for 15 minutes, then at 350° for 30 minutes.

Spring Temptation Pie

1 cup boiling water
1 (3 ounce) package lemon gelatin
1 cup orange or lemon sherbet
2 cups whipped topping
2 cups miniature marshmallows
1 (8 ounce) can crushed pineapple, drained (optional)
1 (9 inch) prepared graham cracker crust

Stir boiling water into gelatin in medium bowl for 2 minutes or until completely dissolved. Stir in sherbet; mix well until melted. Refrigerate 25 minutes or until gelatin mixture is slightly thickened. Fold in whipped topping, marshmallows, and pineapple. Pour into crust. Freeze until firm (overnight is best).

Makes 6 to 8 servings.

Sugar-free: Use sugar-free gelatin and unsweetened pineapple.

Maryanz Sugar-Free Pie

1 (6 ounce) package sugar-free gelatin
2 cups boiling water
1 (12 or 16 ounce) package frozen unsweetened berries
2 baked pie shells
Sugar-free whipped topping

Mix gelatin with 2 cups boiling water (do not add any more water). In blender, put frozen berries; add hot gelatin and mix thoroughly, then pour into pie shells and chill in refrigerator. When solid add whipped topping.

Diabetic Fruit or Berry Pie

3 to 4 cups fruit or berries
6 ounces frozen apple juice (do not dilute)
1 teaspoon cinnamon
2 tablespoons cornstarch
2 tablespoons margarine
2 unbaked piecrusts

OVEN 350°

In saucepan cook fruit or berries, apple juice, and cinnamon until boiling. Remove from heat. Add cornstarch that has been mixed with a little cool water. Stir while adding cornstarch. Pour into piecrust. Top with 2 tablespoons margarine. Add top crust. Bake at 350° for 40 to 45 minutes or until crust is done.

No-Sugar-Added Pineapple Cream Pie

1 can crushed pineapple, with juice
1 (8 ounce) container fat-free sour cream
1 (3 ounce) box vanilla sugar-free
   pudding mix
1 graham cracker crust

Pour pineapple with juice into bowl. Mix in sour cream. Slowly mix in pudding mix. Pour into graham cracker crust and chill at least 2 hours.

Cookies

Easter Story Cookies

1 cup whole pecans
Zippered baggie
Wooden spoon
1 teaspoon vinegar
3 egg whites
Pinch salt
1 cup sugar
Tape
Bible

OVEN 300°

Place pecans in baggie and let children beat them with wooden spoon to break into small pieces. Explain that after Jesus was arrested He was beaten by the Roman soldiers. Read John 19:1–3.

Let each child smell vinegar. Put 1 teaspoon vinegar into mixing bowl. Explain that when Jesus was thirsty on the cross He was given vinegar to drink. Read John 19:28–30.

Add egg whites to vinegar. Eggs represent life. Explain that Jesus gave His life to give us life. Read John 10:10–11.

Sprinkle a little salt into each child's hand. Let each taste it, then brush the rest into the bowl. Explain that the salt represents the salty tears shed by Jesus' followers, and the bitterness of our own sin. Read Luke 23:27.

So far the ingredients are not very appetizing. Add 1 cup sugar. Explain that the sweetest part of the story is that Jesus died because He loves us. He wants us to know and belong to Him. Read Psalm 34:8 and John 3:16.

Beat with mixer on high speed for 12 to 15 minutes until stiff peaks form. Explain that the color white represents the purity in God's eyes of those whose sins have been cleansed by Jesus. Read Isaiah 1:18 and John 3:1–3.

Fold in broken nuts. Drop dough by teaspoons onto waxed-paper-covered cookie sheet. Explain that each mound represents the rocky tomb where Jesus' body was laid. Read Matthew 27:57–60.

Put cookie sheet in oven, close door, and turn oven off. Give each child a piece of tape and seal oven door. Explain that Jesus' tomb was sealed. Read Matthew 27:65–66.

Go to bed! Explain that they may feel sad to leave the cookies in the oven overnight. Jesus' followers were in despair when the tomb was sealed. Read John 16:20, 22.

On Easter morning, open the oven and give everyone a cookie. Notice the cracked surface and take a bite. The cookies are hollow! On the first Easter Jesus' followers were amazed to find the tomb open and empty. Read Matthew 28:1–9.

"He has risen"—you can be a victor from the dark domain because He arose!

Pecan Sandies

1 cup butter or margarine
⅓ cup sugar
2 teaspoons water
2 teaspoons vanilla
1 cup flour
1 cup chopped pecans
Powdered sugar

OVEN 325°

Cream butter and sugar; add water and vanilla; mix well. Add flour and pecans. Chill 3 to 4 hours. Shape into balls or fingers. Bake for 20 minutes at 325°. Cool and roll in powdered sugar.

Makes up to 5 dozen.

Pecan Pie Cookies

1 cup flour
½ cup oats
½ cup butter, softened
¾ cup brown sugar
3 eggs
¾ cup light corn syrup
1 cup broken pecans
1 teaspoon vanilla
¼ teaspoon salt
1 tablespoon flour

OVEN 350°

Mix together 1 cup flour, oats, butter, and brown sugar until they resemble fine crumbs. Press into bottom of well-greased 9x9-inch pan. Bake 15 minutes. While crust bakes, beat together eggs, corn syrup, pecans, vanilla, salt, and 1 tablespoon flour. Pour over hot crust. Bake 25 to 30 minutes. Cool and cut.

Makes 16 cookies.

Smorbakelser (Swedish Butter Cookies)

1 cup butter
2 egg yolks
½ cup sugar
1 teaspoon almond extract
1 teaspoon vanilla
2 cups flour

OVEN 400°

Cream butter, egg yolks, sugar, and extracts together until light and fluffy. Add flour and mix well. Dough will be soft but not sticky. Roll out (do not over-flour surface) and cut with cookie cutter, or use in cookie press. Bake for 8 to 10 minutes. They burn easily, so be careful.

Forgotten Kisses

2 egg whites
¼ teaspoon cream of tartar
1 cup sugar
1 teaspoon vanilla
1 (16 ounce) package chocolate chips

OVEN 375°

Beat egg whites until foamy; add cream of tartar and beat until stiff peaks form. Beat in sugar and vanilla; fold in chocolate chips. Drop by teaspoonfuls onto ungreased cookie sheet. Place in oven and shut off heat; leave in oven 5 hours or overnight, without opening the door and peeking.

You can substitute crushed peppermint sticks or cinnamon imperials for chocolate chips.

Makes 40 cookies.

Chewy Chocolate Cookies

1 package (2-layer size) chocolate cake mix
2 eggs
1 cup Miracle Whip
1 cup chocolate chips
½ cup chopped walnuts (optional)

OVEN 350°

Mix cake mix, eggs, and dressing in large bowl with electric mixer on medium speed until blended. Stir in remaining ingredients. Drop rounded teaspoonfuls onto greased cookie sheet. Bake 10 to 12 minutes or until edges are lightly browned.

Makes 4 dozen.

Chocolate Butterfinger Balls

Mix together and roll into balls:
2 cups crunchy peanut butter
3 cups crisp rice cereal
1 stick margarine
1 pound powdered sugar

Melt in double boiler:
1 large Hershey bar
1 (16 ounce) package chocolate chips
1 teaspoon vanilla
1 slab paraffin wax

Dip balls into chocolate mixture. Place on sheets of waxed paper and chill.

Thin Chocolate Chip Cookies

1½ cups sugar
2 sticks (1 cup) margarine
2 eggs
2 teaspoons vanilla
2½ cups Grape-Nuts Flakes cereal
1 cup chocolate chips
⅛ teaspoon salt
1 teaspoon baking soda
2 cups flour

OVEN 350°

Cream sugar and margarine together; add eggs and stir; add vanilla and stir. Add cereal and chocolate chips; stir together. Put salt and baking soda into flour and add to creamed mixture, a small amount at a time. Stir well. Drop by teaspoonfuls onto cookie sheet and bake for 20 minutes or until golden brown. Bake less time for smaller cookie.

Krispie Chocolate Cookies

1 cup butter
1 cup sugar
1 cup brown sugar
2 eggs
1 teaspoon vanilla
1 teaspoon salt
1 teaspoon baking soda
2½ cups flour
1½ cup oats
1½ cups crisp rice cereal
2 cups chocolate chips

OVEN 350°

Cream together butter and sugars. Beat in eggs and vanilla. In separate bowl, combine salt, baking soda, and flour. Mix into creamed mixture. Stir in oats and crisp rice cereal, then chocolate chips. Drop by spoonfuls onto cookie sheets and bake 10 minutes.

Big Chocolate Chip Cookies

1 cup margarine
1 cup brown sugar
1 egg
1 teaspoon vanilla
2 cups flour
1 teaspoon baking soda
½ teaspoon salt
1 cup rolled oats
1 (12 ounce) package chocolate chips
½ cup chopped nuts (optional)
½ cup raisins (optional)

OVEN 350°

Combine margarine, brown sugar, egg, and vanilla. Add flour, baking soda, and salt. Add oats, chocolate chips, nuts, and raisins; mix well. Measure ¼ cup dough for each cookie, making each cookie 3 inches around and ½ inch thick. Bake on lightly greased cookie sheet for 15 minutes. Let cool 5 minutes before removing.

Chocolate Chip Coconut Cookies

⅓ cup shortening
⅓ cup butter
½ cup sugar
½ cup brown sugar
1 egg
1 teaspoon vanilla
1½ cups flour
½ teaspoon baking soda
½ teaspoon salt
1 (6 ounce) package chocolate chips
¼ package coconut
1 to 2 cups oats

OVEN 375°

Mix shortening, butter, sugar, brown sugar, egg, and vanilla. Blend in flour, baking soda, and salt. Mix in chocolate chips, coconut, and oats. Drop rounded teaspoonfuls 2 inches apart onto ungreased baking sheet. Bake 8 to 10 minutes. Cool slightly before removing from baking sheet.

World's Greatest Chocolate Chip Cookies

1 cup oil
1 cup margarine, softened
1 cup brown sugar
1 cup sugar
1 egg
1 teaspoon vanilla
3½ cups flour
1 teaspoon salt
1 teaspoon cream of tartar
1 teaspoon baking soda
1 cup quick oats
1 cup crisp rice cereal
6 ounces butterscotch or peanut butter chips
1 (12 ounce) package chocolate chips

OVEN 350°

Blend oil and margarine. Cream with sugars, egg, and vanilla. Sift together dry ingredients. Mix with oats, crisp rice cereal, and chips. Bake on greased cookie sheet for 12 minutes or until lightly browned.

Chocolate Chip Cookie Balls

1 box Duncan Hines devil's food cake mix
1 egg
¾ cup vegetable oil
1½ cups chocolate chips
½ cup chopped pecans

OVEN 350°

Mix all ingredients together. Roll in 1-inch balls. Place on ungreased cookie sheet. Bake 5 to 7 minutes. Cool on rack. Store in airtight container.

Makes about 2 dozen.

Chocolate Chip Cream Cheese Cookies

4 egg yolks
2 cups butter (do not substitute)
2 cups sugar
2 (8 ounce) packages cream cheese
2 tablespoons almond extract
4 cups flour
Pinch salt

OVEN 375°

Combine eggs, butter, and sugar. Add cream cheese and almond extract. Combine flour and salt and add to creamed mixture. Drop by spoonfuls onto cookie sheets and bake until edges turn light brown, about 10 minutes.

Double Chocolate Mint Chip Cookies

1 (10 ounce) package mint-flavored semisweet chocolate morsels, divided
1¼ cups flour
¾ teaspoon baking soda
½ cup butter, softened
½ cup firmly packed brown sugar
¼ cup sugar
½ teaspoon vanilla
1 egg
½ cup chopped nuts (optional)

OVEN 375°

Melt ¾ cup mint chips over boiling water (or microwave: melt on high 1 minute and stir; repeat). Stir until smooth. Cool to room temperature. In bowl, combine flour and baking soda; set aside. In large bowl beat butter, brown sugar, sugar, and vanilla until creamy. Add melted morsels and egg; beat well. Gradually blend in flour mixture. Stir in remaining morsels and nuts, if desired. Drop by rounded tablespoonfuls onto ungreased cookie sheets. Bake for 8 to 9 minutes. Allow to stand 2 to 3 minutes before removing from cookie sheets; cool completely.

Pudding 'n' Chocolate Chip Cookies

2 packages vanilla pudding mix (instant or regular)
2 cups baking mix
½ cup vegetable oil or applesauce
2 eggs
6 tablespoons milk
1 cup chocolate chips

OVEN 350°

Mix ingredients in order given. Drop onto ungreased cookie sheet by teaspoonfuls. Bake for 8 to 10 minutes.

Very Best Oatmeal Pan Cookies

1 stick margarine
1 cup brown sugar
1 egg
2¼ cups oats
2 teaspoons baking powder
½ teaspoon salt
1 teaspoon vanilla

OVEN 425°

Mix ingredients and press into greased pan, about ½ inch thick. Bake until brown, about 10 minutes. Cut while still warm.

Chocolate Chip Treasure Cookies

1 (14 ounce) can sweetened condensed milk
½ cup butter, softened
1½ cups graham cracker crumbs
½ cup flour
2 teaspoons baking powder
1½ cups flaked coconut
2 cups mini semisweet chocolate chips
1 cup chopped pecans
1 cup raisins

OVEN 375°

Beat condensed milk and butter. Add mixture of graham cracker crumbs, flour, and baking powder. Mix well. Add remaining ingredients. Drop by spoonfuls onto greased cookie sheets. Bake 9 to 10 minutes until lightly brown.

Makes 48 or more cookies, depending on size.

Oatmeal-Raisin Cookies

1 cup shortening
2 cups brown sugar
2 eggs
1 teaspoon baking soda
1 teaspoon salt
2 cups flour
2 cups oats
1 cup raisins

OVEN 375°

Cream shortening, sugar, and eggs. Mix in sifted baking soda, salt, and flour. After this is mixed well, add oats and raisins and mix well. Drop by teaspoonfuls onto cookie sheet. Bake for 10 to 12 minutes.

Makes 4 dozen.

Powdered Oatmeal Cookies

1½ cups shortening
3 cups brown sugar
3 eggs, beaten
1½ teaspoons vanilla
2¼ cups flour
¾ teaspoon salt
1½ teaspoons baking powder
1½ teaspoons baking soda
4½ cups oats
Powdered sugar

OVEN 350°

With mixer beat shortening, brown sugar, eggs, and vanilla. Mix together flour, salt, baking powder, baking soda, and oats; mix together with other ingredients. Chill overnight. Make balls and roll in powdered sugar. Grease cookie sheet. Bake for 8 to 10 minutes.

Oatmeal Chocolate Chip Cookies

1½ cups flour
2½ cups oats
1 teaspoon salt
¾ cup brown sugar
¾ cup sugar
1 cup shortening
2 eggs
1 teaspoon vanilla
1 teaspoon baking soda
1 cup chocolate chips
½ cup chopped nuts

OVEN 400°

Mix together flour, oats, and salt. Cream sugars and shortening; add eggs, vanilla, and baking soda dissolved in hot water. Add chocolate chips and nuts. Bake until light brown.

No-Bake Oatmeal Fudge Cookies

½ cup margarine
½ cup milk
2 cups sugar
1 tablespoon cocoa
3 cups oats
¾ cup peanut butter
1 tablespoon vanilla

Mix margarine, milk, sugar, and cocoa. Bring to rolling boil. Boil 1 minute. Remove from heat and add rest of ingredients. Mix well; drop by tablespoonfuls onto waxed paper. Let cool and eat.

Cocoa Oatmeal Chocolate Chip Cookies

1¾ cups boiling water
1 cup quick-cooking oats
1 cup brown sugar
1 cup sugar
½ cup margarine
2 eggs
1¾ cups flour
1 teaspoon baking soda
1 teaspoon baking powder
1 tablespoon cocoa
¾ cup chopped nuts
1 (12 ounce) package chocolate chips

OVEN 350°

Pour water over oats; let stand 10 minutes. Add sugars and margarine. Stir until melted. Add eggs. Add dry ingredients. Mix well. Add half of chips. Pour into greased and floured 9x13-inch pan. Sprinkle nuts and rest of chips on top. Bake about 40 minutes.

Oatmeal Drop Cookies

2 cups sifted flour
1½ cups sugar
1 teaspoon baking powder
½ teaspoon baking soda
½ teaspoon salt
1 teaspoon cinnamon
3 cups rolled oats
1 cup raisins
¾ to 1 cup chocolate chips (optional)
1 cup oil
2 eggs
½ cup milk

OVEN 375°

Sift flour, sugar, baking powder, baking soda, salt, and cinnamon. Mix in oats and raisins, also chocolate chips if desired. Add in order oil, eggs, and milk. Mix until thoroughly blended. Drop by teaspoonfuls onto cookie sheet. Bake for 10 minutes.

Makes about 6 dozen.

Oatmeal Cookies

2 cups sugar
½ cup sweetened condensed milk
1 stick butter
3 tablespoons cocoa
½ cup peanut butter
2½ cups oats
2 teaspoons vanilla

Cook sugar, milk, butter, and cocoa for 1½ minutes (bring to boil). Remove from stove; put in peanut butter and stir well. Add oats and vanilla. Stir well. Drop by spoonfuls on waxed paper. Cool until firm.

Holiday Fruit Drop Cookies

1 cup shortening
2 cups brown sugar
2 eggs
½ cup sour milk or ⅔ cup buttermilk
3½ cups flour
1 teaspoon baking soda
1 teaspoon salt
1 cup chopped nuts
2 cups dates, cut into small pieces, or 1 cup candied cherries and 1 cup dates
2 cups candied cherries, cut into small pieces

OVEN 400°

Mix shortening, sugar, and eggs well. Stir in milk. Blend dry ingredients and stir into shortening mixture. Add nuts, dates, and cherries. Chill 1 hour. Heat oven. Drop dough by spoonfuls on greased baking sheet or make into balls. Bake 8 to 10 minutes.

Makes 8 dozen.

Christmas Cookies

2 cups sugar
½ teaspoon salt
1 cup shortening
1 ounce baking ammonia
1 tablespoon vanilla
2 cups sweetened condensed milk
4 cups flour, just enough to stiffen

OVEN 350°

Mix all ingredients together. Roll out about ½ inch thick; cut out with favorite cookie cutter. Bake 10 minutes. Decorate with vanilla icing and sugar sprinkles.

Makes about 11 to 12 dozen.

Baker's Note: Baking ammonia can be purchased through a baking catalog such as King Arthur Flour's Baking Catalog.

Christmas Eve Cookies

1 cup sugar
½ cup butter
½ cup shortening
1 egg, separated
2 cups flour
½ teaspoon salt
1½ tablespoons cinnamon
1½ cups chopped nuts

OVEN 325°

Grease and flour 10x15-inch pan. Cream sugar, butter, and shortening. Add egg yolk and dry ingredients. Press into pan. Beat egg white until foamy and spread very thinly over batter. Press on nuts. Bake for about 30 minutes. Cut into squares. Place on pretty plate with sprig of holly and red bow.

Holly Cookies

⅓ cup butter
16 marshmallows
1 teaspoon green food coloring
1 teaspoon vanilla
2½ cups cornflakes
Red cinnamon candies

Melt butter and marshmallows in double boiler. Blend in food coloring and vanilla. Place cornflakes in large bowl; pour mixture over cornflakes and mix lightly with fork. Drop cookies on waxed paper or form into wreath. Sprinkle with cinnamon candies and allow to set. No refrigeration needed.

Sour Cream Christmas Cookies

1 cup shortening
1 cup margarine
2 cups sugar
2 eggs
2 teaspoons baking soda
¾ teaspoon salt
1 teaspoon baking powder
2 teaspoons vanilla
1 teaspoon lemon juice
1 teaspoon nutmeg
6 cups flour
1 cup sour cream
1 cup buttermilk

OVEN 375°

Melt shortening and margarine together; cream with sugar, eggs, baking soda, salt, and baking powder; mix well. Add vanilla, lemon juice, and nutmeg. Alternately add flour, sour cream, and buttermilk. Chill overnight, uncovered. Roll and cut on floured surface. Bake for 5 to 8 minutes, or until soft in middle.

Peanut Oatmeal Cookies

1 cup flour
½ teaspoon baking soda
½ cup margarine or butter
½ cup peanut butter
⅓ cup sugar
⅓ cup packed brown sugar
½ cup shredded carrot
2 egg whites
½ teaspoon vanilla
1 cup rolled oats

OVEN 375°

In bowl stir together flour and baking soda. In large mixer bowl beat margarine with electric mixer on medium speed for 30 seconds. Add peanut butter, sugar, and brown sugar; beat until fluffy. Add carrot, egg whites, and vanilla; beat well. Add dry ingredients to beaten mixture; beat well. Stir in oats. Drop dough by rounded teaspoonfuls, 2 inches apart, onto ungreased cookie sheet. Bake about 10 minutes or until done. Remove cookies from cookie sheet. Cool on wire rack.

Ribbon Christmas Cookies

2 sticks butter
1¾ cups sugar
1 egg
1 teaspoon vanilla
2½ cups flour
1¼ teaspoons baking powder
¼ teaspoon salt

Add below ingredients to taste:
A few drops green food coloring
Mint extract
Semisweet chocolate chips
Walnuts
Maraschino cherries
A few drops red food coloring

OVEN 375°

Cream butter and sugar. Add egg and vanilla; mix well. Mix together dry ingredients and add to creamed mixture. Divide into 3 parts. Chill part 1; add green food coloring and mint extract. Part 2: Add semisweet chocolate and walnuts. Part 3: Add maraschino cherries (and red food coloring if needed). Place aluminum foil in bread pan. Pack dough in pan one part at a time then chill overnight. Pull dough out of pan by holding onto foil. Cut in half lengthwise, then slice about ¼ inch thick. Bake for 8 to 10 minutes.

Easy Peanut Butter Cookies

1 (14 ounce) can sweetened condensed milk
¾ to 1 cup peanut butter
1 egg
1 teaspoon vanilla extract
2 cups biscuit baking mix

OVEN 350°

In large mixer bowl, beat sweetened condensed milk, peanut butter, egg, and vanilla until smooth. Add biscuit mix; mix well. Chill at least 1 hour. Shape into 1-inch balls. Place 2 inches apart on ungreased baking sheets. Flatten with fork. Bake 6 to 8 minutes or until lightly browned (do not overbake). Cool. Store tightly covered at room temperature.

Kourabiedes (Greek Christmas Cookies)

1 pound unsalted butter or margarine
3 tablespoons powdered sugar
2 egg yolks
1 teaspoon vanilla
5 cups flour, sifted
Powdered sugar for topping

OVEN 375°

Cream butter until light and fluffy. Beat in sugar. Add egg yolks and vanilla. Gradually work in sifted flour to make soft dough. You will need to discard spoon and use your hands after certain point, something children love to do. With floured hands shape into small crescents or oval shapes about ½ inch thick. Place 1 inch apart on ungreased cookie sheet. Bake for about 20 minutes or until bottoms are very lightly browned. Place cookies on plate and sift sugar over tops and sides. Cool thoroughly before storing.

Grandma's Peanut Butter Cookies

1 cup butter or margarine
¾ cup brown sugar
¾ cup sugar
1 teaspoon vanilla
2 eggs, beaten
1 cup peanut butter, creamy or crunchy
1 cup flour
1 cup bran
¾ cup rolled oats
2 teaspoons baking soda

OVEN 350°

Melt butter or margarine; beat together with sugars, vanilla, eggs, and peanut butter. Combine flour, bran, oats, and baking soda. Stir flour mixture into butter mixture. Drop by teaspoonfuls onto ungreased cookie sheet. Bake for 15 to 18 minutes.

Quick and Easy Peanut Butter Cookies

1 cup peanut butter (creamy or crunchy)
1 egg
1 cup sugar

OVEN 350°

Spray two cookie sheets with vegetable cooking spray. Mix ingredients together and drop by spoonfuls; bake about 8 to 12 minutes. Do not brown cookies on top as they will burn on bottoms.

Makes 36.

Variations: You may add nuts, M&M's, raisins, oats, or coconut.

Cocoa Peanut Butter Cherries

½ cup peanut butter
½ cup butter
1½ cups sugar
2 eggs
3 teaspoons cocoa
1 teaspoon vanilla
1 cup flour
1 cup chopped pecans

OVEN 350°

Grease and flour 9x13-inch pan. Melt peanut butter and butter in bowl over hot water. Add remaining ingredients and stir until blended. Bake for 25 to 30 minutes; cool and cut into squares.

Makes about 2 dozen.

Peanut Butter Cornflake Cookies

1 cup sugar
1 cup light corn syrup
1½ cups peanut butter
1 teaspoon vanilla
8 cups cornflakes

Put sugar and syrup in saucepan; heat to full boil. Remove from heat and add peanut butter and vanilla. Beat until smooth. Pour over cornflakes; stir until flakes are completely coated. Drop by teaspoonfuls onto waxed paper.

Makes 3 dozen.

Peanut Clusters

1 pound chocolate almond bark
1 (12 ounce) package chocolate chips
1 cup chunky peanut butter
1 large (12 to 16 ounce) package salted peanuts

Melt almond bark in microwave (about 3 minutes; adjust time for your microwave). Add chocolate chips; stir until melted. Add peanut butter and nuts; mix well. Drop by spoonfuls onto waxed paper. Chill until set.

Pumpkin-Butterscotch Cookies

1½ cups pumpkin
½ cup margarine
1 cup sugar
½ teaspoon salt
1 teaspoon vanilla
1 cup chopped walnuts
1 egg
2 cups unsifted flour
1 teaspoon salt
1 teaspoon baking powder
1 teaspoon cinnamon
1 package butterscotch chips

OVEN 375°

Mix all ingredients in order given; drop by spoonfuls onto greased cookie sheet. Bake for 12 to 14 minutes.

Makes 4 dozen.

Variations: Raisins, pecans, or coconut may be substituted for butterscotch chips.

Also, 3 ripe bananas can be substituted for pumpkin.

Pumpkin Cookies

1 cup margarine
2 cups sugar
2 cups pumpkin
1 cup chopped nuts or raisins
2 teaspoons vanilla
2 teaspoons cinnamon
2 teaspoons baking powder
2 teaspoons baking soda
4 cups flour

OVEN 375°

Mix together margarine, sugar, pumpkin, nuts (or raisins), and vanilla. Sift together other ingredients and mix together with pumpkin mixture. Drop onto greased cookie sheet. Bake for 12 to 15 minutes.

Pumpkin Nut Cookies

¼ cup shortening
½ cup sugar
1 egg, beaten
½ cup cooked pumpkin
1 cup sifted flour
2 teaspoons baking powder
½ teaspoon salt
1¼ teaspoons cinnamon
⅛ teaspoon ginger
¼ teaspoon nutmeg
½ cup raisins
½ cup chopped nuts

OVEN 350°

Cream shortening; add sugar until light and fluffy. Add egg and pumpkin; mix well. Sift flour, baking powder, salt, and spices together. Stir in dry ingredients and mix. Add raisins and nuts. Drop by teaspoonfuls onto greased cookie sheet. Bake for 15 minutes.

Makes 2 dozen.

Snickerdoodle Cookies

1 cup soft shortening (or half butter and half shortening)
1½ cups sugar
2 eggs
2¾ cups flour
2 teaspoons cream of tartar
1 teaspoon baking soda
¼ teaspoon salt
2 tablespoons sugar
2 teaspoons cinnamon

OVEN 400°

Mix shortening, sugar, and eggs. Sift together flour, cream of tartar, baking soda, and salt. Stir into creamed mixture. Roll dough into balls the size of small walnuts. Mix 2 tablespoons sugar and cinnamon. Roll balls into mixture. Place 2 inches apart on ungreased cookie sheet. These cookies puff during baking but will flatten out. They are still soft when done. Bake for 8 to 10 minutes.

Sugar Drop Cookies

2½ cups flour
1½ teaspoons baking powder
¾ teaspoon salt
1 cup sugar
¾ cup vegetable oil
2 eggs
1 teaspoon vanilla
Assorted colored sugars

OVEN 350°

In small bowl combine flour, baking powder, and salt; set aside. In large bowl combine sugar and vegetable oil; mix well. Beat in eggs and vanilla. Gradually add flour mixture. Drop by rounded teaspoonfuls onto ungreased cookie sheet. Shape into balls; roll in colored sugar. Bake 8 to 10 minutes.

Soft Sugar Cookies

2½ cups Wondra flour
1 teaspoon baking powder
½ teaspoon salt (optional)
¾ cup butter or margarine, softened
1 cup sugar
2 eggs
1 teaspoon vanilla

OVEN 350°

Mix together flour, baking powder, salt, and butter or margarine. Add sugar, eggs, and vanilla. Mix together and chill in refrigerator 1 hour. Roll out to ½ inch thick. Cut into desired shapes. Bake for 8 to 10 minutes.

Cutout Sugar Cookies

1 cup (2 sticks) butter, softened
1½ cups sugar
2 eggs
1½ teaspoons vanilla
4½ cups flour
1 teaspoon salt
1 teaspoon baking soda
1 teaspoon baking powder
½ teaspoon nutmeg
1 cup dairy sour cream

OVEN 375°

Cream butter and sugar until light and fluffy. Beat in eggs and vanilla. Sift dry ingredients together and add alternately with sour cream, mixing well. Chill until firm enough to roll out on lightly floured surface, ½ inch thick. Cut with cookie cutter. Place on ungreased cookie sheet. Sprinkle with plain or colored sugar. Bake 8 to 10 minutes. Place on wire rack to cool.

Makes 5 to 6 dozen.

Sugar Cookies

1¾ cups oil
2 eggs
Vanilla or almond extract to taste
4½ to 5 cups flour
2 cups powdered sugar
2 teaspoons cream of tartar
1 teaspoon baking soda

OVEN 350°

Mix together oil and eggs; flavor to taste with vanilla or almond extract. In separate bowl, mix flour, powdered sugar, cream of tartar, and baking soda. Add oil mixture and stir well. Drop by spoonfuls onto cookie sheet. Flatten with glass or fork. Bake about 10 minutes. Sprinkle with cinnamon sugar before baking or decorate after baking.

Best Date Cookies

1 cup brown sugar
⅔ cup butter (or half butter and half shortening)
1 egg
1 teaspoon salt
1 teaspoon baking soda
¼ cup milk
2 cups flour
1 cup chopped dates
½ cup chopped nuts

OVEN 375°

Mix together ingredients and drop onto cookie sheet. Bake for 15 minutes.

Date Cookies

½ cup butter
½ cup light brown sugar
½ cup sugar
½ teaspoon vanilla
1 egg
2 cups flour
¼ teaspoon baking soda

Filling:
1 (7¼ ounce) package chopped dates
¼ cup sugar
½ teaspoon salt
⅓ cup water
1 cup chopped nuts

OVEN 375°

Cream butter; add brown sugar, ½ cup sugar, vanilla, and egg; beat until light. Add flour and baking soda. Chill until firm. Mix dates, ¼ cup sugar, salt, and water. Simmer 5 minutes, stirring often. Add nuts. Divide dough in 2 equal parts. Roll each part on floured waxed paper into 9x13-inch rectangles. Spread with filling; wrap in the waxed paper. Chill overnight. Cut into ⅛-inch slices. Bake for 10 minutes.

Makes 5 to 6 dozen.

Jan Hagel Cookies

½ pound butter
1 cup sugar
1 egg yolk
½ teaspoon cinnamon
2 cups flour
1 egg white
Chopped almonds or walnuts

OVEN 375°

Mix in order given, except egg white and nuts. Spread mixture on greased cookie sheet. Brush egg white on top of dough and sprinkle with chopped nuts. Bake for 20 minutes. Cut into strips while still warm.

Zucchini Oat Cookies

1 cup brown sugar
1 cup white sugar
⅓ cup, less 1 tablespoon, oil
1 egg
1 cup zucchini, finely chopped or ground
2 cups plus 1 tablespoon flour
½ teaspoon salt
1 teaspoon baking soda
1 teaspoon cinnamon
1 cup quick oats
½ cup chopped nuts

OVEN 350°

Lightly grease or spray cookie sheet. Mix together sugars, oil, egg, and zucchini. Sift and add flour, salt, baking soda, and cinnamon. Add oats and nuts. Bake for 10 to 12 minutes.

Ginger Snaps

2¼ cups flour
2 teaspoons baking soda
1 teaspoon ground ginger
1 teaspoon ground cinnamon
½ teaspoon ground cloves
¼ teaspoon salt
1 cup light brown sugar
¾ cup solid shortening
¼ cup molasses
1 egg

OVEN 375°

Sift together first six ingredients and set aside. Combine remaining ingredients and beat well. Add dry ingredients to beaten mixture. Form 1-inch balls. Roll in sugar if desired. Place 2 inches apart on ungreased cookie sheet. Bake for approximately 10 minutes.

Makes about 4 dozen.

Orange Slice Cookies

2 cups brown sugar
4 eggs, beaten
2 cups flour
2 teaspoons baking powder
1 teaspoon salt
20 orange slices
1 cup chopped nuts (optional)

OVEN 420°

Mix sugar and eggs in bowl. Add flour, baking powder, and salt. Cut orange into slices. Dip pair of scissors in flour and cut sliced oranges in zigzag ridges along peeling side. Add oranges to sugar mixture and mix well. Place in greased baking pan and smooth out. Bake for 30 to 35 minutes. Cut into small pieces and roll in powdered sugar while hot. May add nuts if desired. Store in very tight container.

Cream Wafers

1 cup butter
2 cups flour
⅓ cup whipping cream

OVEN 370°

Mix ingredients. Cover and chill. Roll dough to ⅛ inch thick. Cut into 1-inch circles. Roll both sides in sugar. Put on ungreased cookie sheet. Pierce 4 times with fork. Bake 7 to 9 minutes. Remove from pan; cool.

Filling:
¼ cup butter
¾ cup powdered sugar
1 teaspoon vanilla
Food colorings of choice

Mix first three ingredients. Divide and color with food colorings. Spread small amount on one cookie and top with another cookie.

Color filling with Christmas colors, Easter colors, or those to match a party color theme.

Jell-O Instant Pudding Cookies

1 stick margarine
½ cup sugar
1 (3.4 ounce) package instant pudding mix
2 eggs, slightly beaten
1½ cups flour
½ teaspoon baking soda
¼ teaspoon salt

OVEN 350°

Cream together margarine and sugar. Add pudding mix, eggs, flour, baking soda, and salt. Mix together well. Drop by teaspoonfuls onto baking sheet. Bake for 12 minutes or until lightly browned. Add nuts or frost if you like.

Makes 3 dozen.

No-Bake Cookies

½ cup milk
½ cup butter
¼ cup cocoa
2 cups sugar
1 teaspoon vanilla
½ cup peanut butter
3 cups oats

Combine milk, butter, cocoa, sugar, and vanilla in saucepan. Bring to boil over medium heat. Cook for 1 minute; do not stir. Remove from heat. Stir in peanut butter and oats. Drop by spoonfuls onto waxed paper. Let stand until cool.

Makes 4 dozen.

Easy Cookies

2 cups sugar
4 tablespoons cocoa
½ cup milk
1 stick margarine
½ cup peanut butter
3 cups quick-cooking oats
½ cup chopped nuts (optional)

In saucepan mix first four ingredients; bring to boil over medium heat and, using wire whisk, cook 2 minutes. Remove from heat. Stir in peanut butter and oats (and nuts if desired). Drop quickly onto waxed paper or cookie sheet (according to desired size).

Melting Moments Cookies

1 scant cup flour
½ cup cornstarch
½ cup powdered sugar
¾ cup margarine, softened
1 teaspoon vanilla

OVEN 370°

Sift together flour, cornstarch, and powdered sugar. Add margarine and vanilla. Stir all together. Form into round bite-size balls. You may flatten the balls if you wish. Bake for 10 to 12 minutes.

Sugar-Free Applesauce Cookies

4 cups oat flour (make in blender or food processor)
2 cups oats
2 teaspoons baking soda
2 teaspoons cinnamon
½ teaspoon nutmeg
½ teaspoon cloves
1 cup cooking oil
2 eggs
4 cups unsweetened applesauce

Optional:
1 cup unsweetened carob chips
½ cup chopped nuts
½ cup chopped dates

OVEN 400°

Mix dry ingredients together, then add oil, eggs, and applesauce. Mix together. Drop by spoonfuls onto ungreased cookie sheet. Bake 8 to 10 minutes.

Makes 6 dozen.

C.C. Cookie (Crispie)

1 cup sugar
1 cup brown sugar
1 cup margarine
1 cup oil
2 eggs
1 teaspoon vanilla
4 cups flour (or substitute 1 cup oats for ½ cup flour)
2 teaspoons baking soda
1 teaspoon salt
4 teaspoons cream of tartar
1 cup or small bag chocolate chips

OVEN 350°

Cream together sugars, margarine, and oil. Add eggs and vanilla. Beat. Place flour on top, making hole in center. In hole, add baking soda, salt, and cream of tartar. Mix lightly; then add chocolate chips. Bake 10 to 12 minutes.

Aunt Viola's Buttermilk Cookies

4 teaspoons baking powder
1 cup buttermilk
1 cup shortening
4 cups brown sugar
4 eggs
6 cups flour

OVEN 350°

Dissolve baking powder in buttermilk. Mix ingredients together. Drop onto lightly greased cookie sheet. Bake for 10 minutes.

No-Bake Candy Cookies

½ cup butter
2 cups sugar
½ teaspoon salt
2 tablespoons cocoa
½ cup milk
½ cup peanut butter
3 cups quick oats

Melt butter in heavy pan. Stir in sugar, salt, cocoa, and milk. Bring to boil; boil for exactly 2 minutes. Remove from heat and stir in peanut butter then oats; mix thoroughly and drop by rounded teaspoonfuls onto waxed paper. Cool then chill. Store in tight container.

Raisin-Filled Sugar Cookies

2 cups margarine
4 cups sugar
2 shakes nutmeg
2 teaspoons vanilla
6 eggs
½ teaspoon salt
4 teaspoons baking powder
12 cups flour
2 cups buttermilk
2 teaspoons baking soda
2 teaspoons lemon juice

Filling:
2 boxes raisins
4 cups water
1 cup sugar
¼ cup flour (approximately, to thicken)

OVEN 400°

Mix and cream together margarine, sugar, nutmeg, vanilla, and eggs until blended. Put salt and baking powder in flour; set aside. Next pour buttermilk in container and add baking soda; stir; then add lemon juice. Alternate buttermilk mixture and flour mixture until thoroughly mixed. Roll out and cut with large cookie cutter. Put 1 tablespoon filling on each cookie and cover with another cookie. Bake at 400° for 15 to 20 minutes.

Filling: In blender, chop raisins in water; then cook with sugar and flour to thicken. Cool.

Cookies in a Jiffy

1 (9 ounce) package yellow cake mix
⅔ cup quick-cooking oats
½ cup butter or margarine, melted
1 egg
½ cup M&M's or butterscotch chips

OVEN 350°

In mixing bowl, beat first four ingredients. Stir in M&M's or chips. Drop by tablespoonfuls 2 inches apart onto ungreased baking sheet. Bake for 10 to 12 minutes or until lightly browned. Immediately remove to wire rack to cool.

Makes 2 dozen.

Buried Cherry Cookies

1 cup sugar
½ cup margarine
1 egg
1½ teaspoons vanilla
1½ cups flour
⅓ cup cocoa
¼ teaspoon baking soda
¼ teaspoon baking powder
¼ teaspoon salt
1 (6 ounce) jar maraschino cherries, drained, juice reserved

Frosting:
½ cup real chocolate chips
¼ cup sweetened condensed milk
2 teaspoons cherry juice

OVEN 350°

Cream sugar and margarine. Beat in egg and vanilla. Add dry ingredients and mix. Shape dough into 1-inch balls. Press down center with thumb. Put cherry in. Melt together frosting ingredients. Cover dough with frosting. Bake for 8 to 10 minutes.

Pizza Cookies

½ cup butter
¾ cup sugar
¾ cup brown sugar
2 eggs
2¼ cups flour
1 teaspoon baking soda
1 teaspoon salt
1 teaspoon vanilla
1 (12 ounce) package chocolate chips
1 cup chopped nuts

Frosting:
1 (6 ounce) package chocolate chips
1 (6 ounce) package butterscotch chips

OVEN 370°

In small bowl, mix together butter, sugars, and eggs. Add flour, baking soda, and salt. Add vanilla, 12 ounces chips, and nuts. Spread in two 14-inch pizza pans. Bake for 25 minutes. Remove from oven and sprinkle remaining chips over hot cookies. Let set 5 minutes then spread chips to make frosting.

Pizza Cookies

½ cup margarine
½ cup peanut butter
1½ cups flour
½ cup sugar
½ cup brown sugar
1 egg
1 teaspoon vanilla
1 (6 ounce) package chocolate chips
2 cups miniature marshmallows
Mini M&M's

OVEN 370°

Mix together first seven ingredients. Press pizza pan. Bake 10 minutes. Remove from oven and sprinkle with chocolate chips and mini marshmallows. Return to oven and bake 5 to 8 minutes more. Do not overbake. Take out and sprinkle with mini M&M's.

Variation: To make in jelly roll pan, double ingredients.

Pizza Cookie

Cookie Dough:

1⅓ cups flour
½ teaspoon baking powder
½ teaspoon baking soda
½ teaspoon salt
⅓ cup margarine, melted
1 cup packed light brown sugar
1 egg
1 tablespoon hot water
1 teaspoon vanilla

Toppings:

½ cup chopped nuts
1 cup chocolate chips
½ cup M&M's
½ cup jelly beans
1 cup butterscotch chips
1 cup peanut butter chips
1 cup miniature marshmallows

OVEN 350°

In large bowl combine flour, baking powder, baking soda, and salt. Stir in melted margarine and brown sugar. In separate bowl, combine egg, hot water, and vanilla. Stir into flour mixture. Grease 12-inch pizza pan. Flour hands and press dough evenly into pan. Sprinkle with selected toppings and top with miniature marshmallows. Bake 18 minutes.

Snowmen Cookies

Nutter Butter cookies
White chocolate almond bark
Mini chocolate chips, for eyes

Melt almond bark and spread chocolate on cookies. Place 2 mini chocolate chips side by side for eyes.

Brownie Waffle Cookies

⅓ cup margarine or butter
1 (1 ounce) packet Nestle Choco Bake
½ cup sugar
1 egg, lightly beaten
½ teaspoon vanilla
¾ cup flour
½ teaspoon baking powder
¼ teaspoon salt
2 tablespoons milk
1 cup finely chopped walnuts

Stir butter and chocolate over low heat until melted. Cool slightly. Add sugar, egg, and vanilla; beat well. Sift flour, baking powder, and salt together. Add to chocolate mixture along with milk and ⅔ cup nuts. Mix well and drop by rounded teaspoonfuls onto greased preheated waffle baker. Sprinkle a few of remaining nuts on top and bake 5 to 6 minutes.

Makes 18 cookies.

Gobs (Cake Version of Oreo Cookies)

2 cups sugar
1 cup shortening
3 eggs
1 cup milk
1 cup boiling water
2 teaspoons baking powder
1 teaspoon vanilla
4 cups flour
2 teaspoons baking soda
½ teaspoon salt
1 cup cocoa

OVEN 350°

Cream together sugar, shortening, and eggs. Add rest of ingredients in large bowl and beat until blended well. To bake, drop by teaspoonfuls onto greased cookie sheet. Bake at 350° for 10 to 15 minutes.

FILLING:
2 cups powdered sugar
1 egg white
1 teaspoon vanilla
½ cup shortening
2 tablespoons flour
2 tablespoons milk
Food coloring of choice (optional)

Cream well by hand or with beater. Put filling in between two cookies, as you would a sandwich.

Cowboy Cookies

2 cups sifted flour
1 teaspoon baking soda
½ teaspoon salt
½ teaspoon baking powder
1 cup shortening
1 cup sugar
1 cup brown sugar
2 eggs
2 cups rolled oats
1 teaspoon vanilla
1 cup semisweet chocolate chips

OVEN 350°

Sift together flour, baking soda, salt, and baking powder. Set aside. Blend shortening and sugars. Add eggs and beat until light. Add flour mixture and mix well. Add rolled oats, vanilla, and chocolate chips. Drop by teaspoonfuls onto greased cookie sheet. Bake 15 minutes.

Makes 11 dozen (can be doubled).

Delicious Cookies

1 cup chopped nuts
1 cup coconut
1 cup quick-cooking oats
1 cup crisp rice cereal
1 cup butter
1 cup oil
1 cup brown sugar
1 cup sugar
2 eggs
3½ cups flour
1 teaspoon cream of tartar
1 teaspoon baking soda
½ teaspoon salt

OVEN 350°

In bowl mix nuts, coconut, oats, and crisp rice cereal; set aside. Cream together butter, oil, and sugars. Beat in eggs. Sift and add flour, cream of tartar, baking soda, and salt. Add first mixture. Drop by teaspoonfuls on cookie sheet and flatten with fork. Bake for 8 minutes.

Coffee Cake Cookies

4 cups flour, divided
1 tablespoon dry quick yeast
1 teaspoon salt
¼ cup sugar
2 sticks margarine
2 eggs, beaten
1 cup scalded milk
¼ cup warm water

Filling:
2 tablespoons melted butter
½ cup brown sugar
1 teaspoon cinnamon

Glaze:
1½ cups powdered sugar
2 tablespoons butter
1 teaspoon vanilla
1 to 2 tablespoons warm water

OVEN 350° to 370°

Mix 2 cups flour with yeast and set

aside. Mix salt, sugar, margarine, eggs, and 2 cups flour; add scalded milk, warm water, and 2 cups of flour mixed with yeast. Mix lightly. Cover and refrigerate overnight.

Divide dough in two. Roll out and brush each half with melted butter. Sprinkle each with mixture of sugar and cinnamon. Roll up from long side. Slice each roll into 12 rolls. Bake for 12 to 15 minutes in greased 9x13-inch pan. Mix glaze ingredients and frost with glaze.

Angel Cookies

1 box angel food cake mix
½ cup water
1 (8 to 12 ounce) bag dry mixed fruit, finely chopped

OVEN 400°

Combine cake mix and water. Stir in fruit. Line cookie pan with foil. Drop by teaspoonfuls onto foil. Bake 8 to 10 minutes. Bake until puffy and golden in color. Cool well before trying to remove from foil.

Praline Cookies

Graham crackers
1 cup margarine or butter
1 cup brown sugar
1 teaspoon vanilla
1 cup pecans, slightly chopped

OVEN 350°

Layer rows of separated graham crackers on cookie sheet. Combine margarine or butter and brown sugar; bring to rolling boil then turn off heat. Add vanilla and pecans. Pour quickly over crackers and spread immediately. (It doesn't look like enough caramel, but it is.) Bake 10 minutes. Take out of pan and place on waxed paper. Cookies set quickly so take them out immediately.

Springerle Cookies

4 eggs
2 cups sugar
2 teaspoons crushed aniseed
3 to 3½ cups sifted flour
½ teaspoon baking powder
2 teaspoons anise extract (optional)
3 to 4 tablespoons whole aniseed to sprinkle in pan

OVEN 300°

Beat eggs until light. Gradually stir in sugar; beat well after each addition. Stir in aniseed. Sift flour with baking powder. Add enough flour to make dough stiff enough to roll out to ⅓ inch thick. These cookies are usually stamped with wooden mold or roller with picture on it. If you do not have a mold, cut into bars. Grease cookie sheet lightly and sprinkle with aniseed. Place cookies on sheet. Bake for 15 minutes or until lower part of cookies are pale yellow; tops will be white.

Makes 5 dozen.

Sour-Milk Jumbles

1 cup shortening
2 cups sugar
3 eggs, well beaten
6 cups flour
2 teaspoons baking powder
½ teaspoon baking soda
¾ teaspoon ground nutmeg
1 cup sour milk

OVEN 370°

Cream shortening with sugar. Add beaten eggs. Mix and sift dry ingredients; add to creamed mixture alternately with sour milk. Roll out thick (about ¼ inch) on floured surface. Cut with desired cookie cutters. Lightly grease cookie sheet if not using Teflon sheets. Sprinkle cookie tops with granulated or colored sugar. Raisins can also be pressed into center of each cookie. Bake for approximately 8 to 10 minutes.

Lemon Snowballs

1 cup shortening
1⅓ cups sugar
4 teaspoons grated lemon rind
2 eggs
6 tablespoons lemon juice
2 tablespoons water
3½ cups flour
½ teaspoon soda
1 teaspoon salt
½ teaspoon cream of tartar
½ cup finely chopped nuts

OVEN 350°

Thoroughly mix first four ingredients. Stir in lemon juice and water. Sift together rest of ingredients and stir in. Form into walnut-size balls. Place about 1 inch apart on ungreased baking sheet. Bake about 10 minutes. Remove from baking sheet and roll in powdered sugar.

Ginger-Molasses Cookies

2¼ cups margarine, softened
1 cup, minus 1 tablespoon, molasses
3 cups sugar
3 eggs
7¾ cups flour
1 tablespoon ginger
2 tablespoons baking soda
1 tablespoon cinnamon
1½ teaspoons salt

OVEN 350°

Mix together margarine, molasses, sugar, and eggs. Sift together flour, ginger, baking soda, cinnamon, and salt; add to molasses mixture. Roll into 1-inch balls. If desired, roll balls in cinnamon-sugar mixture. Place on ungreased cookie sheets. Bake 8 to 10 minutes, until light brown.

Old-Fashioned Molasses Cookies

1 cup sugar
1 cup shortening
1 teaspoon salt
1 cup molasses
½ teaspoon ground cloves
1 teaspoon cinnamon
½ teaspoon ginger
4 teaspoons baking soda
1 cup sour milk
5 to 6 cups flour

OVEN 400°

Mix sugar, shortening, and salt together. Add molasses and beat. Add cloves, cinnamon, ginger, and soda and beat. Add milk, then enough flour to make soft dough (try 5 cups first and form sample cookie). Add last cup of flour as needed. Drop by teaspoonfuls onto cookie sheet. Bake 8 to 10 minutes.

Chocolate Peppermint Creams

Cookies:
3 cups flour
1¼ teaspoons baking soda
½ teaspoon salt
¾ cup butter
1½ cups packed brown sugar
2 tablespoons water
2 cups chocolate chips
2 eggs

Peppermint Filling:
3 cups powdered sugar
⅓ cup butter, softened
¼ teaspoon peppermint extract
¼ cup milk
5 drops green food coloring

OVEN 350°

Cookies: Sift flour, baking soda, and salt together. In large saucepan, over low heat, melt butter with brown sugar and water. Add chocolate chips and stir until melted. Remove from heat; cool slightly. Beat in eggs. Add flour mixture and mix well. Drop by teaspoonfuls on greased cookie sheets. Bake for 8 to 10 minutes. Cool.

Filling: Blend ingredients together with mixer in small bowl. Pair cookies together with 1 teaspoon filling.

Makes approximately 3 dozen filled.

Note: Chocolate chips, butter, and water can be heated in microwave for 2 minutes on high, until chocolate melts (microwaves may vary). Add brown sugar, mixing well.

Molasses Cookies

¾ cup shortening
1 cup brown sugar
1 egg
¼ cup molasses
1 teaspoon cinnamon
2¼ cups flour
¼ teaspoon salt
2 teaspoons baking soda
½ teaspoon cloves
1 teaspoon ginger

OVEN 350°

Cream shortening and sugar. Add egg and molasses and beat. Add dry ingredients. Mix well. Chill thoroughly. Roll into small balls. Dip in granulated sugar. Place sugar side up 2 inches apart on greased cookie sheets. Bake for 12 to 15 minutes.

Sugarless Spice Cookies

2 cups raisins
2 teaspoons cinnamon
½ teaspoon nutmeg
⅓ cup butter or shortening
1¼ cups water
2 eggs
2 cups sifted flour
½ teaspoon salt
1 teaspoon black walnut extract or vanilla
1 teaspoon baking soda
1 teaspoon baking powder
6 packets artificial sweetener

OVEN 350°

Boil together raisins, cinnamon, nutmeg, butter or shortening, and water for 3 minutes. Set aside to cool; then add eggs, flour, salt, walnut or vanilla extract, baking soda, baking powder, and artificial sweetener. Mix together. Spray cookie sheets with cooking spray. Drop by teaspoonfuls onto cookie sheets. Bake for 12 to 15 minutes.

Dessert Bars

Chocolate Chip Blonde Brownies

2 cups brown sugar
⅔ cup butter, melted
2 eggs
2 teaspoons vanilla
1 to 2 cups flour
¼ teaspoon baking soda
1 teaspoon baking powder
¼ teaspoon salt
½ cup chopped nuts (optional)
1 package chocolate chips

OVEN 350°

Add brown sugar to melted butter; cool. Add eggs and vanilla to mixture and blend well. Add sifted ingredients gradually (flour, soda, baking powder, and salt). Stir in chopped nuts. Pour mixture into greased 8x12-inch pan. Sprinkle chocolate chips on top. Bake in 350° oven for 20 to 25 minutes. (Do not overbake.) Cut into squares.

Chocolate Chip Cookie Dough Brownies

2 cups sugar
1½ cups flour
½ cup cocoa
½ teaspoon salt
1 cup vegetable oil
4 eggs
2 teaspoons vanilla
½ cup chopped walnuts (optional)

Filling:
½ cup butter
½ cup packed brown sugar
¼ cup sugar
2 tablespoons milk
1 teaspoon vanilla
1 cup flour

Glaze:
1 cup (6 ounces) semisweet chocolate chips
1 tablespoon shortening
¾ cup chopped walnuts

OVEN 350°

In mixing bowl, combine sugar, flour, cocoa, and salt. Add oil, eggs, and vanilla; beat at medium speed for 3 minutes. Stir in walnuts if desired. Pour into greased 9x13-inch baking pan. Bake at 350° for 30 minutes or until brownies test done. Cool completely. For filling, cream butter and sugars in mixing bowl. Add milk and vanilla; mix well. Beat in flour. Spread over brownies; chill until firm. For glaze, melt chocolate chips and shortening in saucepan, stirring until smooth. Spread over filling. Immediately sprinkle with nuts, pressing down slightly.

Yield: 3 dozen.

Black and White Brownies

2 eggs
1 cup sugar
⅓ cup butter, melted
⅔ cup flour
¾ teaspoon baking powder
¼ teaspoon salt
⅔ cup or 1½ ounces coconut
½ teaspoon almond extract or vanilla
2 squares melted chocolate or ½ cup melted chocolate chips (peanut butter or butterscotch chips are good substitutes)

OVEN 350°

Beat eggs and sugar. Blend in butter. Sift together dry ingredients. Stir into creamed mixture. Mix coconut and extract into one-third of batter. Blend chocolate in remaining batter. Pour chocolate batter into greased 8x8-inch pan. Spread vanilla batter on top. Bake at 350° for 25 to 30 minutes. Cool; cut into squares.

Cream Cheese Brownies

1 (18.3 ounce) package brownie mix

Filling:
1 (8 ounce) package cream cheese, softened
1 egg
⅓ cup sugar
⅛ teaspoon salt

OVEN 350°

Prepare brownie mix according to package directions. Spread in 9x13-inch pan and set aside. Combine cream cheese, egg, sugar, and salt for filling. Space large spoonfuls of filling on top of batter. Use butter knife to form swirl designs. Bake at 350° for 30 to 35 minutes.

Caramel Brownies

⅔ cup evaporated milk, divided
1 (14 ounce) package caramels
1 box German chocolate cake mix
¾ cup margarine, melted
1½ cups chopped walnuts or pecans
1 (12 ounce) package chocolate chips

OVEN 350°

Combine ⅓ cup evaporated milk and caramels. Microwave for 6 to 7 minutes on medium. Stir after 3 minutes. Set aside. Grease 9x13-inch pan. In large bowl combine cake mix, melted margarine, ⅓ cup evaporated milk, and nuts. Stir by hand until mixed. Press half of dough into pan (reserve half for topping). It barely covers bottom of pan. Bake at 350° for 6 minutes. Sprinkle chocolate chips over hot crust. Pour caramel from spoon over chocolate chips until nearly covered. Press bits of reserved dough between fingers and make thin layer on top of caramel and chips. Bake 15 to 18 minutes at 350°. Cool and cut.

Hershey Syrup Brownies

½ cup margarine
1 cup sugar
1 cup flour
½ teaspoon baking powder
4 eggs
1 teaspoon vanilla
1 (16 ounce) can chocolate syrup
1 cup chopped nuts (optional)

OVEN 350°

Blend margarine and sugar; mix in flour and baking powder; add eggs and vanilla. Beat. Add syrup. Mix nuts in after syrup or sprinkle on top. Pour into 11x15-inch pan and bake for 30 minutes.

Frosting:
1⅓ cups sugar
6 tablespoons milk
6 tablespoons margarine
1 cup chocolate chips

Boil ingredients for 1 minute; beat and spread on brownies.

Brownies

8 eggs
4 cups sugar
2 cups flour
1½ sticks margarine
¾ cup corn oil
6 tablespoons cocoa
2 teaspoons vanilla
1 cup chopped pecans

OVEN 350°

Beat eggs first; then mix dry ingredients; add rest. Beat well. Bake at 350° for 30 minutes.

Icing:
1 (1 pound) box powdered sugar
1 stick margarine
2 tablespoons cocoa
1 teaspoon vanilla

Mix and spread on warm brownies.

Simply Delicious Brownies

1 stick margarine
1 cup sugar
2 tablespoons cocoa
1 cup self-rising flour
1 large egg (or 2 small eggs), beaten
1 teaspoon vanilla

OVEN 400°

Melt margarine in 7½-inch baking pan; set aside. Blend together sugar, cocoa, and flour. Mix in beaten egg and vanilla. Mix well. Pour batter in 7½-inch baking pan with margarine. Bake in oven at 400° for 15 minutes.

Buttermilk Frosted Brownies

1 stick margarine
3½ tablespoons cocoa
½ cup oil
1 cup water
2 cups sugar
2 cups flour
½ cup buttermilk
2 eggs
1 teaspoon baking soda
1 teaspoon vanilla
2 cups chopped nuts (optional)

OVEN 350°

Combine margarine, cocoa, oil, and water in pan; bring to boil, mixing well. Add sugar and dissolve; then add flour, buttermilk, and eggs. Add soda, vanilla, and nuts. Pour into jelly roll pan and bake at 350° for 20 minutes.

Frosting:
1 stick margarine
3½ tablespoons cocoa
⅓ cup evaporated milk or 5 tablespoons buttermilk
1 (1 pound) box powdered sugar
1 cup chopped nuts
1 teaspoon vanilla

Combine margarine, cocoa, and milk; bring to boil. Remove from heat and add powdered sugar, nuts, and vanilla. Beat and frost while brownies are still warm.

Brickle Brownies

1 cup butter, softened
¾ cup sugar
¾ cup brown sugar
1 egg
2¼ cups flour
1 teaspoon baking soda
½ teaspoon salt
1 (8 ounce) package Heath Bits 'O Brickle

OVEN 350°

Mix butter, sugar, brown sugar, and egg. Stir in flour, soda, and salt; dough will be stiff. Stir in Heath Bits 'O Brickle. Pour into 9x13-inch ungreased pan. Bake at 350° for 25 minutes. Let cool completely! Cut into squares.

Hint: You can substitute chocolate chips for Heath Bits 'O Brickle.

Old-Fashioned Frosted Brownies

3 tablespoons butter
1½ cups sugar
3 eggs
3 squares baking chocolate, melted
1½ cups flour
Pinch salt
⅔ teaspoon baking powder
⅔ cup milk
½ cup chopped walnuts

OVEN 350°

Cream butter and sugar; add eggs and beat until smooth. Add chocolate (should be cooled but still liquid). Mix together flour, salt, and baking powder. Add flour mixture and milk alternately to chocolate mixture. Add walnuts. Bake in jelly roll pan or two 8x8-inch pans at 350° for 30 minutes.

Frosting:
4 tablespoons butter
1 (1 pound) box powdered sugar, sifted
4 tablespoons cocoa with a little hot coffee
1 teaspoon vanilla
Chopped walnuts (optional)

Cream together butter and sifted powdered sugar; add cocoa and coffee a little at a time. Add vanilla; beat until smooth and spreading consistency. Spread on cooled brownies. Top with chopped nuts if desired.

Chocolate Cookie Bars

1¾ cups flour
¾ cup sugar
¼ cup cocoa
1 cup butter
2 cups semisweet chocolate chips, divided
1 (14 ounce) can sweetened condensed milk
1 teaspoon vanilla
1 cup chopped nuts

OVEN 350°

In medium bowl, stir together flour, sugar, and cocoa; cut in butter until crumbly (mixture will be dry). Press firmly on bottom of 9x13-inch baking pan. Bake 15 minutes. Meanwhile in medium saucepan, combine 1 cup chocolate chips, milk, and vanilla. Cook over medium heat, stirring constantly, until chips are melted. Pour over crust; top with nuts and remaining chocolate chips. Bake 20 minutes.

Milk Chocolate Chip and Peanut Butter Bars

½ cup (1 stick) butter or margarine
½ cup creamy peanut butter
¾ cup sugar
¾ cup packed light brown sugar
1 teaspoon vanilla
3 eggs
1¾ cups flour
1½ teaspoons baking powder
½ teaspoon salt
2 cups milk chocolate chips

OVEN 350°

Grease 9x13-inch baking pan. In large bowl, beat butter and peanut butter; add sugar, brown sugar, and vanilla; beat until well blended. Add eggs; beat well. Stir together flour, baking powder, and salt; add to creamed mixture, beating until blended. Stir in milk chocolate chips. Spread batter in prepared pan. Bake 40 minutes or until browned. Cool and cut into bars.

Chocolate Revel Bars

3 cups quick-cooking rolled oats
2½ cups flour
1 teaspoon baking soda
1 teaspoon salt
1 cup butter or margarine
2 cups packed brown sugar
2 eggs
4 teaspoons vanilla, divided
1½ cups semisweet chocolate pieces
1 (14 ounce) can sweetened condensed milk
2 tablespoons butter or margarine
½ teaspoon salt
½ cup chopped walnuts

OVEN 350°

Combine oats, flour, soda, and salt. Beat 1 cup butter for 30 seconds. Add brown sugar and beat until fluffy. Add eggs and 2 teaspoons vanilla; beat well. Stir dry ingredients gradually into beaten mixture, stirring until well combined. In saucepan heat chocolate, sweetened milk, 2 tablespoons butter, and ½ teaspoon salt over low heat, stirring until smooth. Remove from heat. Stir in nuts and 2 teaspoons vanilla. Put two-thirds of oat mixture in bottom of ungreased 10x15-inch baking pan. Spread chocolate over mixture. Dot with remaining oat mixture. Bake at 350° for 25 to 30 minutes. Cool on wire rack. Cut into bars.

Makes 72 bars.

Rice Krispie Treats

1 cup sugar
1 cup light corn syrup
1 cup peanut butter
5 to 6 cups crisp rice cereal

Bring sugar and syrup to boil. Remove from heat. Add peanut butter; mix together. Add crisp rice cereal and stir. Place in 9x13-inch pan. Let cool.

Easy Bars

3 eggs
¾ cup white sugar
¾ cup brown sugar
1 cup oil
1 heaping teaspoon baking soda
2 teaspoons vanilla
1 teaspoon salt
2 tablespoons peanut butter
2 scant cups flour
2 cups quick-cooking oats

OVEN 350°

Combine ingredients and bake at 350° for 15 minutes or until center is done. While still hot drip icing over bars.

Icing:
1 cup powdered sugar
1 teaspoon vanilla
Water

Combine powdered sugar and vanilla; add water until thin enough to drip.

Variations:
1 tablespoon salad dressing or 2 tablespoons honey
1 cup raisins
1 cup nuts
Peanut butter chips or chocolate chips

O'Henry Bars

1 cup sugar
1 cup light corn syrup
1 cup peanut butter
6 cups crisp rice cereal

Topping:
1 cup butterscotch chips
1 cup chocolate chips

Combine sugar and syrup in saucepan and bring just to boil. Stir in peanut butter. Then stir in crisp rice cereal and spread in 9x13-inch pan. Melt butterscotch and chocolate chips together, then spread on top.

Nutritious Crispy Bars

½ cup butter or margarine
4½ cups miniature marshmallows
1 teaspoon vanilla
½ cup crunchy peanut butter
4 cups crisp rice cereal
½ package chocolate chips
1½ cups puffed rice (optional)
½ cup dried bananas
½ cup dried apricots
¼ cup raisins
1½ cups granola cereal
¼ cup dried apples

Melt butter or margarine and marshmallows until creamy. Add vanilla and peanut butter. Remove from heat. Mix dry ingredients in bowl. Stir in melted marshmallow mixture. Press in pans and chill. Then cut and serve.

Chocolate Nut Caramel Bars

2 cups chocolate chips
2 tablespoons vegetable shortening
40 caramels
5 tablespoons margarine
2 tablespoons water
1 cup chopped peanuts

Melt over hot water chocolate chips and 2 tablespoons vegetable shortening. Stir until smooth. Pour half into 8x8-inch pan, spreading evenly. Refrigerate until firm. Combine caramels, margarine, and 2 tablespoons of water over heat until smooth. Add nuts and pour over chocolate mixture that has hardened. Then reheat remaining half of chocolate mixture and oil and cover caramel layer. Refrigerate several hours until hard.

Peanut Butter Cereal Bars

½ cup sugar
½ cup light corn syrup
¾ cup peanut butter
1 teaspoon vanilla
3 cups Special K cereal
1 package butterscotch chips
2 squares baking chocolate

Boil together sugar and syrup just until sugar dissolves. Remove from stove and add peanut butter and vanilla. Mix thoroughly and add Special K cereal. Spread thinly in buttered pan. Melt butterscotch chips and chocolate squares and frost bars with this. Allow to cool. Cut into bars.

Chessy Peanut Butter Bars

1 stick margarine
½ cup peanut butter
1 cup self-rising flour
1½ cups sugar
2 eggs, well beaten
½ teaspoon vanilla

OVEN 350°

In double boiler over low heat, melt margarine; add peanut butter; stir well. Add flour, sugar, eggs, and vanilla; stir well. Spread evenly into square baking pan. Bake at 350° until golden brown. Cool; then cut into squares.

Peanut Butter and Jelly Bars

1 box vanilla cake mix
½ cup (1 stick) margarine or butter, softened
2 eggs
1 (12 ounce) jar strawberry jelly (1 cup)
1 (10 ounce) package peanut butter chips

OVEN 375°

Grease 9x13-inch pan. Mix cake mix (dry), margarine, and eggs in large bowl using spoon (mixture will be stiff). Spread evenly in pan. Spread jelly evenly in pan to within ½ inch of edges. Sprinkle with peanut butter chips. Bake about 25 minutes or until golden brown around edges. Cool completely. Cut into 2½-inch bars. For ease in cutting use sharp or wet knife.

Quick Peanut Butter Bars

1 cup sugar, less 2 tablespoons
⅔ cup light corn syrup
1½ cups creamy peanut butter, less 2 tablespoons
3¾ cups Cheerios cereal

Cook sugar in corn syrup until dissolved, very short time. Add peanut butter and mix until smooth. Stir in Cheerios and spread in greased 9x13-inch pan. You may add frosting before cutting into bars.

Spicy Pumpkin Bars

1¾ cups sugar
4 large eggs, beaten until frothy
1 cup corn oil
2 cups (16 ounces) pumpkin
2 cups flour
2 teaspoons baking powder
1 teaspoon salt
2 teaspoons pumpkin pie spice
1 cup golden raisins

OVEN 350°

Add sugar to eggs and beat for 2 minutes. Beat in oil and pumpkin. Sift dry ingredients over raisins and fold dry mixture into egg mixture. Do not overmix. Pour into greased and floured 9x13-inch pan. Bake in oven for 35 to 40 minutes or until done through. Cool on rack and cut into 24 squares.

Pumpkin Bars

4 eggs
1⅔ cups sugar
1 cup oil or applesauce
2 cups cooked pumpkin
2 cups flour (may use 1 cup whole wheat and 1 cup white)
2 teaspoons baking powder
1 teaspoon baking soda
2 teaspoons cinnamon
½ teaspoon nutmeg
¼ teaspoon ginger
⅛ teaspoon ground cloves
1 teaspoon salt
½ cup raisins (optional)

OVEN 350°

Beat eggs, sugar, oil, and pumpkin until light and fluffy. Stir together dry ingredients. Add to pumpkin mixture and mix well. Spread batter in ungreased 10x15-inch pan. If desired, sprinkle batter with raisins. Bake at 350° for 30 minutes.

Yields 24 bars.

When cool, frost with canned cream cheese frosting or make frosting by mixing together:

1 (3 ounce) package cream cheese, softened
½ cup butter
1 teaspoon vanilla
2 cups powdered sugar

Mixed Nut Bars

1 cup butter or margarine, softened
1 cup brown sugar
1 egg yolk
2 cups flour
¼ teaspoon salt
1 teaspoon vanilla
1 (12 ounce) package butterscotch bits
½ cup light corn syrup
2 tablespoons butter
1 tablespoon water
1 (13 ounce) can mixed nuts (one with fewer peanuts is best)

OVEN 350°

Mix 1 cup butter or margarine, brown sugar, egg yolk, flour, salt, and vanilla until crumbly. Press into ungreased 9x13-inch pan. Bake at 350° for 20 to 25 minutes. Melt in double boiler butterscotch bits, corn syrup, 2 tablespoons butter, and water. Pour over base and cover with nuts, press. Refrigerate until set. Cut into squares.

Pecan Pie Bars

1 package yellow cake mix
½ cup margarine or butter, softened
1 egg
1 cup chopped pecans

Filling:
⅔ cup reserved cake mix
½ cup brown sugar
1½ cups dark corn syrup
1 teaspoon vanilla
3 eggs

OVEN 350°

Generously grease bottom and sides of 9x13-inch pan. Reserve ⅔ cup dry cake mix. In large mixing bowl combine margarine, remaining cake mix, and 1 egg. Mix until crumbly. Press into pan. Bake at 350° for 15 to 20 minutes until light golden brown. Mix together filling ingredients and pour over partially baked crust. Sprinkle with pecans. Return to oven and bake for 30 to 35 minutes until filling is set. Cool. Cut into bars.

Davy Crockett Bars

2 cups flour
1 cup sugar
1 teaspoon salt
1 teaspoon baking powder
1 teaspoon baking soda
1 cup brown sugar
1¾ to 2 cups quick-cooking oats
1 (6 ounce) package chocolate chips
1 cup chopped nuts (optional)
2 eggs
1 cup vegetable oil
1 teaspoon vanilla

OVEN 350°

Mix flour, sugar, salt, baking powder, and baking soda. Mix in brown sugar, oats, chocolate chips, and nuts if desired. Combine eggs, oil, and vanilla; add to oat mixture, then stir into dry mixture. Press into ungreased jelly roll pan. Bake at 350° for 15 minutes or until lightly browned. Do not overbake. Cool slightly before cutting.

Green Tomato Bars

4 cups green tomatoes, finely chopped
1 cup brown sugar
¾ cup soft margarine
1 cup brown sugar
1½ cups flour
1 teaspoon baking soda
1 teaspoon salt
2 cups oats
½ cup nut meats

OVEN 375°

Simmer for 20 to 25 minutes.

Mix margarine with remaining six ingredients and press 2½ cups of mixture in bottom of 9x13-inch pan. Spread tomato mixture on top. Spread on remaining crumbs. Bake at 375° for 30 to 35 minutes.

Créme de Menthe Bars

⅓ cup butter
1 cup sugar
4 eggs
1 can Hershey's syrup
1 cup flour

OVEN 350°

Cream together butter and sugar. Add eggs, Hershey's syrup, and flour. Spread in greased and floured 9x13-inch pan. Bake 20 to 25 minutes at 350°. Cool.

Filling:
4 cups powdered sugar
2 tablespoons milk
1 cup butter, softened
1 teaspoon peppermint extract
2 ounces (½ cup) crème de menthe
Dash green food coloring

Combine and spread on top of first layer. Refrigerate for 2 hours.

Topping:
1 (12 ounce) package semisweet chocolate chips
4 tablespoons oil

Melt semisweet chocolate chips and oil. Beat. Spread on top. Better if refrigerated.

Cheerio Bars

1 cup light corn syrup
1 cup sugar
1 cup peanut butter
1 cup peanuts, dry roasted or salted
1 cup coconut
6 to 8 cups Cheerios

Bring syrup and sugar to boiling point. Add peanut butter, peanuts, and coconut. Mix in Cheerios. Spread in pan. Refrigerate.

Honey Bars

1 egg
¾ cup oil
¼ cup honey
1 cup sugar
½ teaspoon salt
1 teaspoon cinnamon
2 cups flour
1 cup chopped nuts

Icing:
1 cup powdered sugar
1 tablespoon water
2 tablespoons milk
2 teaspoons vanilla

OVEN 300°

Beat egg, oil, honey, and sugar. Add salt, cinnamon, and flour. Mix well. Fold in nuts. Pat dough out on cookie sheet. Bake 20 minutes at 300°. While hot, top with icing. To make icing, combine all ingredients.

Cinnamon Coffee Bars

¼ cup soft shortening
1 cup packed brown sugar
1 egg
½ cup hot coffee
1½ cups flour
1 teaspoon baking powder
¼ teaspoon baking soda
¼ teaspoon salt
1 teaspoon cinnamon
½ cup raisins
¼ cup chopped nuts

OVEN 350°

Cream together shortening, brown sugar, and egg. Stir in hot coffee. Sift together dry ingredients. Add to first mixture. Blend in raisins and nuts. Spread in greased 9x13-inch pan. Bake at 350° for 18 to 20 minutes.

Glaze: Mix together 1 cup powdered sugar, 1 teaspoon vanilla, 1½ tablespoons milk; spread on hot bars. Cool and cut.

Makes about 2 dozen bars.

Quick Graham Bars

½ cup (1 stick) margarine
1 cup sugar
2 eggs, beaten
2½ cups graham cracker crumbs
2 cups miniature marshmallows
1 (12 ounce) package semisweet chocolate chips
3 tablespoons peanut butter

Melt margarine; add sugar and eggs; bring to boil. Boil until thick, 2½ to 3 minutes, stirring occasionally. Cool slightly. Add graham cracker crumbs and marshmallows and mix thoroughly. Press into 9x13-inch greased pan. Melt chocolate chips with peanut butter. Spread over graham cracker crust. Refrigerate until chocolate starts to harden. Cut into squares. Will keep in freezer for several months.

Makes 30 squares.

Filled Date Bars

Filling:
3 cups (1 box) pitted dates, chopped
⅓ cup sugar
1½ cups water

Cook over low heat 10 minutes. Cool.

Crust:
¾ cup shortening
1 cup brown sugar (dark is best)
1¾ cups sifted flour
½ teaspoon baking soda
1 teaspoon salt
1 cup rolled oats

OVEN 400°

Work crust together with hands like pie dough. Pat half into greased and floured 9x13-inch pan. Spread filling; pat remaining crumbs on top. Bake at 400° for 20 to 30 minutes. When cooled, sprinkle with powdered sugar and cut.

Holiday Cherry Cheese Bars

Crust:
1 cup walnut pieces, divided
1¼ cups flour
½ cup firmly packed brown sugar
½ cup butter-flavored shortening
½ cup flaked coconut

Filling:
2 (8 ounce) packages cream cheese, softened
2 eggs
2 teaspoons vanilla
⅔ cup sugar
1 (21 ounce) can cherry pie filling

OVEN 350°

Grease 9x13-inch pan. Set aside. Chop ½ cup nuts coarsely, for topping. Set aside. Chop remaining ½ cup finely.

Crust: Combine flour and brown sugar. Cut in shortening until fine crumbs form.

Add ½ cup finely chopped nuts and coconut. Mix well. Remove ½ cup; set aside. Press remaining crumbs in bottom of pan. Bake for 12 to 15 minutes, until edges are slightly browned.

Filling: Beat cream cheese, eggs, vanilla, and sugar in small bowl with electric mixer at medium speed until smooth. Spread over hot baked crust. Return to oven. Bake 15 minutes.

Spread cherry pie filling over cheese layer. Combine reserved coarsely chopped nuts and crumbs. Sprinkle over cherries. Return to oven and bake 15 minutes. Cool; refrigerate several hours. Cut into bars.

Lemon Coconut Squares

CRUST:
1½ cups sifted flour
½ cup brown sugar
½ cup butter

OVEN 300°

Mix and pat into bottom of buttered 9x13-inch pan. Bake at 300° for 15 minutes.

FILLING:
2 eggs, beaten
1 cup brown sugar
1½ cups coconut
1 cup chopped nuts
2 tablespoons flour
½ teaspoon baking powder
¼ teaspoon salt
½ teaspoon vanilla

OVEN 350°

Combine filling ingredients and pour into baked crust. Bake at 350° for 15 minutes.

FROSTING:
1 cup powdered sugar
1 tablespoon butter, melted
Juice of 1 lemon

Mix and spread over filling while still warm.

Cashew Caramel Crunch Squares

1 (14 ounce) bag caramels
2 tablespoons butter
2 tablespoons water
6 cups Kellogg's Cocoa Krispies cereal
1 cup cashews
1 cup white chocolate chips

Grease 9x13-inch pan. Put caramels, butter, and water into large saucepan or microwave-safe bowl. Place over medium-low heat and cook for 18 minutes, stirring occasionally, or microwave on high for 3 to 4 minutes, stirring every minute, until caramels melt and mixture is smooth. Stir in cereal and nuts; let cool 1 minute; then stir in white chocolate chips. Press into prepared pan and let cool. Invert onto cutting board. Cut into 2-inch squares.

Makes 24 squares.

Tea Time Tassies

1 cup margarine or butter
3 ounces cream cheese
1 cup flour
Chopped nuts

OVEN 325°

Cream together margarine or butter and cream cheese. Add flour; mix well; chill 1 hour. Shape into 24 balls; press into ungreased mini-tart pans. Sprinkle with chopped nuts.

Filling:
1 beaten egg
1 tablespoon butter, melted
1 teaspoon vanilla
½ cup chopped nuts (optional)
¾ cup brown sugar

Combine filling ingredients and fill tart shells. Bake at 325° for 25 minutes.

Yields 2 dozen small tarts.

Pecan Tarts

½ cup butter or margarine
1 (8 ounce) package cream cheese
1 cup flour

OVEN 350°

Let butter and cream cheese soften at room temperature, then mix well; add flour, mix and chill 1 hour. Press dough into tart cups.

Filling:
1 teaspoon butter, melted
¾ cup brown sugar
1 large or 2 small eggs
1 teaspoon vanilla
½ to 1 cup chopped pecans

Mix all ingredients well; fill tart shells three-quarters full. Bake at 350° for 15 minutes, then 250° for 30 minutes until brown. Cool and eat.

Felix King's "Poison" Berry Tarts

1 cup flour
½ cup butter, softened
¼ cup powdered sugar
1 (3 ounce) package vanilla pudding mix
Raspberries or strawberries

OVEN 350°

Mix flour, butter, and powdered sugar. Divide dough into 12 equal pieces. Press each piece against bottom and sides of ungreased medium muffin cups. Do not allow dough to extend above tops of cups. Bake tart shells 8 to 10 minutes, or until golden brown. Cool. Carefully remove shells from cups with top of knife.
Filling: Follow directions for pudding on package. Spoon pudding into cooled tart shells, using about 3 to 4 tablespoons in each. Top with berries.

Makes 1 dozen tarts.

Peppermint Stick Bars

3 cups sugar
1 cup shortening
2 cups milk
3 cups flour
3 teaspoons baking soda
¾ cup cocoa
4 medium eggs
1 cup white chocolate chips
4 to 6 peppermint sticks, crushed

OVEN 300°

Cream sugar and shortening together, then add milk, alternating with combined sifted flour, baking soda, and cocoa. Add eggs. Put in greased 9x13-inch pan. Bake 30 minutes or until done.

Topping: Before last 2 minutes of baking time, sprinkle white chocolate chips on top of brownies. Spread chocolate and immediately sprinkle with crushed peppermint sticks on top.

Candies

Chocolate Fudge

3 cups semisweet chocolate chips
1 (14 ounce) can sweetened condensed milk
Dash salt
1 cup chopped walnuts
1½ teaspoons vanilla

In heavy saucepan, over low heat, melt chips with sweetened condensed milk and salt. Remove from heat; stir in walnuts and vanilla. Spread evenly into foil-lined 8- or 9-inch square pan. Chill 2 hours or until firm. Turn fudge onto cutting board, peel off foil, and cut into squares. Store, loosely wrapped, at room temperature.

Makes about 2 pounds.

Fudge

1 can vanilla or chocolate ready mix frosting
1 (18 ounce) jar peanut butter
Chopped nuts (optional)

Mix together frosting and peanut butter. Chill. Add nuts.

Quick 'n' Easy Fudge

2 (8 ounce) boxes semisweet chocolate squares
1 (14 ounce) can sweetened condensed milk
2 teaspoons vanilla
1 cup chopped walnuts

Melt chocolate and milk in microwave; stir often. Add vanilla and nuts; stir; pour into buttered 9x9-inch pan. Refrigerate and serve.

Chocolate Fudge

3 cups sugar
6 tablespoons cocoa
⅛ teaspoon salt
1 cup milk
3 tablespoons light corn syrup
3 tablespoons butter
1½ teaspoons vanilla
¾ cup chopped nuts

Combine sugar, cocoa, salt, milk, and syrup in saucepan. Cook until mixture forms soft ball when dropped in cold water. Remove from heat and add butter, vanilla, and nuts. Beat until mixture loses part of its shine. Pour into buttered pan. Let harden and cut into squares.

Makes 1½ pounds.

Powdered Sugar Peanut Butter Fudge

1 pound powdered sugar (10x)
½ cup milk
1 (12 ounce) jar creamy peanut butter
1 (7 or 8 ounce) jar marshmallow creme

Mix together sugar and milk in saucepan. Bring to rolling boil on high heat. Reduce heat to medium and boil 5 minutes, stirring continuously. Remove from heat and add peanut butter and marshmallow creme. Mix thoroughly. (Work fast or it will harden in pan.) Pour into buttered pan. When cooled cut into bite-size pieces.

Chocolate-Scotch Fudge

1 (12 ounce) package chocolate chips
1 (12 ounce) package butterscotch chips
1 cup condensed milk (recipe below)
1 teaspoon vanilla
1 cup chopped nuts

Heat chips and milk together, stirring often. When melted, add vanilla and chopped nuts. Pour into buttered pan, 9x13-inch or smaller. Put into refrigerator. When cooled cut into pieces.

Condensed milk:
½ cup warm water
1 cup plus 2 tablespoons instant non-fat dry milk
¾ cup sugar

Pour water into blender. Add dry milk and sugar. When blended, use or store in refrigerator. Will keep several months in refrigerator.

Peanut Butter Fudge

3 cups sugar
¼ cup butter
⅔ cup evaporated milk
3 tablespoons peanut butter
1 teaspoon vanilla
3 teaspoons miniature marshmallows

Boil together sugar, butter, and canned milk until mixture forms hot ball in cold water. Add peanut butter, vanilla, and marshmallows; beat and pour into well-greased pan.

Easy Peanut Butter Fudge

1 stick margarine
1 (12 ounce) jar peanut butter (1½ cups)
1 teaspoon vanilla
1 pound powdered sugar

Melt margarine; add peanut butter, vanilla, and powdered sugar. Mix well with hands. Spread in greased 9-inch square pan.

Marshmallow Crème Peanut Butter Fudge

3 cups sugar
1 cup milk
1 pint marshmallow creme
1½ cups peanut butter
1 teaspoon vanilla

Cook sugar and milk to soft ball stage. Remove from heat. Add other ingredients. Mix then refrigerate until hard. Cut and serve.

Chocolate-Drizzled Peanut Butter Fudge

1½ cups sugar
1 cup (5 ounces) evaporated milk
¼ cup butter
1 jar marshmallow creme
1 cup chunky peanut butter
1 teaspoon vanilla
2 squares (1 ounce each) semisweet baking chocolate

Grease 8- or 9-inch square pan. Melt sugar, milk, and butter. (Can microwave on high for 6 minutes, stirring after 3 minutes.) Cook 4 to 6 minutes more or until small amount of sugar forms soft ball when dropped in water, or until temperature reaches 236°. Add remaining ingredients except chocolate; beat until well blended. Pour into pan. Cool 30 minutes. Melt chocolate in microwave for 1 to 2 minutes. Stir after 30 seconds. Drizzle over top.

Pecan Peanut Butter Fudge

2 cups sugar
⅔ cup evaporated milk
1 cup peanut butter
1 small jar marshmallow creme
1 cup pecans

Bring sugar and milk to soft ball stage (about 4½ minutes on reduced heat after it comes to boil). Add peanut butter. Mix well. Add marshmallow creme. Mix well. Add nuts and pour into 9x9-inch buttered dish.

No-Cook Peanut Butter Fudge

1 cup butter-flavored shortening
1 cup peanut butter
1 tablespoon vanilla
4 cups powdered sugar
Walnuts

Melt shortening; add peanut butter, stirring until melted also; add vanilla. Pour melted mixture into powdered sugar; mix well. Put in 8x8-inch pan and decorate with walnuts.

Peanut Butter Fudge

2 cups sugar
⅓ cup milk
1 pint marshmallow creme (or 2 cups miniature marshmallows)
1 cup peanut butter
1 teaspoon vanilla

Combine sugar and milk in saucepan and cook to soft ball stage (234°). Remove from heat. Add marshmallow creme, peanut butter, and vanilla. Mix well. Pour into buttered 6x10-inch pan. Cool and cut into squares.

Fantasy Fudge

3 cups sugar
¾ cup margarine
⅓ cup (small can) evaporated milk
1 (12 ounce) package chocolate bits
1 (7 ounce) jar marshmallow creme
1 teaspoon vanilla
1 cup nuts

Butter 8-inch square pan. Put sugar, margarine, and milk in heavy saucepan. Bring to full boil; boil 5 minutes; remove from heat. Beat in remaining ingredients, just until well blended. Pour into pan. Cool; cut into squares.

Sour Cream Fudge

2 cups sugar
½ teaspoon salt
1 cup dairy sour cream
2 tablespoons butter or margarine
½ cup broken pecans or other nuts

Combine sugar, salt, and sour cream in heavy saucepan. Cook, stirring occasionally (over not too high heat, as it will scorch), until a little dropped into cold water forms a soft ball (or 236° on candy thermometer). Add butter or margarine. Let cool at room temperature without stirring until mixture is lukewarm (110°). Beat mixture until it loses gloss; add nuts. Spread in buttered 9x9-inch pan. When firm, cut into squares.

Makes a small amount, about 24 pieces, but is very rich.

Note: Boiling time is approximately 6 or 7 minutes. Follow directions exactly.

Two-Tone Fudge

2 cups brown sugar
1 cup sugar
1 cup evaporated milk
½ cup butter
1 (7 ounce) jar marshmallow fluff
1 teaspoon vanilla
1 (6 ounce) package butterscotch chips
1 cup chopped nuts
1 (6 ounce) package chocolate chips

Combine sugars, milk, and butter. Bring to full boil over medium heat, stirring constantly. Boil 10 minutes over medium heat, stirring occasionally (if using candy thermometer, cook to soft ball stage). Remove from heat and add marshmallow fluff and vanilla. Stir until mixture is smooth. To half add butterscotch chips and ½ cup nuts; stir until smooth. Pour evenly in pan. To other half add chocolate chips and ½ cup nuts; stir until smooth. Pour over butterscotch mixture.

Blue Ribbon Peanut Brittle

3 cups sugar
1 cup light corn syrup
½ cup water
1 teaspoon salt
1 pound raw peanuts
1 teaspoon baking soda
1 teaspoon vanilla

Boil together in heavy saucepan sugar, syrup, water, and salt, until it reaches 240°. Add peanuts and cook to 290°. Remove from heat and add baking soda and vanilla. Stir well and pour onto buttered sheet pan. Break into pieces when cool.

Peanut Brittle Candy

¼ cup water
3 cups sugar
1 cup light corn syrup
4 cups raw peanuts
3 teaspoons baking soda

Mix water, sugar, and syrup. Bring to boil; add peanuts and boil about 10 minutes (on medium-high heat) or until golden brown. Remove from heat and stir in baking soda. Mixture will foam and turn white. Stir until it is color you want. The more it is stirred, the darker it gets. Pour out onto buttered heavy-duty aluminum foil or cookie sheet. Spread as thin as you can. Cool and break into pieces.

Peanut Butter Treats

½ cup butter, softened
½ cup brown sugar
½ cup sugar
1 egg
½ cup creamy peanut butter
½ teaspoon vanilla
1¼ cups flour
¾ teaspoon baking soda
½ teaspoon salt
36 miniature Reese's peanut butter cups

OVEN 370°

Combine butter, sugars, egg, peanut butter, and vanilla; beat until smooth. Combine flour, baking soda, and salt; add to creamed mixture. Roll in small balls and place each in miniature muffin tins. Bake for 8 to 9 minutes. Remove from oven and immediately put Reese's cup in each. Cool in pan. Can be stored in refrigerator for 1 week.

Peanut Butter Cornflake Treats

1 cup sugar
1 cup corn syrup
2 cups peanut butter
4½ cups cornflakes

Boil together sugar and syrup for 1 minute. Add peanut butter and cornflakes. Drop by tablespoonfuls onto buttered cookie sheet and cool in refrigerator.

Peanut Butter Chessy Cakes

1 stick butter
1 cup peanut butter
2 cups brown sugar
3 eggs
2 cups flour
1 teaspoon vanilla
2 cups chopped nuts (optional)

OVEN 350°

Mix butter, peanut butter, and brown sugar. Mix in eggs and flour. Add vanilla and nuts if desired. Bake at 350° for 40 minutes.

Homemade Peanut Butter Cups

1 cup peanut butter
1 (1 pound) box powdered sugar
¼ pound butter, melted and cooled
1 cup crushed graham crackers
Hershey chocolate bar (1½ ounce)

Mix together peanut butter, sugar, butter, and graham crackers. Mix well. Use your hands to pat into 9x13-inch pan. It is a dry mixture, so take your time. Melt chocolate and spread on top. Cut into squares.

Candied Pecans

¼ cup butter or margarine
½ cup brown sugar
1 teaspoon cinnamon
2 cups pecan halves
Salt (optional)

Use heavy skillet or pan. Cook ingredients over medium-low heat, stirring constantly until nuts are coated and sugar is golden brown (about 5 minutes). Spread on aluminum foil; sprinkle lightly with salt if desired. Cool.

Spiced Pecans

1 egg white
1 teaspoon cold water
1 pound pecan halves
½ cup sugar
¼ teaspoon salt
1 teaspoon cinnamon
½ teaspoon nutmeg
½ teaspoon (scant) cloves

OVEN 270°

Beat egg white and water until frothy. Add nuts and mix thoroughly. Mix dry ingredients; coat nuts. Bake on buttered cookie sheet for 1 hour, stirring every 15 minutes. Dry on paper towels. Store in airtight container.

Southern Salted Pecans

⅓ cup butter
1 tablespoon salt
4 cups pecans

OVEN 200°

Melt butter in large skillet. Stir in salt and pecans. Pour into 9x13-inch pan and bake for 1 hour, stirring every 15 minutes. Drain on absorbent paper towel.

Sugar and Spice Pecans

1 cup firmly packed brown sugar
⅓ cup boiling water
½ teaspoon cinnamon
½ teaspoon ginger
⅛ teaspoon allspice
⅛ teaspoon nutmeg
2 cups pecan halves
¼ teaspoon maple flavoring

Lightly butter 10x15-inch jelly roll pan. In heavy 3-quart saucepan, combine brown sugar, water, and spices. Bring mixture to full boil over medium-high heat, stirring occasionally. Boil without stirring for 5 minutes. Remove from heat. Add nuts and flavoring. Stir until coating on nuts begins to sugar, approximately 2½ to 3 minutes. Pour into prepared pan and quickly separate nuts. Cool completely. Store in airtight container in cool, dry place.

Microwave Caramel Corn

1 cup brown sugar
¼ cup light corn syrup
1 stick butter
¼ teaspoon salt
½ teaspoon baking soda
1 teaspoon vanilla
½ cup popcorn, popped

Bring brown sugar, corn syrup, butter, and salt to boil in 2-quart microwave-safe bowl. Boil for 2 minutes. Add baking soda and vanilla; stir. Pour mixture over popped corn; microwave on high for 1 minute. Stir well and repeat 3 additional minutes, stirring after each minute. Cool on cookie sheet.

Caramel Popcorn

2 sticks butter
½ cup light corn syrup
2 cups brown sugar
¼ teaspoon cream of tartar
¼ teaspoon salt
1 teaspoon vanilla
1 teaspoon baking soda
8 quarts popped corn

OVEN 220°

Mix butter, syrup, and sugar; bring to boiling point. Let boil 6 minutes and keep stirring. Take off heat and add cream of tartar, salt, vanilla, and baking soda. Stir until foamy and quickly pour on popped corn, stirring while pouring. Spread this in large flat pans and bake for 1 hour. Stir 2 or 3 times. Store in tightly closed containers. Can be made in advance and kept in refrigerator. Peanuts or any nuts can also be added as desired.

Potato Candy

⅔ cup hot cooked potatoes
2 teaspoons butter, melted
1 (1 pound) box powdered sugar, sifted
2½ tablespoons cocoa
1 teaspoon vanilla
Dash salt
2 cups (½ pound) moist coconut

Put potatoes through ricer. Add butter and powdered sugar; beat until well blended. Add cocoa; beat thoroughly. Mix in vanilla, salt, and coconut. Drop by teaspoonfuls onto waxed paper. Refrigerate to harden. Hardened candy should be kept in tightly covered container once it has set.

Makes 1½ pounds.

Mashed Potato Candy

½ cup mashed potatoes
2½ (1 pound) boxes powdered sugar
2 sticks margarine
Peanut butter

Beat together potatoes, sugar, and margarine. Roll out into ¼-inch-thick square. Spread with peanut butter and roll up like jelly roll. Cut into 1-inch pieces.

Baked Potato Candy

1 medium potato, baked (not red or yellow potato)
1 pound powdered sugar
Creamy peanut butter

Cool potato until you can hold it in your hand. Remove peel and mash well with fork in medium-size bowl. Add powdered sugar gradually, stirring well until stiff dough forms. Turn out on board covered with powdered sugar. Roll into rectangle about ¼ inch thick. Spread with peanut butter. Roll into tight roll, using spatula to help lift dough, beginning with long side. Let dry for about 1 hour, then slice into ¼-inch slices and spread out on plate with waxed paper between layers. Cover lightly. Dough can be tinted with food coloring, or 2 tablespoons cocoa may be added before rolling.

Haystacks

2 packages butterscotch pieces
1 can potato sticks
1 cup salted peanuts

Melt butterscotch pieces in pan at low temperature. Add potato sticks and peanuts. Stir until well coated. Drop by teaspoonfuls onto waxed paper to form clusters.

Chow Mein Haystacks

6 ounces butterscotch morsels
½ cup chunky peanut butter
1 cup miniature marshmallows
1 (3 ounce) can chow mein noodles

In top part of double boiler over hot, not boiling, water, melt together butterscotch morsels and peanut butter. Add marshmallows, stirring constantly until mixture is smooth. Gently fold in noodles. Blend well. Drop mixture by teaspoonfuls onto waxed paper. Let cool until set.

Ohio Buckeyes

2 sticks margarine, melted
2 cups peanut butter
4 cups powdered sugar
1 teaspoon vanilla
2x2-inch piece of paraffin
3 cups chocolate chips (not imitation chocolate)

Cream together all ingredients except paraffin and chocolate. Chill in refrigerator for a few hours, then roll into balls approximately ¾ inch in diameter. Chill balls in refrigerator at least 8 hours. Melt paraffin and chocolate in double boiler. Using toothpick, dip each ball into chocolate mixture, twirling off excess chocolate. Place on waxed paper to set up.

No-Bake Chocolate Dainties

2 cups sugar
1 stick margarine
½ cup evaporated milk
2 cups quick-cooking oats
⅓ cup cocoa
½ cup coconut
1 teaspoon vanilla

Mix sugar, margarine, and milk together. Boil 4 minutes. Remove from heat and stir in oats, cocoa, coconut, and vanilla. Beat and drop by spoonfuls onto waxed paper. Let sit until cool.

Ding-a-Lings

1 package almond bark
1½ cups Peanut Butter Crunch cereal
1¼ cups cashews
1¼ cups mixed nuts
1½ cups miniature marshmallows

Melt almond bark. In large bowl combine Peanut Butter Crunch, cashews, mixed nuts, and marshmallows. Pour almond bark over and drop by spoonfuls onto waxed paper.

Caramel Apple Pieces

½ cup brown sugar
4 teaspoons flour
4 tablespoons butter
4 teaspoons milk
1 teaspoon vanilla
4 medium apples, cored and cut into ⅛-inch pieces (peel if for small children)
Chopped nuts (optional)

In small saucepan mix together brown sugar, flour, butter, and milk. Stir constantly on medium heat until thick and bubbly. Remove from heat and add vanilla. Let cool. Spoon caramel sauce over apples. Sprinkle with chopped nuts if desired.

Sweet Things

1 cup chopped dates
1 cup fat-free condensed milk
1 cup chopped pecans
Reduced-fat Ritz crackers

Frosting:
1 (3 ounce) package fat-free cream cheese
½ cup reduced-fat margarine
1½ cups powdered sugar
1 teaspoon vanilla

OVEN 320°

Mix dates and milk in saucepan. Cook on medium heat until thick. Mix in pecans. Spread Ritz crackers on cookie sheet and cover with date mixture. Bake for 8 minutes. Mix together frosting ingredients. Frost. Cover and refrigerate.

Graham Gems

¼ cup sugar
½ teaspoon salt
½ cup flour
2 teaspoons baking powder
1 cup whole wheat flour
1 cup milk
2 tablespoons sour cream
1 egg, beaten

OVEN 420°

In mixing bowl, stir together first five ingredients; make well in center. In another bowl combine milk, sour cream, and egg. Add to first ingredients, stirring just until blended. Pour into greased muffin cups. Bake for 15 to 20 minutes until lightly browned. Serve with butter, margarine, or honey.

Meringue Surprises

2 egg whites
1 teaspoon vanilla
⅛ teaspoon salt
½ cup sugar
6 ounces chocolate chips

OVEN 300°

Combine egg whites, vanilla, and salt. Beat until stiff. Beat in sugar gradually until stiff and satiny. Fold in chocolate chips. Drop by teaspoonfuls onto greased cookie sheet and bake 30 minutes.

Divinity Candy

2 cups sugar
½ cup light corn syrup
½ cup hot water
¼ teaspoon salt
2 egg whites
¾ cup chopped nuts
1 teaspoon vanilla

Mix together sugar, syrup, water, and salt. Cook until hard ball forms in water. Beat egg whites until stiff; pour hot syrup slowly over whites. Beat on high speed for 5 minutes; then add nuts and vanilla. Spoon onto waxed paper.

Peppermint Divinity

2⅔ cups sugar
⅔ cup light corn syrup
½ cup water
2 egg whites
2 teaspoons peppermint extract
Red food coloring
⅔ cup broken nuts (optional)

Heat sugar, corn syrup, and water in 2-quart saucepan over low heat, stirring constantly until sugar is dissolved. Cook, stirring constantly, to 260° on candy thermometer, or until small amount of mixture dropped into very cold water forms hard ball. Remove from heat. Beat egg whites until stiff peaks form; continue beating while pouring hot syrup in thin stream into egg whites. Add peppermint extract and food coloring. The mixture should hold its shape. Add nuts if desired. Drop by spoonfuls onto waxed paper.

Rice Krispie Candy

½ cup sugar
½ cup light corn syrup
¾ cup peanut butter
3 cups crisp rice cereal

Bring sugar and corn syrup to boil. Remove from heat; add peanut butter, mix well, and stir in cereal. Drop by spoonfuls onto waxed paper.

Party Favorites

Chocolate chips
Ritz crackers
Peanut butter

Put water in pan and put another pan on top, creating double boiler. Put chocolate chips in top pan and heat until melted. Spread peanut butter on cracker; place another cracker on top. Dip into chocolate. Place on waxed paper to dry, then refrigerate.

Corn Pop Squares

¼ cup margarine
1 package marshmallows
1 teaspoon vanilla
1 package M&M's (to taste)
6 cups Corn Pops cereal

Melt margarine and marshmallows in microwave. Add vanilla. Reserve a few M&M's for sprinkling on top. Mix M&M's and Sugar Pops with marshmallow mixture; put in 8x11-inch dish to cool and harden. Cut into squares and serve.

English Toffee

1 cup sugar
1 cup butter
1 teaspoon vanilla
6 (1½ ounce) Hershey bars
Chopped pecans

Cover cookie sheet with foil and spray with nonstick cooking spray. Cook sugar and butter to hard crack on medium heat until mixture turns brown. Add vanilla. Pour onto foil and spread out ⅛ to ¼ inch thick. Break up Hershey bars; lay on top of hot toffee. Spread. Sprinkle with nuts. Cool and break into pieces.

Old-Time Taffy

1 cup sugar
1 cup dark corn syrup
2 tablespoons apple cider vinegar
Lump of butter, the size of a peanut
½ teaspoon baking soda

Place first four ingredients in pan; bring to boil. Boil until mixture forms hard ball in cup of cold water. Then add baking soda; stir well. Pour onto buttered pan and, when cooled, pull until shiny and ready to cut.

Strawberry Candies

1 (12 ounce) package coconut
1 (14 ounce) can condensed milk
1 teaspoon almond extract
1½ cups chopped almonds (optional)
2 packages strawberry gelatin (maybe more)

Mix coconut, milk, extract, nuts, and 1 package gelatin. Mixture will be sticky. Shape into candies that look like strawberries; roll in one box of gelatin (may need more). Green icing can be piped on top for leaves. Chill before eating.

Variation: Use blueberry gelatin or another favorite flavor.

Index

APPETIZERS

PIES